Eros and Chaos

On The Hudson
Jung
BOOK SERIES

The Jung on the Hudson Book Series was instituted by the New York Center for Jungian Studies in 1997. This ongoing series is designed to present books that will be of interest to individuals of all fields, as well as mental health professionals, who are interested in exploring the relevance of the psychology and ideas of C. G. Jung to their personal lives and professional activities.

For more information about this series and the New York Center for Jungian Studies contact: Aryeh Maidenbaum, Ph.D., New York Center for Jungian Studies, 41 Park Avenue, Suite 1D, New York, NY 10016, telephone (212) 689-8238, fax (212) 889-7634.

For more information about becoming part of this series contact: Betty Lundsted, Nicolas-Hays, P. O. Box 2039, York Beach, ME 03910-2039, telephone (207) 363-1558, email: nhi@ici.net.

Eros and Chaos

THE SACRED MYSTERIES
AND DARK SHADOWS OF LOVE

VERONICA GOODCHILD

Foreword by Dianne Skafte

NICOLAS-HAYS, INC.
YORK BEACH, MAINE

First published in 2001 by
Nicolas-Hays
P.O. Box 2039
York Beach, ME 03910-2039

Distributed to the trade by
Weiser Books
Box 612
York Beach, ME 03910
www.weiserbooks.com

Library of Congress Cataloging-in-Publication Data
Goodchild, Veronica.
  Eros and Chaos : the sacred mysteries and dark shadows of love / Veronica Goodchild.
    p. cm. -- (Jung on the Hudson book series)
  Includes bibliographical references and index.
  ISBN 0-89254-054-0 (pbk. : alk. paper)
  1. Love. 2. Jungian psychology. I. Title. II. Series
BF175.5.L68 G66 2001
152.4'1—dc21

                                                              00-066850
VG

Cover art is *Lovers (Mithuna)*. Reddish sandstone, H. 74 cm. India, Madyha Pradesh, Khajuraho style, 11th century. Photo copyright © 2001 The Cleveland Museum of Art. Leonard C. Hanna, Jr., Fund, 1982-64.

Typeset in 11.5 Palatino

Printed in the United States of America

08 07 06 05 04 03 02 01

 8   7   6   5   4   3   2   1

The paper used in this publication meets the minimum requirements of the Amercian National Standard for Information Sciences—Permanence of Paper for Printed Library Materials Z39.48-1992 (R1997).

For Robert—my husband,
Lover of my soul
With whom the mysteries and shadows of love
have their unknown origins,
enjoy their daily round
and journey beyond time . . .
There is no greater gift.

A very special place in my heart goes to my children,
Sarah and Tim,
star travelers and old souls,
who were present before I saw them,
and whose knowing and being
have taught me much about the art of
loving

CONTENTS

FOREWORD

by Dr. Dianne Skafte

Dr. Goodchild and I are deep in conversation with a woman who expresses intense desire to leave her job. Its stressful, conflictual atmosphere sickens her, and she longs to work more creatively on her own. "But I have to wait until I get the right opportunity before I can follow my desire," she sighs.

I am about to nod my head emphatically when Dr. Goodchild leans forward and says, "No, you have it backward. Put the whole force of your being behind your desire. Then the opportunities will open." For a moment the space between us fractures. We feel the jolt of something more powerful than the words themselves. Our companion is staring at Dr. Goodchild with a stunned look, and all three of us know that her life course has just shifted.

Who can explain those uncanny moments when words bypass ordinary consciousness and penetrate directly to the soul? Those moments happen often around Dr. Goodchild, I have noticed. She has the special ability to mobilize courage in another person with a single sentence—or even a glance—almost through direct transmission. Reading *Eros and Chaos*, I perceive the deeper sources of her strength as a teacher. Here is a guide who asks you to venture only where she herself has stepped. We know, through her own knowing, how it feels to love wholly and be abandoned, to love partly and abandon another, to love not at all. And if Fate permits, we may even find the true beloved on a windy beach after one thousand years of separation. Dr. Goodchild shares accounts from her own life and therapeutic practice, and also from the realm of mythology, story, and legend. In the eerie yellow light of ancient tales, we detect the universal contours of our own experience.

Veronica Goodchild knows from the beginning that entering "those fateful places that undo us" is not easy. She reminds us that our tendency to flinch from the chaotic edge of things is understandable, particularly in a culture that worships rationality, predictability, and control. But as former beliefs and societal structures dissolve before our eyes, we learn that making friends with the great unknown is our best—perhaps our only—course of action. Dreams, imagination, rapport with nature, aesthetic sensibility, and engagement with anomalous phenomena are among the guides that Dr. Goodchild invokes for our journey into the unknown. Marginalized peoples, our sufferings and symptoms, and even the death of Princess Diana can lead us into domains where new life flourishes.

I read this book with pen in hand so that I may take notes from the marvelous quotations in every chapter. Dr. Goodchild allows the voices of depth psychologists, mystics, poets, and ordinary folk to join our dialogue. One also is treated to narratives of the author's own dreams, most of which include astonishing imagery. I am especially taken by her description of "the Eye of the Divine" as it gazes with gentle, compassionate vision, opening and closing, bringing worlds into being and allowing others to pass away. There is a sense of both infinite mercy and utter indifference to the fate of the cosmos. I shudder a little each time I follow the transmutations of this dream, for I feel the icy brush of something far beyond my ken. Only one who has lived close to archetypal presence could usher us into a living experience of its terror and beauty.

Eros and Chaos is certain to change the way we think about sorrow, desire, yearning, revelation, and many other stations of the soul. The fall into dissolution is painful and terrifying, make no mistake. Yet Veronica Goodchild demonstrates—through her words and the passion behind them—that if we surrender ourselves to love's inexorable pull, we enter into union with a sacred *something* that holds us close. I now better understand why the woman at our table can be knocked out of her accustomed groove by a few simple words. Those words carry invisible tornadoes brought back from the cosmic edge of chaos. And I happen to know, on the best authority, that the other face of chaos is love.

→ everyday shamanism

I am a Star following her way like you

—from a Mithraic liturgy

ACKNOWLEDGMENTS

My life and vocation are inextricably bound with the following people whose love, presence, and commitment have helped make real incarnation possible:

Walter Odajnyk, my first analyst, who taught me the reality of the psyche. In our work together, I became conscious of love as a divine force, as that presence that informs all our relationships, and that in ways both terrible and beautiful reveals to us the face of our calling.

Patricia Finley, who helped me refine the experience of powerful archetypal energies into a lived life, and who was present through the births of my two children.

Ray Walker, teacher, "supervisor," analyst, colleague, and friend, who for some twenty years has been unfailingly and ruthlessly faithful to the journey of my soul.

Ash*tiana Sundeer, shaman, earthkeeper, guardian of the ancient mysteries, visionary, and psychic, who helped me over the years with great irreverence, humor, and depth to remember the beauty, wisdom, and value of being a woman, and who reawakened a secret from the stars.

St. John, gnostic mystic, devotee and guardian of cosmogonic love, who at various times came to me when I might have forgotten, and who stood by me while I wrote this book.

To Flicker, longtime dearest friend, deep gratitude and love, especially for the endless hours of conversations on the mysteries and vicissitudes of life.

And to my parents Jean and Ronald, who gave me life, who let me go, and who were there after many years of my being away, standing like sentinels, true witnesses to the ancient truth that "love endureth all things." With my parents I am deeply grateful for the fact that love has had the chance to mature.

I wish also to acknowledge Dr. Cathy Rives at Pacifica Graduate Institute, and Dr. Robert Sardello, who served as the first readers of this text, before it went through its many changes into its present form. Cathy asked questions that helped me clarify my initial ideas. Robert Sardello's response to my first draft led to changes and additions that clarify and deepen the writing. I wish also to thank Dr. Christine Downing, who generously and gracefully read a later version, which led to some further refinements. A feeling of deep gratitude goes to Dr. Dianne Skafte, friend and colleague, whose oracular sensibilities go always to the heart of things.

And again my husband Robert, whose fierce loyalty, great humor, and deep loving helped me trust the voice of my own creativity. From ancient streams Robert—together with his keen poetic sensibility—emerges as a true witness and guardian of the soul of the work, whether it be teaching, or writing, or simply the artistry of a life.

An earlier and much briefer version of chapter 2, titled "Eros and Chaos: The Mysteries and Shadows of Love," first appeared in *Pathways into the Jungian World: Phenomenology*

and Analytical Psychology, Roger Brooke, editor (London & New York: Routledge, 2000).

The section on Princess Diana in chapter 5 first appeared, with minor alterations, as "Death of a Princess: In Memoriam, Diana, Princess of Wales" in *Quadrant: The Journal of the C. G. Jung Foundation for Analytical Psychology* (vol. XXIX:2, Summer 1999, pp. 57–71), published by the C. G. Jung Foundation for Analytical Psychology, Inc., 1999. Reprinted by permission.

PROLOGUE

It is early Spring. We are on a flight from Los Angeles to London to enjoy a short, two-week vacation in Cornwall, on England's Celtic West Coast. We are perhaps halfway into the long ten-hour flight, which crosses the continental U.S.A. before journeying over the Atlantic ocean. We have had drinks and dinner, and now the lights are dimming for the movie. I wonder what it is. The credits begin, and I see that it's a film I have already seen: Shine. *I decide to try to sleep instead. I nestle up against my husband's body, my head in the nook of his shoulder. I close my eyes and try to relax. Immediately I half open them, in the act of getting myself comfortable and settled. I glance at the movie screen, and see the credits still going up. I wonder if I'll watch the movie after all. I turn to my husband and ask if he is going to watch it. He replies that he did watch it; it is already over; see, the credits are on the screen. He tells me that I fell into such a deep sleep that he did not dare move for fear of waking me. It is in fact two hours later. What seemed to me to be the closing and opening of my eyes in a matter of seconds, was in real time (chronological time) the length of the movie. I simply cannot believe it.*

As I struggle with the feeling of utter disbelief, a memory comes to me of what has just happened in that two-second interval that stretched over two hours. I had found myself in a barely furnished room in which were several figures, mostly men as I recall, in long white robes that were tied at the waist. One of them was standing behind what appeared to be a simple, wooden desk on which was placed a very large open manuscript, all hand written in italic script and illustrated with richly colored paints. No one spoke a word, because here in this place the communication was all achieved telepathically, a kind of field communication. As I stood before this one figure I was drawn into a vibration of what I can only describe as unconditional love. The energy of this unconditional love seemed to be emanating off him as if he were constituted by it, and such that any being in his presence would be filled with the gentle, undulating, merciful, compassionate rays that formed his being. Here there was no judgment, no criticism, only complete acceptance of one's own being. It was as if in this presence, my own vibrational form was moved to match the higher and more refined resonance of this being of love. I cannot say with any certainty that this being was what we might call an angel; he appeared to have human form. However, it was clear that he resided in another dimension that was not Earth, but clearly could intersect with Earth. Perhaps it is a parallel place, a parallel universe. No demand of any kind was made upon me. The emphasis was on the experience, the feeling of being filled with a profoundly moving, compassionate sensibility brought into my field by this emissary from the realms of cosmic love.

One thing I am absolutely sure of—though I cannot prove—is that this experience was not a dream. I know that in the proverbial twinkling of an eye, while my physical body remained on the airplane, I traveled or was taken to this place, met with these beings, and was transformed. Of the actual two-hour interval I have no recollection. I neither stirred nor resettled myself during that time as I usually do while trying to sleep in an uncomfortable upright position on a long overnight flight. All that remains of that period of time is the witnessing presence of my husband who observed that my physical body remained motionless while I appeared to go into a death-like sleep.

The next two weeks were filled with a gentle glow. I felt extraordinarily loving toward my mate, which naturally delighted him. Although the comparative density of my normal state returned, and continues to return, if I recall this experience I can put myself right back into its beautiful presence, and I can fully remind myself that this kind of compassionate love resides in the universe, and that it visits us, and that it longs for us to be able to incarnate and live it here and now on Earth.

I tell this story by way of prologue to my text for three reasons. Two of these reasons have to do with the content of this work and the third reason has to do with the style of the work—how it is being written—which is inseparable from the content, and which I discuss in the last section of this Prologue.

OF LOVE AND SHADOWS

This book is about the very difficult phenomenon of love, a difficulty that arises because love cannot be separated from its shadows. Since I argue that love is best figured in the form of eros, and that the shadows of love lead one into the domain of chaos, my discussion of love and its shadows is situated within the context of eros' relation with chaos. This view radically challenges the more familiar coupling of chaos and order, a paradigm that is at the root of many of our personal, cultural, and collective crises.

Love always evokes its shadows. We cannot love, then, unless we are able to come to terms with our shadows, with our own darkness, and be in relationship to it. I also regard love as an achievement of maturity, an achievement of consciousness that necessarily involves an awareness, following the work of C. G. Jung, that there are other centers of being in the psyche beside the conscious ego personality. So although many children seem to have a natural facility for love, I am not going to focus on the complexity of their experience in this book as it is not their task to bear the burden of consciousness, of loving consciously. That task is ours.

Although the story that begins this work does not include within itself its shadow, its shadow can be said to reside in the fact that I am unable to remain within the compelling and refined state of love, the state that I fully experienced with the being of love in that unknown land. Much of the time—probably like most people—I fall back into those chaotic states of ignorance, fear, and inconsiderateness, those falling apart places that so often have at their origin the vulnerable gaping wounds inherited from childhood, culture, or incarnational destiny, that prevent our ability to love and simultaneously keep us humble and very human.

Paradoxically, it is these humiliating gaping wounds that also potentially open us to the divine realms and a larger destiny, and to that difficult work of loving. In moments of grace—that admittedly I have worked twenty some odd years toward achieving, by seeking to know and differentiate myself—I am able to love with soft eyes, sweetly, passionately, fiercely, kindly, sexually, erotically, darkly, and pathetically. I especially love the word "pathetic," because it means in its root "filled with soul."

I also tell the story in the Prologue because it raises the specter of an anomalous or ontologically ambiguous experience. What is the nature of such an experience as I had on the airplane, an event that seemed neither dream nor situated in the outer world? In moments of chaotic breakdown—of either an individual or collective nature, when our familiar and cherished positions become unraveled—or alternatively, in those delicate moments of deep loving, we are perhaps most open to such experiences. Are we on such an unraveling edge, both personally and culturally? In this book I suggest that we are on such a frontier, and that what appears to be breaking through in our personal and cultural moments of breakdown is the archetypal and cosmic field of eros—love. In this regard, my experience on the airplane is, itself, the kind of event that we have relegated to the shadows, and these experiences are now seeking reentry into our lives.

As a Jungian psychotherapist and teacher for twenty years, I know that dreams and fantasies are considered real, psychically real, and are to be taken with the utmost seriousness and consideration as providing symbolic clues to the nature of one's psychological reality. But other kinds of experiences that do not fit our prevailing scientific and technological paradigms of reality tend to remain marginalized in depth psychology's (or our culture's) shadows. Such experiences put in question the familiar psyche/world, inner/outer, either/or, real/not real dichotomies. This marginalizing of certain events that do not fit our collective view of what is real is all the more curious because Jungian psychology, and certainly many of Jung's own experiences, also challenge these prevailing dichotomies. But then Jung always said that he thanked God he was Jung and not a Jungian! Mention a UFO encounter, a crop circle, a past life memory, an experience of bi-location, or a visitation by an angel, even a lucid dream, and eyebrows tend to start rising—even among Jungians.

Yet with the emergence of quantum physics in this century, an emergence that parallels that of Jungian psychology, a whole new worldview has come into being; one that is noncausal, discontinous, synchronistic, and potentially very creative. We tend to remain stuck in the old Newtonian, causal, mechanistic worldview, however, as being the only take on reality. Yet there is also a move in our time to speak out about anomalous kinds of experiences, such as near death encounters (NDEs), and visitations with fairies, angels, and beings from other planets, dimensions, or time frames, all experiences challenging the old, familiar paradigms. Such experiences open up a third ontological domain, a distinctive realm of being, residing somewhere between our sensory world and our intellectual capacities. This subtle landscape is more consonant with the imaginal experiences of soul than the dualistic distinctions and divisions of mind versus matter.

The word *imaginal* derives from the Islamic scholar, Henri Corbin (1972), who in recovering the multi-tiered cosmos of

Sufi mysticism, calls this in-between but nevertheless entirely real dimension the *mundus imaginalis*. He makes a clear distinction between its ontological reality to which individuals may go, and the term *imaginary*, which, by contrast, is equated with the *unreal* (p. 1). Jung's emphasis on psychic reality, or the reality of the psyche—a world that he describes, too, as neither spirit nor matter,[1] but perhaps the place where spirit and matter both "touch and do not touch"[2]—is perhaps more precisely equivalent to Corbin's *mundus imaginalis*.

Jung, however, can be confusing about the nature of this imaginal soulscape or psychic reality, at times suggesting that it is an inner world of dreams, fantasies, images, ideas, and affects, an approach to psyche that preserves a Newtonian-Cartesian inside/outside, psyche/world separation. At other times Jung, especially in his later work on alchemy, synchronicity and its parallels in quantum physics—work that seems to reveal a hidden yet glowing acausal and nonlocal connection between inner and outer—revisions his theory of the nature of the archetype. In this work the archetype is no longer described as exclusively an inner psychic structure that arranges our perceptions and experiences. Rather, it is described as psychoid, that is, as a factor that extends seamlessly from the inner world into nature, matter, and the cosmos. More accurately the psychoid aspect of the archetype is like an invisible field that surrounds and holds psyche and matter together. What I wish to emphasize in this book is that

---

1. C. G. Jung, *Letters I* (Princeton: Princeton University Press, 1973), p. 200. In a letter to Henry Murray on 10 September 1935, Jung writes: "I'm chiefly concerned with the psyche itself, therefore I'm leaving out body and spirit." For Jung, body and spirit are metaphysical realities ("mere aspects of the psyche") belonging to the disciplines of medicine and theology respectively. "Psychic experience is the only immediate experience," he says in this letter.
2. C. G. Jung, *The Structure and Dynamics of the Psyche*, Collected Works 8 (Princeton: Princeton University Press, 1969b), §418.

this psychoid field as "the invisible in things" is an a priori reality structured by cosmogonic love, and that in our times it is increasingly trying to draw our attention to its presence.

Synchronistic events, for example, are crucially important to Jung as they seem to point to this basic underlying unity of all being, what Jung also describes as the *unus mundus*, a unity that sometimes appears as a material fact, and sometimes as a psychological event, but more often as a subtle body field or presence that is neither outer fact nor inner event, yet curiously embraces both. Indeed, it is my view that the god Eros lurks in this compelling desire of matter and spirit for each other to recover a lost wholeness. It could be that Jung's guide, Philemon, is, as Jung hints at, both a dream or fantasy figure and also an imaginal being, an inhabitant of the *mundus imaginalis*, a being from another dimension. Such an observation suggests that Jung's psychology recovers a multi-tiered cosmos, an observation that has perhaps not yet been made explicit enough in his work.

In Jung's worldview there are inner psychological events and images that require introspective reflection and "as if" symbolic understanding. The outer world is other and different from this world. And then there is another domain, the psychoid realm that discloses the *unus mundus* or *mundus imaginalis*, that we can travel to as Corbin describes, or that at extraordinary moments perhaps intersects with our world. Genuine synchronicities reveal this world, as do perhaps certain active imagination processes, certain dreams and visions, and the phenomenon of UFO encounters. My story in this prologue, that I felt emphatically was not a dream, may have been one of these visits to another dimension, for one of the curious features of the journey, like the UFO encounter or a journey to the *mundus imaginalis*, is that we cannot tell how we got there.

It could also be that the inner world of dreams, the psychoid realm of the archetype, the *mundus imaginalis* of Corbin, the world of synchronicities as illustrated for example by UFOs, and the outer world of our daily concerns, reflect five qualitatively different tiers or dimensions of being and reality. My point here is not to clarify or distinguish in any precise way what these levels are, but only to point out that the issue of what constitutes psyche, soul, or the imaginal, their "where" and their inhabitants, is a complex one, and that there are in all likelihood potentially different domains that intersect each other and to which we have access. It is this possibility of multi-leveled vibrational fields of being to which I wish to draw attention, for I fear it is not adequately addressed in Jung's psychology. Such awareness might make room for experiences that otherwise often remain hidden or unacceptable for people.

I wish, therefore, to approach the complex realm of love and its shadows through stories that couple chaos and eros, rather than the more familiar linking of chaos and order, while simultaneously making space in my text for accounts of events that reach into parallel and synchronistic worlds that ask to be witnessed and addressed. In any case, love, like most of the important experiences in life, is always a matter of fate and synchronicity which we can never make or cause to happen. An underlying theme in this text, therefore, is that the whole project of depth psychology—not to mention its parallel in quantum physics and string theory—has opened up a realm of experience and experiencing with which we have hardly begun to come to terms, and for which our familiar, rational modes of apprehending are entirely inadequate. Love and its attendant shadows are perhaps the most important factors in a life that reach into this mysterious and unknown territory.

FROM COMPLEX TO COSMOS:
RECOLLECTIONS AND REFLECTIONS

The style of this book is as important as the content. I intend to forge a link between my own experience and its moments of chaos and breakdown, moments of woundings and passions, and those transpersonal and imaginal realms that come through these fractures in my own being. Said in another way, I am attempting a visionary writing, a work that blends deeply felt experience of the topic and its cultural and archetypal elaborations with its articulation. Hence the format will be a blend of experiences (including dream, vision, and reverie), which are set in italics, and reflections.

In this study, I shall probably err on the side of unashamedly letting my passion about my topic be my guide, as I try to let the juiciness of the chaos/eros fields of experience find their own enlivening or devastating expressions. I do not intend to indulge in mere sentiment or confession. But I also do not intend to write with a misplaced notion of objectivity, which would falsely separate me from my subject.

My aim is to cooperate as much as possible with a feeling-mind, and with a metaphorical consciousness, that is, a consciousness that is both differentiated but not split off from what also wants to be spoken, a consciousness that is participatory, and one that opens the imaginal depths of the world. In being related to the material, in wrestling with it, my aim is to let the material transform me, as much as to bring new aspects of these age-old themes to light. In this sense, writing this book is a vocation, a calling, a creative act—with its own demons and limitations—of the individuation process. I am not distanced from my theme; on the contrary, I am grabbed by these potent archetypal, indeed cosmic, realities through my own joys and wounds, my own love and its failures, and my deep concern for the crisis of love in our times. This is perhaps both the book's strength and its flaw, its value and its inadequacy, its eros and its chaos.

In the same way, I invite the reader to enter this text via his or her own wounds, which will transform the text for each reader, making it perhaps something quite other than either I intended, or it intended for me. I suppose the greatest compliment a reader of a text could give is that the material grabbed her, and in so doing, changed her in some way, making the act of reading, like writing, an act of transformation. But perhaps we never even approach a piece of writing unless something in it already draws us near. Certainly we do not remain with a subject, or do not learn anything from it, if there is no emotional involvement. In this regard, eros or its absence informs all our relations, and all our learning.

So, I shall be guided by my experiences and allow my enthusiasm for my topic to be my companion. My own individuation process has been about an increasing uncivilizing of my being and attitudes. Like many women of my generation, I have been an adaptive father's daughter who has been in search of her own authentic expression, her own feminine voice, in life and in work. Thus I must try not to lose my position and perhaps fall into the fantasy of producing a perfect piece of scholarship. To do that would be a betrayal of that to which I ethically feel called to be true. I cannot therefore so much write about my topic as much as out of, and with it, in a spirit of love with its shadows, a writing with passion and with eros as my companion.

One of the difficulties of writing this book for me has been the willingness to risk staking out a position, taking a firm stand. Jungians—especially therapists or analysts—are mostly taught to consider possibilities and to hold ambiguities in awareness, to stand back and to reflect back, to be present to the other and to keep our own views out of the situation as much as possible, rather than to impose them. It is certainly not considered good therapy to impose anything!

Such psychological attitudes, however, become like a noose around your neck when it comes to writing. In committing to a written text, you have to take a stand, otherwise you give neither yourself nor your reader anything to grapple with. As an author, you might change your mind ten minutes after the text is fixed at the printers forever, but if you waffle or stay on the fence there remains nothing substantial, or even quirky enough, with which the reader can be engaged. This is why authors write more than one book! They are always trying to catch up with their new ideas. In my own case, I had to eventually edit out a tendency to support my ideas with too many references to other authors as "authorities." I was hiding behind others, and keeping myself from making my claims, and inhibiting myself from putting across my own views. I think that one has to risk taking on a certain kind of boldness—even exhibitionism—in committing one's ideas to paper and hoping that others will read them.

On the other hand, we do not always know where our ideas come from, whose they are, who supports them finding a form, or for whom they are intended, even though it is our hands at the keyboard. In the end, a book may or may not find its way to a publisher, may or may not find its way into the world. I like to think of a book as a living being that also has a life apart from its author, and that, like *The Red Violin*, has its own incarnational destiny. We cannot finally be the judge of our own work. But we can be responsive to those ideas that visit us and try to be responsible with what they seem to seek from us. For the rest, we must let go and trust in that Something that seems to urge us on, even though in the end our frail efforts may fall into oblivion. One of Jung's strongest commands was "not to imitate." This vital injunction is both a blessing and a curse, for in its freedom lies a terror from which we can be protected if we make the spirit of his work into a dogma or a theoretical system. Writing, much like love, involves a tremendous risk, one that opens us to chaos!

Vocation and Dream

Standing on the shores of the Sea of Galilee in Israel when I was 18, watching the sun go down on the mountains of Tiberias on the opposite shore, the world disclosed itself as a veil, a beautifully colored garment, clothing a deeper mystery that penetrated it. Later on, while floating in the Dead Sea surrounded by ancient caves (that only much later I came to know housed the Essene community), I felt that I knew this place, that the landscape activated some memory code in the cells of my soul. During the summer, I changed my course of study at the university that I was about to enter, from law to theology. Back in England, later that year, studying the gospel of St. John in Greek, I was profoundly moved by this gnostic mystic and his preoccupations with love, which I didn't really understand, but which nonetheless caused reverberations somewhere deep inside me. Twenty-three years later, I had the following dream.

I am part of a group once again studying this gospel, trying to penetrate its mystery, feeling called down into the foundational depths of my being, that layer beneath everything I know, and everything I have been taught. In the dream, the rest of the study group moves on, but I am compelled to remain with the text as if trying to decipher some esoteric level to it. The dream evoked a numinous feeling response. It also propelled me toward further graduate studies, for it inspired in me a desire to develop my thinking and learning, beyond being a clinician in the therapy room. During the summer before I began my doctoral program I went to the island of Patmos in Greece, to feel near to St. John, the one who had been so tormented by his cosmic visions, who had appeared so recently in my dream. I felt inchoately certain that my writing would eventually have something to do with the mysteries of cosmic love. I found an icon of this saint that, along with pictures of Sappho, Aphrodite, my lover, and my children, and crystals and rocks from different beaches in the world, have been on my personal altar, presences accompanying my work.[3]

Growing up in an Anglican clergyman's household, my life in one form or another has been a struggle with love, with love and its many vicissitudes, with love and its failures and disappointments. Depth psychology too delves into this rich

---

3. Author's Dream Journal, March 1992.

terrain in its theories and particularly in its praxis. Jung's work, with its emphasis on religious experience and the reality of the dream, was the link for me between my Christian background (with its contrasting emphasis on ideals), and my need to come to terms with this force, this "mighty daimon," as Socrates (in Plato's *Symposium*) refers to love, or the "sweetly bitter," as Sappho speaks of eros, that fuels the cosmos, and brings everything into being.

In my analytic work both as a therapist and a patient I have time and again been humbled by the fact that the fall into love always brings up love's shadows, as if the purpose of love's penetrating gaze is to bring up everything opposite to itself, only to reveal further its mysteries.

My book then is a working of the major issues of my life, and more specifically, an amplification of the above mentioned dream. It is an offering—my best effort for now, on behalf of a vision, that like St. John, was granted to me—that I give back now with gratitude to all those real people, and to those inhabitants of the land of soul, who have loved me, and held me, and made it possible for me to journey so abundantly into the second half of my life.

The treatment of my topic, *Eros and Chaos: The Sacred Mysteries and Dark Shadows of Love,* unfolds in a series of essays which are best imagined as amplifications or variations of its central theme. In chapter 1, I begin by challenging the popular prejudice that links chaos and order, and suggest rather that we consider chaos's relation with eros. The breakdown of order in the West and the emergence of new paradigms of reality, especially in the last one hundred years, open us to this possibility. The appearance of Freud's and Jung's psychology of the unconscious (Freud's sexual, and Jung's symbolic, dare we say, 'erotic,' theory) dramatically reveals the presence of mythic Eros. Indeed, in my view, the archetypal figure of Eros ruled Jung's life, and often—both as much by its presence as in its absence—is central to our own.

Throughout my work, I am writing in one way or another on the observation that if loving is so key to us—arguably the one experience we would rather not leave this life without having known—how is it we're so incompetent at it. My view is that we cannot separate love from its shadows, and that until we do face this union of eros with its dark partner chaos, we will not become better at this mystery of loving. Love, then, is difficult and demanding, perhaps the most difficult accomplishment of all. But the mythic figure of Eros is not an easy figure. He spans an arc from the sublime to the disastrous, from bliss to despair, which intuitively makes sense if we reflect even momentarily on our experiences with love and the messes it can create in our lives.

In West Africa the god Gba'adu, who embraces all existence, including dark and deathly chaotic forces, is viewed as the ultimate mystery of existence. Sadly in the West, our god of light and love has become dissociated from these darker forces, and though, in fact, death and destruction seem all too often to have the upper hand, we are largely severed, in a conscious way, from the unraveling and regenerative forces of chaos. Simultaneously, the full riches and creative mysteries of erotic love are all too often denied or inaccessible to us.

I elaborate these ideas on the mysteries and shadows of love in chapter 2, through the lens of two mythic tales that couple chaos and eros: the Orphic creation myth, and the Indian myth of Vak and her visionaries. I further argue that the fall into love, or the dissolution of love into chaotic and painful states, perhaps has as its goal a more refined and conscious living of eros and its shadows, and the reconnection of human life within a wider cosmic field.

In chapter 3, I explore the suffering shadows of love, particularly the themes of abandonment and abandoning, through the image of the Orphan. I am particularly struck by how suffering invites us to surrender into the unknown, and to sunder our attachments to old structures that no longer serve the soul. In such a fall or wounding we can also find our true vocation, a call that connects us with our vertical fate or destiny.

Chapter 4 explores chaos and the marginalized feminine via the image of what I call clitoral consciousness, an image that arose in a dream. Chaos has often been associated with the feminine, and with women's experience in particular, in a derogatory manner. In this chapter I emphasize how the sensual, erotic, dark, rhythmic, and transformative dimensions of the feminine have been eclipsed in a patriarchal consciousness that values linear, rational thinking. A reconnection to these lost realms often requires a painful descent, an abandoning of the collective fathers to journey to dark, underground, instinctual worlds.

In chapter 5, I focus on the chaotic and numinous in psychotherapy, drawing particular attention to how the evolution—even reduction, perhaps devolution—of Jung's psychology to a depth psychology that overvalues theory and method, lies in danger of losing its original purpose. This initial intent, in allying itself with the esoteric traditions of alchemy, mysticism, and the mystery traditions, was aimed at the transformation of consciousness itself. This initiatic journey maintains our relationship with the larger cosmos, rather than aiming to correct early childhood aberrations, and waters the soul in the chaotic and unfathomable mysteries of cosmic Eros.

In the final chapter, I show that the collapse of the usual boundaries separating spirit and matter opens the world as a *unus mundus*, which Jung and von Franz explore in their later texts on synchronicity. This radical insight is still largely unexplored. I try to amplify what remains implicit in Jung's and von Franz's writings, that the synchronistic, *unus mundus* field is a level of reality pulsating with cosmogonic love. Here, spirit and matter meet in an in-between realm, a subtle locale of visionary and chthonic experience never before created. A UFO encounter illustrates such an experience. This *kairos* of psychophysical union is a call that, if we fail to heed, puts us in danger of continuing the split between psyche and

world (with all the terrible ecological and psychological consequences for modernity) that has increasingly marked our
history during the last two thousand years.

The book finishes with an Epilogue that summarizes
the themes of my work. I claim that the collapse into chaos
that marks our times, both personally and collectively, invites
us to situate our ways of knowing and being in the service of
love, its mysteries and shadows, rather than in a restoration
of order.

Chapter 1

CHAOS AND ORDER
Challenging a Familiar Paradigm

The great problem of our time is that we don't understand what is happening to the world. . . . Our values are shifting, everything loses its certainty. . . . Who is the awe-inspiring guest who knocks at our door portentously?

—C. G. Jung (1975), p. 590.

The problem of love is the most important in human life. Also the most important is the most difficult to talk about . . . . But no doubt such a discussion belongs to our age of reorientation.

—C. G. Jung (1973), pp. 38–39.

This book arises from a desire to challenge an all-too-familiar paradigm in our times—that chaos gives rise to order—and to show that chaos is a harbinger of eros, and not of order. When chaos and eros are twinned in this fashion, they challenge our reigning paradigms of control and domination over the world, and introduce a more complex and subtle way of knowing and being, one that is perhaps nearer to our felt experience. In particular this book illustrates that chaos linked with eros invites us into the epiphanies of love and its shadows, invites us into reveries on the mysteries of, and obstacles to, our loving and being loved, and resituates us within the larger fabric of creation. A key point in my work is to show that in our contemporary world, chaos is a vocation, calling us into the *unus mundus*, into a world of synchronicities, where the desire of spirit for matter is witnessed.

We live in an age of breakdown, breakdown of the order we have constructed in the West. During this century, we have been witnessing the gradual eclipse of a worldview, and the birthing of another *zeitgeist* that is slowly making its presence felt. The limitations of causal, linear, ego-conscious thinking—limitations well documented in the sciences during this century, in quantum, field, string, and chaos theories, and in depth psychology by the symptom, the dream, synchronicity, and some levels of the transferential relationship in therapy—invite us to take note of the irrational, unpredictable, unrepeatable, and nonlinear.

As the physicists Bentov (1977), Wolf (1994), Goswami (1995), and the Jungian scholar and analyst von Franz (1992) indicate, physics and depth psychology invite us into a new synthesis, for matter acts as if it has consciousness, and consciousness itself appears to reach deeply into the structure of matter. In all likelihood, these two poles constitute a unitary reality. The breakdown of our prevailing worldview might be seen then as an invitation into chaos, and into love, those fateful places that undo us so, into those cracks between the worlds where new life emerges. The call into chaos and into love is the call into that place where spirit and matter seek expression through us, and unite and dissolve into an ungraspable mystery, allowing us to approach more intimately the wholeness of ourselves and things.

Most of the ancient Mystery traditions involved an initiation or preparation for the embodied soul to be able to withstand, or suffer, a cosmological disclosure, and to witness a divine revelation. Today we might speak of this as an experience of the Self, an experience of the ego's relation to its eternal source, the archetypal experience of the *fenestra aeternitatis*, the window onto eternity that simultaneously allows the divine into time-bound reality. In such experiences, often imaged as an unspeakable secret inviting, even demanding, silence, the human being seems to participate in, and be transformed by the same kind of cosmogonic love that holds the universe together—the planets in their orbits and the stars in their constellations. In such experiences, humankind is resituated within the larger fabric of creation that embraces and contains the individual as a part. In such experiences, so-called psychological projections are dissolved, and the soul is liberated into a cosmology of relations fulfilling the divine destiny to unite once again the unknowable mysteries of spirit and matter as different faces of a transpersonal whole.

Could it be that the chaos of our world, losing its way in breakdowns on all levels from the personal to the political, from the cultural to the geophysical, signals that moment of deadly peril where collective consciousness seeks its own destruction and dissolution, in order to birth a relation to this complex Mystery, a connection that we can only approach, that we can only forge, with an attitude born of a willingness to suffer, and of a love that can only emerge from our grief?

Love is a high achievement. Rilke (1954) writes of love "being difficult . . . the work for which all other work is but preparation" (p. 54). And the poet, H. D. (1988) similarly says, "yet to sing love, love must first shatter us" (p. 33).* The central claim of Robert Romanyshyn's (1999) recent book, *The Soul in Grief: Love, Death, and Transformation*, is that we grieve because we have dared to love, and by grace we can love again because we have allowed ourselves the time to grieve. The author Isabel Allende (1994), in her wrenching account of her daughter Paula's death, recorded within the context of her own (Isabel's) stirring life story—a piece of writing in which she sought to keep her sanity during the long days and nights of Paula's slow and silent withdrawal behind the veil—writes:

> Perhaps we are in this world to search for love, find it and lose it, again and again. With each love, we are born anew, and with each love that ends we collect a new wound. I am covered with proud scars (p. 314).

---

* From "Eros, Section 7" by H. D. Doolittle, from *Selected Poems*, copyright © 1957 by Hilda Doolittle. Reprinted by permission of New Directions Publishing Co.

In the same way that the heavenly bodies of star and planet and swirling, unformed, chaotic gases find their home within the vast reaches of the dark night of the cosmos, so too certain mythologies image Eros/Aphrodite as birthing out of the silver egg of unformed, dark chaos, or the Indian goddess Vak emerging out of the chaotic, dark, watery depths, with a golden jar of amrita in hand, singing creation into being from her heart. These stories impress upon us the union of the mighty primordial forces of chaos and eros, both in the natural and psychological terrains.

In the West, we have tended to emphasize chaos's relation with order, from the Genesis story through psychological fiction to contemporary theories of chaos in the physical sciences. In my work, I show that chaos can be viewed as guardian and intimate companion of divine and chthonic love, not the matrix out of which order is created. When we make order out of chaos, we kill eros as part of the divine creation, and annihilate our love affair with the world. Our contemporary ecological and environmental crises mirror in no small way the devastating effects of a heritage based on order, which perhaps is bound more with our power needs to control, and which ignores the soul's desire for the chaos of creativity and feeling.

The move from an order/power-based consciousness to a chaos/love-based awareness can also be seen as a move from a hierarchically ordered universe that excludes its unwanted shadows, to a soul-making cosmos based on mutual regard and participation. Archetypally, this shift can be imaged as a move away from what Jung (1959) describes as the archetype of the Hostile Brothers of the Christian Aeon, to the *coniunctio* depicted, for example, in the image of the mystical and reciprocal connection of the adept/soror, or brother/sister relationship of the alchemical traditions. Astrologically, the move is from the Age of Pisces to the Age of Aquarius. C. G. Jung (1975) speaks of an evolving consciousness that can endure opposites, and face its shadows, as the achievement of the Holy Spirit, meaning a "restitution of the original oneness of the unconscious on the level of consciousness" (p. 135).

It is both notable and grievous that chaos retained its connection with order, but lost its more vital relationship with love. Surely this is no accident. I suggest in this book that love is dangerous and so is chaos. Each evokes the image of the numinous Other, our highest spiritual longings, and our deepest earthly yearnings, and still more profoundly, the urge to unite these cosmic and human vibrations of spirit and matter within the cells and souls of our bodies. These realities of chaos/eros may even be missed completely because we tend to either disparage the idea, or we don't allow ourselves to long for the dark complexities that make up their realms. We reduce the body to biological drives and split off spirituality into ethereal realms. What is avoided in such a reductive splitting, perhaps out of an ancient terror, is the *tremendum* of the daimonic powers of sexuality, the numinosity of the chthonic realms, and the fundamental Otherness to the ego of these archetypal powers.

Yet if we continue to refuse to confront the dangers of Otherness, we perpetuate the split in consciousness that marks these times as hanging so precariously in the balance. Then the secrets demanding silence continue to come in the back door of our culture as violations of relationships and rapes of the soul, rather than as disclosures of the unapproachable and dark mysterious beauty of love.

It might be argued that there is danger in apparently dismissing and devaluing order. This is not my intention. When the landscape of order retains its cosmological connection, I have no trouble with its usage. In such usage, for example, we might speak of an apparent acausal orderedness underlying unpredictable synchronistic phenomena. Such orderedness unites psyche and matter in a numinous revelation of meaning that presents itself to us from quite beyond our conscious knowledge.

Or, we might speak of the Tao as a holistically ordered interconnectedness of all being, a state in which one's psychological disposition is in an acausal mirror symmetry with events in the outside world. Jung (1970) describes this as "bringing heaven and earth into harmony" (§604). Richard Wilhelm's famous Rainmaker story, often referred to by Jung, is an example. In this story, a Rainmaker in a Chinese village brought rain, not by any magic, but by taking on the disturbed and inharmonious conditions of the village. When he managed to recover his own harmony in meditation, "Naturally, the rain came."[1]

Another objection that might be raised concerns the relation of order and meaning. They are not, however, the same. Jung (1975, p. 494, and von Franz, 1974, p. 165) distinguishes them. For example, something could be constructed in an orderly arranged patterning, like a fly, but its meaningfulness in terms of the total context might be less apparent. The same might be said of my book. I am depending on at least a certain orderly presentation—a theme to be worked, chapters that discretely amplify different aspects of my central theme—to achieve a coherence that will allow it to be read. But how significant is my text? Does it mean anything? There could be a wide divergence of views about that. I myself am not precisely sure about its meaning. I am mostly wanting to explore a theme that stirs me profoundly, and to invite the reader to reflect on my theme, to participate in its textures and nuances, its images and range of affects, and to allow the words and language to evoke my topic as much as anything I might "say" about it. So in this respect, I might say that this piece of writing, this *essai* (attempt) has meaning for me. Whether I achieve that to any degree for others is quite another matter.

---

1. C. G. Jung, *Mysterium Coniunctionis* (Princeton: Princeton University Press, 1970b), §604, n. 211, pp. 419–420.

Although order and meaning are not equivalent, it remains true that Jung heavily emphasizes meaning. Meaning is his myth. He (1969a) writes, for example, "a psychoneurosis must be understood, ultimately, as the suffering of a soul which has not discovered its meaning" (§497). Jung, in fact, ascribes cosmological meaning to humankind's consciousness, in its purpose of reflecting the world. He says this gives humans a *raison d'être* of significant proportions, for without meaning—that he claims, arguably, only the human creature is capable of—the world dissolves in meaninglessness.

Now whether we agree with this point of view, or not, meaning, in this context, is not merely an abstraction. It is more of a contemplation, a reflection, a wonder-ing, like the word *theoria* in its original sense, endowing us with a cosmic purpose. In fact, Jung is implying here that consciousness is a second field of creation, comparable, if not equal, to God's. He (1975) writes in a letter:

> Nobody seems to have noticed that without a reflecting psyche the world might as well not exist, and that, in consequence, consciousness is a second world-creator, and also that the cosmogonic myths do not describe the absolute beginning of the world but rather the dawning of consciousness as the second Creation (p. 487).

Similarly, von Franz (1974) writes of the West African divinity, Fa, as the god who discloses the meaning of one's life to individuals one at a time (p. 267). Or we might describe Eros as the god who is behind the individuation process, in which the mystery and meaning, meaning-as-mystery, of one's life becomes increasingly apparent. We all know, too, accounts of spirit guides, etheric doubles, guardian angels, daimonic presences of one kind or another (richly described in antiquity) who enrich our lives and bring a numinous presence beyond the everyday, or into the everyday.

But like so much of our language, concepts such as order and meaning in patriarchal culture have dried up and lost their souls, and only retained their personas. Order too often smacks of an impersonal imposition in a negative sense, or a doctrinaire attitude without regard for the exigencies of an individual's life; or perhaps order masks itself as intellectualism divorced from the subtleties of spirit, or the passion of feeling.

In like manner, meaning can get blind overusage, especially in the field of psychology, and begin to break with the complexities of felt, bodily experience. It can become a construction of the ego's desire to appropriate the unconscious for its own ends, so that perhaps it can feel safe and on top and in control of feeling states, such as despair and meaninglessness. Hillman (1972), in lamenting what the scientific worldview has done to our words, writes: "This contemporary representative of the Enlightenment . . . would reduce language by stripping away all ambiguities, emotional undertones, and historical associations to make each word mean one thing and one thing only" (p. 210).

Early on in this century T. S. Eliot complained that too often we have the experience but miss the meaning. Today, I think, the obverse is closer to the truth: we have the meaning—pre-packaged in digestable bites as it were, so evidenced by all the how-to books in pop psychology and pop culture—and miss the experience. Where then is the chaos in the experience, and the eros?

It is such impoverished, one-sided usages that I am referring to when I wish to resituate chaos's relation with love, rather than with order. For our rationally ordered consciousness, invaluable at times, has not made us more wise or more connected with our feelings (in the sense of consciously achieved value judgments), and for all our ego attainments, substantial as they are, we stand on the brink of planetary annihilation, with a brokenness in the hearts and souls of many people.

CHAOS/EROS: LOVE AND ITS SHADOWS

Love is something, more than anything else, we all long for. The word "love" already evokes life's moist possibilities, compared with order's more deadly, dry presence. To love and be loved is arguably the only thing that most of us would rather not exit this life without knowing. In my experience as a therapist, most people come into therapy in search of love, no matter what the presenting problem. Fame, fortune, and even mediocrity may come and go, but love participates in the substance of the universe itself, and is eternal. Love ceases not. Once you have loved and been loved, it can never be taken away; not even at death, such is the imprint in the cells of our souls. Love is that eternal landscape that takes us beyond life, beyond death, even beyond rebirth.

Most near-death experiences (NDEs) reveal love to be one of the most exquisitely beautiful and deeply compelling worlds that comes forward to greet us, and toward which we travel in making that difficult transition. People commonly report about NDEs that they are generally asked two questions about their earthly experiences: What did you learn? And did you love? And the lives of most people who return from NDEs are transformed by the numinosity and deep mystery that lies at the heart of love's compassionate embrace. It is an ecstasy that often becomes a guiding influence in their vocational and personal lives.

Jung's (1961) own account of a near-death experience is impregnated with these mystical impressions. Although these experiences made it difficult for him to return to earthly life, which seemed suddenly gray and like a constricting box, compared with what awaits us on the other side, they also deepened his creative life. In fact, the reality of the visions that accompanied his illness initiated a fruitful period of work. It was as if the power of his transformational experiences freed him to follow the flow of his thoughts and most of his major works were written after this time (pp. 294–297).

So, this theme of love to which my book bears witness refers not only to what goes on between two people, but also to that cosmic force which fuels the individuation process and unites humankind with all creation. My hope is that in this work I am moving in that direction—which highlights eros's link with chaos and thus dislodges its connecton with order, and resituates love beyond the personal, as central as that is, into its larger archetypal and cosmic dimensions.

Why Eros?

There is often considerable confusion over the use of the word *love* (a fact that made me hesitate to employ the term at all, or at least to consider which term to use). This is partly due to our language: in English we have only one word for the vast range and complexity of experience that commonly comes under love's wing—a range that can move from inner needs, to the mastery of emotional states that achieves a relatedness to our affects, to the withdrawal of projections to reveal the mystery of the Other, to the revelation of a divine mystery that perhaps should not be spoken at all—love from a small "l" to a capital "L" as it were.

In Greek, by comparison, we find the classical image of the three modes of love: Eros, Philia, Agape, each focusing on a different facet of this broad terrain and covering a spectrum from sexual to spiritual love (though notably there are no mythologies surrounding Philia and Agape), each, no doubt, making its way at one time or another into the therapy relationship and into life.

Too, there are the various goddesses and gods from around the world who represent the different faces of love and who make their way for better or worse into our lives and into the therapy room. Simply speaking, we might say that Aphrodite is mostly associated with sensuous, sexual love, with that delicious pull toward undifferentiated union of lover and beloved; Hera with conjugal, jealous, or possessive love; Artemis with brotherly or sisterly love; and Quan Yin (or Kwannon) from the East, who is associated with merciful, divine compassion. Each of us knows, I'm sure, these different embodiments of love's complexity.

So why in this work do I speak of love via Eros? I do so for at least three reasons which are important for the vision of love that I am trying to present in this work.

In Hesiod's *Theogony* (where he first appears in ancient Greece), Eros is, after Chaos and Gaea (Earth), one of the three primordial divinities, whose activity and energy is universal and extends to all being. Eros here is an underlying force of creation. In this myth he is also brother to Night and Erebus, and thus is linked with the unconscious, with death, with journeys to the underworld and, inevitably, with love's shadows. As in Apuleius' tale *Psyche and Eros*, in which Psyche's last task is her journey to the underworld, we are reminded that the journey of love always involves what Christine Downing (1975) calls a "psychotics of eros" (p. 635). The original meaning of psychosis is: "I give life." It is those profound, chaotic disturbances of love—betrayal, abandonment, loss, and frustration—that bring renewed life, new depths of love, and often fuels our creativity.

In his Orphic origins, Eros is the creator god who not only sets the rest of the universe in motion, but also as Eros-Phanes ("light-bringer") has links to the creation of consciousness as revelation—an illumined visionary consciousness (rather than the logos of interpretation)—and to the instinctual realms in his theriomorphic forms that also connect him with Dionysus, God of wine, ecstatic experience, and women. So Eros in this guise holds the tension of sexual, instinctual love, and the spiritual forms of love.

In the West we have tended to separate sexual love from divine love, and human love from the transpersonal, an example of the spirit/matter dissociation that has increasingly characterized the Christian era. The love songs of the Troubadours in 12th-century France and later in other parts of Europe, following the gnostic traditions of the Sufi visionary poets, first attempted to address this separation in their valuing of love between individuals as the union of sexual and mystical love. However, their heretical attempts got lost and went underground when they were wiped out in the early 13th century. The continuing dissociation of matter and spirit—that lingers, for example, in Jungian thought in the often thoughtless dismissal of falling in love as a possession, an unconscious projection of the animus/anima complex—and its devastating consequences for modernity, is something I am attempting to address in this book. One story told by Socrates in *Plato's Symposium* suggests that Eros, here son of Penia (which means "need"), represents our desire for the recovery of this lost union or wholeness.

In addition, in the Orphic myth, Eros's dark origins and golden wings link him to Aphrodite, the golden one, who is his mother in some stories and who herself according to others, is born of the foamy waves of watery chaos. Here, Aphrodite is associated with undifferentiated love, while her son Eros represents a more differentiated form of love, even transformative love. This accompaniment of Aphrodite and Eros suggests that love is always flowing back and forth between union and separation, between proximity and distance, between chaos and generation. The fable attributed to Aristophanes in the *Symposium* draws attention to this aspect of love's nature. Originally, human beings were ovoid-shaped doubles who became severed in two by Zeus as a punishment when they revolted against the gods. The result is that humans, with a persistence born of starvation for the lost Other, are forever dying to find their complement. The separation, however, allows for intermittent sexual contact and the pursuit of other important activities, which makes the loss of the original separation bearable even while we continue in our search to heal what has been sundered.

Here, Eros is the only god who allows us, up to a point, to recover our original identity and nature: reunion with our other half (the search for wholeness); reunion with our lost love (the desire for a soul-mate); and reunion with the gods and goddesses (the search for the recovery of the sacred). Embedded within the story is the implication that the desire for reunion is one that allows space and healthy distance, a differentiation of love necessary for every kind of relationship that we embody.

These tales and their various nuances and imaginings present eros in three guises. First, eros is the love that binds together the fabric of the universe, the *fons et origo* of the rhythm of all created being, and covers a range from heaven to hell. Second, eros is the force of love that binds spirit and instinct, the illumination of consciousness infused with love, and the dark, animal, earthy passions of love. And third, eros is a form of differentiated love where the merging of two lovers is balanced by a relation between the lover and the beloved. Because I am deliberately wanting to give the widest possible landscape for love, Eros is the figure whom I choose to symbolize love.

Love is a paradox and evokes all our shadows. The claim in this book is that it is just this great undoing, this peculiar darkened illumination, that is part of love's great gift to us. It is perhaps in this sense that Jung (1961) speaks of eros as the divine origin of all higher consciousness (p. 353). This higher consciousness is one that values the divine spark in nature and the material world as well as the world of spirit. This gnosis is what Jung recovered from his researches into alchemy, and found again in synchronicity; that is, that intermediate, subtle world of the imaginal, the psychically real, where eros and his dark partner chaos roam.

WHY MYTH?

In using myth to act as the container for my central theme and its different facets—by no means exhausted by the chapters in my study—the (usually) unexamined assumption first proposed by Jung that the psyche is constructed in pairs of opposites is being challenged. This binary code in Jung is perhaps most familiar to people in Jung's theory of typology. If, for example, thinking is a person's dominant orientation in consciousness, then feeling is inferior, that is, less developed, and emerges in a more primitive way via the unconscious. Of course, these types are not always so neatly arranged in actual people, but in general the pairings are upheld.

In my book, the linking of chaos and eros is not intended as a pairing of opposites. Rather, chaos/eros is a way of opening up a broad archetypal field best imagined through the ambiguity of myth, rather than the clarity of paired concepts or images. Mythological images seem to hold a greater complexity, variety, and richly textured patterning of life than the usual antithetical pairings hold—birth/death, spirit/matter, light/dark, king/queen. Perhaps myth fills in the space or the range between these too easily described dichotomies. For example, in surveying the stories surrounding Aphrodite, we see how many origins she has, and the many characters with whom she has been connected. Such an array of connections makes it neither simple, nor desirable really, to create neatly ordered pairs. Perhaps pairings gratify the ego's desire for structure, order, and clarity. Although there is nothing wrong with such an orderly presentation of reality, bodily felt experience is usually as wide-ranging, as far-flung, as complex and subtle, as are the multiplicity of Aphrodite's connections. It is this kind of richness of experience that I wish to evoke and describe in my study.

Jung himself was ambivalent about, or at least aware of the limitations of, his view of the psyche as structured in pairs. This ambivalence is seen, for example, in his own description of the Self as both the *complexio oppositorum,* and the Self as the totality of psyche, conscious and unconscious; even that psyche and world are one. Perhaps Jung (1961) was thinking of this when, in the second paragraph of the Prologue to his *Memories,* he writes of myth as being more individual and expressing life more precisely than science. Science tends toward statistical and empirical generalities that do not reflect the quirky details and complex vicissitudes of an individual life (p. 3). Maybe it is a scientific mind that structures in pairs. Maybe it is a scientific mind that structures at all.

Another good example where Jung calls the oppositional nature of psyche—so appealing to the discriminating function of ego-consciousness—into question is provided in his discussion of the fantasy figures, Salome and Elijah. Jung (1961) first suggests that those figures are personifications of

Logos and Eros, but then immediately corrects his definition as excessively intellectual. Rather, he writes, Salome and Elijah comprise events and experiences, living figures in the land of psyche (p. 182). Jung here seems to be saying that although the mind wants to create intellectual abstractions that make sense—and even to box events into neat categories—our experience is always larger than that, and cannot be so neatly confined. Eros himself is always eluding us, hiding somewhere in the dark behind our most enlightened views. He is the breaker of dichotomies and barriers, par excellence! Perhaps in our lives we are always ahead of our theories.

The point Jung is making concerns the radical limitations of all our intellectual theories in the face of the fullness of experience. The full richness and ambiguity of experience seems to demand more than a dichotomous way of thinking. It seems to require the full richness and ambiguity of mythical ways of thinking. Moreover, the kinds of experiences which are ontologically amibiguous, like the one that begins this book, would also seem to demand a way of thinking which is less rigid than the binary oppositions of either/or. Indeed the psychoid nature of the archetype, experiences of synchronicity, Jung's interest in UFOs, and the whole realm of the *mundus imaginalis,* the imaginal, lend themselves more readily to the fluid, spontaneous, associative, and non-fixed character of mythical forms of thinking. Such experiences, Jung writes, are "nothing but a tremendous intuition striving for expression" (1966b §151).

Jung's encounter with Philemon provides such an example. In describing his soul companion and guide, Philemon, Jung almost suggests that although this figure first appeared in a dream, he was this other character existing quite separately from him. Jung (1961) writes:

> He was a mysterious figure to me. At times he seemed to me quite real, as if he were a living personality. I went walking up and down the garden with him, and to me he was what the Indians call a guru (p. 183).

Jung strongly indicates that Philemon inhabits a separate ontological ground than either Jung or a dream figure does. In fact, this impression is strengthened when in conversation several years later, Jung asks a cultivated Indian visitor about his own guru. The Indian, somewhat matter-of-factly, tells him that his guru is the spirit of an eminent scholar of the Vedas who died centuries ago, adding that there are ghostly, as well as living gurus. Jung (1961) writes that he thought immediately of Philemon (p. 184).[2] In other words, Philemon was not just a dream figure; he had a spiritual presence that nevertheless seemed quite real—so real in fact that he walked up and down the garden with Jung in conversation.

It seems clear that in this encounter Philemon is neither a projected psychic experience nor a material external fact. This binary way of thinking, which is at the root of Jung's notion of the psyche as paired in opposites, is undone by the presence of a figure like Philemon. Actually Jung's work is punctuated by openness to such experiences. For example, his comments about UFOs imply a realm of subtle bodies which are neither exactly psychic projections nor material facts; on the other hand, they might be both.[3] This is an ontologically ambiguous realm, the *mundus imaginalis*, which Jung also hinted at as the realm of alchemy. In *Psychology and Alchemy* (1968), he writes:

---

2. See also, C. G. Jung, *Letters I* (Princeton: Princeton University Press, 1973), p. 491. In a letter dated 30 January 1948 to Father Victor White about a dream, Jung writes: "While I stood before the bed of the Old Man, I thought and felt: *Indignus sum Domine* ["I am not worthy, Lord"]. I know Him very well: He [that is, Philemon] was my "guru" more that 30 years ago, a real ghostly guru—but that is a long and—I am afraid—exceedingly strange story. It has been since confirmed to me by an old Hindu."

3. C. G. Jung, "Flying Saucers: A Modern Myth of Things Seen in the Skies," in CW 10 (Princeton: Princeton University Press, 1970a), §589–824. See also, C. G. Jung, *Letters II* (Princeton: Princeton University Press, 1975), p. 3, where Jung speculates that if UFOs are both a psychic projection and have real materiality, then they would be an example of synchronicity.

> But, just because of this intermingling of the physical and
> the psychic, it always remains an obscure point whether the
> ultimate transformations in the alchemical process are to be
> sought more in the material or more in the spiritual realm.
> Actually, however, the question is wrongly put; there was
> no "either-or" for that age, but there did exist an interme-
> diate realm between mind and matter, i.e., a psychic realm
> of subtle bodies whose characteristic it is to manifest them-
> selves in a mental as well as a material form (§394) .

These still largely implicit observations of Jung's need to be
drawn out more explicitly by others. This work is perhaps
beginning to be done.

M.-L. von Franz (1980a) in writing about what we now
call imaginal or psychic reality, always keeps an open mind
about the nature of so-called projected contents and their
ontological status. She greets our achievements in consciousness—specifically the symbolic nature of so-called objective
psychic reality—with a most dubious attitude because it
tends to make us so wooden, and no longer very instinctual
or connected to the whole of life. Simultaneously, she warns
that we should always be most cautious when speaking of
projection, that is, presumably, when we are speaking of the
precise nature of these imaginal realities. The implications of
her argument, too, need to be further drawn out. But this is
probably why she calls for depth psychologists and physicists to work together, and why she feels so urgently that the
phenomenon of synchronicity must continue to be explored.
In other words, could it be that the psyche/matter relation is
calling us to go beyond what depth psychology has so far
achieved or documented?

Romanyshyn (2000a) too, has begun to draw out the
implications for our thinking of these imaginal realities. At
the end of his essay, "Alchemy and the Subtle Body of
Metaphor," he tells a story of bilocation, suggesting that the
ontological status of imaginal figures needs to be addressed
by what he calls neither/nor ways of thinking. In "Angels
and Other Anomalies of the Imaginal Life," Romanyshyn
(2000b) argues that the presence of angels and the golden

dome of heaven in medieval paintings have an ontological validity that undercuts our ways of thinking in terms of facts or concepts.

Has depth psychology, in its attempts to make itself acceptable to a prevailing scientific worldview, been so seduced by the inertia of collective forces that it has participated in castrating those subtle levels of being, like angels, and Philemon, and even striking examples of other worlds trying to intersect our own, such as crop circle phenomona and UFOs? Are realities that defy our categories of the empirical or psychological essentially annihilated? Do psychologists not really believe that there might be inhabitants of parallel universes that share our earthly space, or do they believe and yet only quietly whisper among themselves about it? It is perhaps no accident that, as branches of psychology march confidently in the direction of managed care, that is, psychology without its soul—that the angels, the Philemons, and the appearance of UFOs make their exacting, not to mention disturbing, claim upon us. The marginalized and chaotic underbelly of our prevailing worldview begins its inexorable unraveling of our most cherished achievements. We have hardly begun to acknowledge this challenge.

All these considerations and questions belong here because I wish to emphasize my fundamental claim that chaos linked with love inspires landscapes of experience that more fully embrace the range, depth, and nuance of our experience than consciousness ordered in pairs tends to suggest. Chaos linked with love evokes an expansive mythological landscape, one more conducive to the totality of experience, while it also allows room for an ontological realm or realms, neither precisely psychological nor exactly physical, that tends to get marginalized as much in our psychologies as in our collective empirical attitudes.

In our psychologies, as much as in our lives today, we need—no, we are called—continually to surrender our all-too-easy, and all-too-limited, theories of reality to explore the complex vision of the multidimensional, and multivibrational, nature of the whole. We must constantly be alerted to the rational, causal, scientific perspective that, in spite of all the different kinds of evidence to the contrary that has emerged in the last century, still so informs the structure of our consciousness, and our ways of being, thinking, and living. As long as we can retain an awareness that such a perspective is only one among many, particularly in view of the new claims being made upon us, then a space opens up for us to be open to what calls.

Chapter 2

CHAOS AND EROS
The Mysteries and Shadows of Love

"In a love relation, as Jung once put it,
you risk everything."
—M.-L. von Franz

"Yet to sing love,
love must first shatter us."
—H. D. (1988), p. 33*

Jung's life unfolded itself between two dramatic and deeply profound experiences that he (1961) records in *Memories, Dreams, Reflections*. The first is the earliest childhood dream that he could remember (when he was 3 or 4), the dream of a numinous, underground phallus, erect and sitting on a golden throne. This dream, Jung says, occupied him all his life (p. 11ff). The second experience is a beautiful prayer to the god Eros, recorded as part of his "Late Thoughts," just before the closure of his physical and earthly life (pp. 353–354). In this context, Jung celebrates Eros as that god whose divinity transcends human limits, and who personifies that broad realm of experience in which rational understanding finds scarcely anything it is able to grasp (p. 353).

The early dream situates the "not to be named" phallic, subterranean deity as a god of nature, related to the underworld and to the recovery of the mysteries of the earth. This dark counterpart to the prevailing Christian atmosphere above ground held in its darkly lit aura the source of Jung's creative genius, and as von Franz (1975) notes, symbolized his "unusually large capacity for love, which both enlivened and burdened his existence" (p. 19). This phallic vitality recalls Eros as a primordial deity (along with Chaos and Gaea in Hesiod's *Theogony*), a god whose energy extends to all being, and who lies in the depths of the psyche with an instinctual gnosis, a vast vision, waiting to re-emerge into life.[1]

Jung's later reverie celebrates the earlier "not to be named," now called Eros, as a cosmic creator God of Love, "the father-mother of all higher consciousness," and as that deity, "whose range of activity extends from the endless spaces of the heavens to the dark abysses of hell" (Jung, 1961, pp. 353–354). Here we are reminded of Eros in the Orphic myth, as that illumined consciousness that is never far from its dark origins in instinctual chaos.

These two accounts picture for us the blueprint of Jung's fate, and its unfolding in his lived, blood and flesh, life, a destiny that was fed like an underground stream by a devotion to the "incalculable paradoxes of love," its mysteries and its shadows. In fact, Jung writes of his initial dream: "Who brought the Above and Below together, and laid the foundation for everything that was to fill the second half of my life with stormiest passion? Who but that alien guest who came both from above and from below?" (p. 15).

---

1. C. G. Jung, *Memories, Dreams, Reflections* (New York: Vintage, 1961), p. 13, where Jung points out that the "eye" of the phallus, with the light above it, points to the etymology of the word *phallus*, which in Greek means "shining," or "bright." Please see my reflections on the *lumen naturae* in chapter 6, which is also relevant in this context.

Everything points to this alien guest,[2] who links the highest with the lowest, who refuses to separate the spiritual from the instinctual, and who is present in our visions and in our passions, as that marginalized figure of eros, love, love joined with its shadows. I suggest that this divine figure is now gathering its creative and destructive forces, seeking entryways into our lives, initiating us to a recovery of a lost and forgotten wholeness, and to a healing of all that divides and ails us.

Love is a mystery, a cosmic force, a divine ray that permeates the universe. Love is the quintessential archetype of the Self, an incalculable paradox, "sweetly bitter," as Sappho (in Balmer, 1984), that daring devotee of Aphrodite, writing some six hundred years B.C., describes the awesome force that visits from beyond, making us tremble and yearn (p. 30). Love both transcends human consciousness and yet is that God-factor that is the *sine qua non* of consciousness itself, the essence upon which all life, subtle and manifest, depends, whether we know it or not.

In the human realm, we are perhaps more familiar with love's pain, the failure of love, and its impossibility. Indeed, the consulting room of modern psychotherapy is full of the complaints and woundings linked to love's disappointments, abandonments, and rejections. Whole schools of psychotherapy are based on such failures of love, in one guise or another: incest problems; love made hungry; inadequate mirroring or idealizing; envy.[3] These shadows of love are what we expect to confront in the consulting room. This is the dark *prima materia* into whose black soil the seed of the *lapis*, the

---

2. C. G. Jung, *Letters II* (Princeton: Princeton University Press, 1975), p. 590, and note 6. Jung employs the image of the "guest" again here. (See opening quote at the beginning of chapter 1). The note suggests that the "awe-inspiring guest" might refer to this phallic deity from Jung's earliest dream.

3. These terms are popularly known to be related to the works of Freud, Fairbairn (in Guntrip, 1969), Kohut (1984), and Klein (1975), respectively.

Philosopher's Stone, is invisibly sown. Work on the parental complexes and personal shadow material is meant to clear the way toward healthy self-regard, adult sexuality, and the capacity for a differentiated relationship and meaningful work, the implicit if not stated goals of most treatment. Freud says we learn to love so that we won't fall ill. W. R. D. Fairbairn explicitly states that humankind's search for a love relationship is the fundamental thing in life. M.-L. von Franz tells us that the famous physicist, Wolfgang Pauli, died a premature death from cancer because of his inability to surrender into love's embrace.

Yet most schools of psychoanalytic psychology continue to restrict themselves to the cure of symptoms within a personalistic frame. In this way, such schools render an invaluable service to the child in the adult, in terms of healing early woundings, re-experiencing aborted transferences, and integrating split-off aspects of the personality, thereby allowing for the possibility of an authentic maturational process.

It was clearly Jung's view, however, that psychotherapy, in providing a container for the regressive movement of psychic energy, also allowed for the deep immersion of the conscious ego—beyond its personal history—in the waters of the collective unconscious, which would allow for the rebirth of the personality. For Jung, the whole analytic process was not so much about curing symptoms and enabling adaptation, but rather about discovering through one's pain a link to the infinite, a resituation of one's personal life within its sacred ground. This sacred ground is, as Jung (1961) writes, that "broader area," the "more unknown" (pp. 353–354), the field of cosmogonic love.

And what is it that so often happens in therapy, no matter what you *think* you are there for? An erotically charged transference develops, most likely in the void produced by an undeveloped capacity for relationship, and a simultaneous longing for such soul-to-soul union, for that which has not yet been experienced. But maybe it is erroneous to speak of such causes; perhaps the large field of love looks for any excuse to constellate itself, and what better opening than the intimate sharing of story and soul between two people.

It is perhaps notable that the rise of psychotherapy coincides, historically, with Nietsche's famous claim that God is dead. The God of love, not finding hospitable reception within the domain of Christianity, began looking for more favorable venues. Hillman (1972) writes:

> When we look back upon the past seventy years, or back yet further to the women in the hospitals of Paris and Nancy, we can see the psyche going to therapy in search of eros. We have been looking for love for the soul. That is the myth of analysis (pp. 296–297).

In fact, there is such a great longing in the human soul for a true meeting with another, a meeting in which one knows the other, and one is known by the other, that the transference, and perhaps even the emergence of psychotherapy itself during the past century, could be the search for this kind of mutual revelation, so grievously lacking for many in our time.

On a darker note, of the unethical behaviors between therapist and patient, the literal sexual acting out of the transference is reported to be the most common abuse, an abuse of eros, who perhaps comes in the back door, when the daimonic dimension of love's numen is too poorly appreciated and we become possessed by its power shadow. Or is it that such transgressions also signal a deeper cultural disturbance at the heart of our world? That our neat and all too complacent personalistic, and even archetypal, psychological theories are helpless to address such an issue? The suppression of transpersonal love in the human sphere, and our inability to embody love, either individually or collectively, may lie behind its abuses. It may be that as Hillman (1972) observes, "No approach to the transference mysteries has as yet been adequate" (p. 59). Similarly, two thousand years of Christianity have not exactly made us better lovers!

Actually, as the poet Rilke (1954) reminds us, love is a high achievement, belonging to maturity:

To love is good, too: love being difficult. For one human to
love another: that is perhaps the most difficult of all our
tasks . . . the work for which all other work is but preparation. For this reason young people, who are beginners in
everything, cannot yet know love: they have to learn it. . . .
But learning-time is always a long, secluded time, and so
loving, for a long while ahead and far on into life, is—solitude, intensified and deepened loneness for him who loves.
Love is . . . a high inducement to the individual to ripen, to
become something in himself, to become world, to become
world for himself for another's sake, it is a great exacting
claim upon him, something that chooses him out and calls
him to vast things (pp. 53–54).

Differentiation of self is a prerequisite for relationship, and
this sort of refinement of self often requires lengthy periods
of solitude, working the *prima materia* of one's own soul. As
Lockhart (1987) writes: "The psyche always pushes for
uniqueness because it is only in bringing uniqueness in relation to other unique natures that relationship is possible at
all" (p. 31). But Rilke goes beyond this, suggesting that love
is a vocation that calls us out into the service of life. The
ripening of character that emerges from solitude is not for its
own sake, but for the world's. We are called, not only to be in
relationship with each other, but to celebrate the world as creative individuals, each in our own way. This is a claim made
upon us as humans, that which differentiates us from the
angel and the animal, as Rilke writes elsewhere, and the
implication is that we are ethically bound to respond.

Rilke's attitude seems well suited to approach the vastness of love that Jung writes about in his autobiography.
Jung's psychology is a psychology of the Self, that is, a psychology that devotes itself to the symbolic and mythic
images, affective representations, and patterns of behavior
associated with the faces of the divine, in their many archetypal manifestations. In the realm of psychotherapy, the focus
of attention is traditionally on how these Self images reveal
themselves in the specific life, dreams, and fantasies of an
individual person. The Self, though, cannot be reduced to

psychology, or the practice of psychotherapy, because as Jung (1961) describes, its "range of activity extends from the endless spaces of the heavens to the dark abysses of hell" (p. 353). Perhaps Jung's reluctance to create institutes, except as research facilities, lay in a real fear of dogmatizing psyche into a system, or reducing the Self into a therapy procedure, much as has already happened—invaluable as the therapy procedure can be.

I wonder, too, if perhaps psychology has overburdened the human realm, especially with its prejudice of the soul as residing within, and that until we find our way back out of our therapy cells into relationship with each other, and especially into union with the world, to find again our place as microcosm to macrocosm, such as in ancient times, we will continue to perpetuate a hubris whose dark shadow is the destruction with which we are all too familiar in modern times. The psyche is simply too large just for us!

The love in the transference relationship is often experienced as arising out of a field much larger than the two mere mortals who must endure the onslaught. It is Jung and his colleague Marie-Louise von Franz who have most contributed to our understanding of the archetypal, transpersonal and transpsychic dimensions of this cosmic mystery. Hence their researches into the complex language of alchemy. In Jung's (1966a) essay, "The Psychology of the Transference" (§353–539) he writes of the many transformations of love in the analytic process, using the rich and paradoxical imagery of the secrets of alchemy, as if our preoccupation with love, or perhaps we should say more accurately, love's preoccupation with us, lies disturbingly at the very heart and depth of earthly life.

The therapy process can become the soulscape for an awareness of love and its dark shadows, its vicissitudes from instinct to spirit and back, and for the differentiation of feeling to be embodied and made present in the human sphere. Perhaps this is what Jung (1961) means when he writes in his hymn to Eros that we are both "the victims and instruments of cosmogonic love" (p. 354), and, like Job, if we respond to the invitation to suffer the numinous affects and images of love and its woundings, we too, may be offered a glimpse of its divine face, and be graced with its power to transform the cells of our souls. This kind of transformation inevitably leads us back into the River of Life. As von Franz (1980b) writes: "If we could see through all our projections down to the last traces, our personality would be extended to cosmic dimensions" (p. 14). The implication is that refinement of consciousness through love leads us out of a world divided, leads us out of psychology itself, into a cosmic synchronistic field where the mysteries of psyche and matter, Self and Cosmos, are beheld as One. Nevertheless, such *coniunctio* or unitive experiences often first dissolve into painful chaotic states as an old order begins to break up and pass away.

Chaos and the Primacy of Order

Chaos is usually linked in the Western mind with order, or cosmos—which supercedes it—rather than with eros. In the dictionary, for example, chaos is defined as disorder as opposed to the orderly, harmonious whole of the universe. Or, in contemporary culture, chaos theory tends to delineate two major fields within itself. Hayles (1990) points out two groups in her *Chaos Bound*—the "order-out-of-chaos" group, and the "hidden-order-within-chaos" group (p. 9). Here order is not only linked with chaos but is also superior to it.

The Jungian analyst Van Eenwyk (1997), who has elaborated the correspondences between Jung's theories (especially in relation to the symbol) and chaos research in his book *Archetypes and Strange Attractors*, has also primarily preserved chaos's relation with order. Though at various places in his text he points to the essential component of relationship, eros, and the determining influence of conscious co-operation with the psyche, and though he beautifully lays out the value of chaos in psychological life as essential for growth and the release of new potentials, he nevertheless maintains culture's bias toward linking chaos with order. He writes: "Could it be that by submitting to the chaos of the unconscious it can become deterministic, progressing from order through chaos to higher levels of order?" (p. 100). And in the dedication of his text he again betrays his unexamined assumption that links chaos with order: "For Leah and Claire, living proof that order emerges from chaos"!

In the practice of psychotherapy, too, chaos and order remain companioned, with order taking precedence, and with understanding, interpretation, and meaning employed defensively at the expense of experiencing with the patient empty and dissociative chaotic states. As Schwartz-Salant (1993) writes, here critiquing Jung and the practice of Jungian psychology: "the overall spirit of [Jung's] psychology is that knowledge exists which can put order into chaos" (p. 1). He adds that although states of absence and the void are acknowledged by Jung—for example, picture seven, the "Ascent of the Soul," in the *Rosarium Philosophorum* (p. 2)—Jung, in discussing this alchemical text, too quickly fills in such deep levels of *nigredo* with knowledge *about* such states. Schwartz-Salant suggests that most Jungians are trained to treat Jung's *nekyia* as their own, as if their job is to continue refining his *prima materia*, rather than plunging into such depths of chaos and despair themselves. By contrast, Schwartz-Salant proposes that a sane person's mad or psychotic parts are "like the chaotic waters of mythology," and he adds "they are always crucial to change and regeneration" (p. 3).

Hillman (1972) also acknowledges that the Apollonic voice of reason and order that rules depth psychology's practice will have none of chaos, "those dark nights and confusions which are its nest" (p. 99). But, he notes, by refusing chaos, we are in danger of losing eros, too. Eros "renews itself in affective attacks, jealousies, fulminations, and turmoils. It thrives close to the dragon" (p. 99).

I wonder, too, if there is not something deadening about this order—especially when it is reduced to a constipated, one concept, one-word-only approach—as opposed to chaos—and whether it reflects more our cultural bias spanning the past four hundred years, of control over the inanimate world by an all-powerful ego and a rational consciousness separated and distanced from both the larger cosmic fabric and the deeper levels of psyche, of which we are in fact an intimate thread. Marie-Louise von Franz (1972) writes:

> The God who fashions the world as a dead object is mostly found in civilizations which have a rather developed technical aspect . . . in which consciousness has already . . . developed as an independent power apart from the unconscious . . . (and) the Godhead is no longer immanent in the material world (p. 90).

She adds: "This process has reached its highest form in our civilization" (p. 92).

M.-L. von Franz (1972) relates a story called "The Death of Chaos-Unconscious" (pp. 92–93) from a Chinese philosopher, in which two characters, Heedless and Hasty, want to be kind and shape Chaos into a beautiful, conscious being, but in so doing kill him. In this tale, the molding of chaos into consciousness and order kills and destroys an essential aspect of creation. This story highlights the questionableness of human consciousness, which we can certainly appreciate as we hover precariously on the edge of extinction, with environmental crises, terrorist attacks, and uncontrollable and untreatable diseases, not to mention our personal and interpersonal limitations via our ignorance of potent psychological and cosmic forces. All this, with the acceleration of knowledge over the past several hundred years.

CHAOS AND CREATION

The castration and devaluation of the forces of chaos and its linking with order in the West does not occur in the non-rational, non-scientific mind. In its linguistic roots and in its mythic origins, chaos is a much more pregnant landscape, intimately joined with the whole process and unfolding of creation. In its Indo-European root origins, the word *chaos* has to do with the image of a yawning, gaping chasm—an openness, a possibility, or alternatively, a black hole of the soul. Chaos, as undifferentiated *massa confusa*, is usually that reality out of which a new form or organization is seen to arise, or more accurately, is crafted. So, in many myths, chaos as the formless void, or its many richly imaged variants, such as darkness, initial waters, or inertia, is the primordial substance that precedes the creation of the world by the God, or Goddess, and is the gaping void to which all destroyed worlds return.

> In the beginning God created the heavens and earth. The earth was without form and void, and darkness was upon the face of the deep; and the Spirit of God was moving over the face of the waters. And God said, "Let there be light"; and there was light.[4]

Or, similarly, in Egyptian mythology, from Hermopolis, city of Hermes (Thoth) Master of Writing, Numbers, Measurement, and Time, comes the description of the Nun, the primordial environment. Lucie Lamy (1981) envisages this as:

> a swampy mire, containing four couples of serpents and frogs. Their names are Naun and Naunet, meaning both "the initial waters" and "inertia," Heh and Hehet, meaning "spatial infinity"; Kek and Keket, "the darkness"; and Amun and Amunet, "That which is hidden." The latter couple is sometimes replaced by Niau and Niaut, "the void" (p. 10).

This primal chaos is the dark, substantial, eternal, and infinite source of the Universe. Out of these watery inert depths comes the lotus, in the center of which is the child Re, or Ra, the principle of light itself. Re says of himself, "I am he who opens his eyes, thus the light comes forth. I am he who closes his eyes, thus comes forth obscurity" (Lamy, 1981, p. 11).

---

4. Revised Standard Version of the Bible.

Chaos in these mythologies is intimately bound with the origin and telos of creation, and cannot merely be reduced to one-dimensional concepts such as disorder, disarray, confusion, even meaninglessness, as in our popular imagination.

Nevertheless, these creation stories image the emergence of light out of the dark void, and remain uncomfortably close to the notion of the rising of an orderly consciousness separated from its shadows in chaotic potential.

But there are other creation stories that link chaos and eros, a coupling that we are perhaps less familiar with, and yet one that is closer to the complexities of love and its shadows which is the central theme of my book. I wish to present two of these creation myths—the Orphic tale, and an Indian myth of the goddess Vak—that beautifully and poignantly portray how chaos is the dark void that gives birth to eros. What deep gnosis connects life at its most abundant moments, those erotic wonders, with chaos, the void, life at perhaps its most devastating?

The Orphic Creation Myth

This story, recounted in Graves (1960) *Greek Myths* vol. I (and to which we have already referred in chapter 1) unfolds as follows:

> Black-winged night, a goddess of whom even Zeus stands in awe, was courted by the Wind and laid a silver egg in the womb of darkness; and Eros whom some call Phanes was hatched from this egg and set the Universe in motion. Eros was double-sexed and golden winged and, having four heads, sometimes roared like a bull or a lion, sometimes hissed like a serpent or bleated like a ram (p. 30).

This myth suggests an intimate and mysterious connection between chaos—here imaged as the "womb of darkness"— and eros as the two great primordial forces of the cosmos (one that N. Katherine Hayles [1990] notes in her book, *Chaos Bound*, p. 19, but sadly does not pursue).

Eros as the "golden-winged" also suggests his birth from Aphrodite, the "golden one," who, as Graves points out, is the same wide ruling goddess "who rose from Chaos and danced on the sea" (p. 49). Aphrodite is the one who according to the *Homeric Hymns* (1970) is accompanied by "bright-eyed lions, bears, and quick insatiable panthers" (p. 79), the one who stirs amritic longing in the loins of men, animals, and women. Here chaos is the intimate companion of divine and chthonic love.

In the rich, instinctual imagery of this story we feel viscerally the dangerous links between chaos and eros. We understand all too easily our patriarchal shrinking from such awesome powers. Love does not arise out of light, out of consciousness. It bypasses these safer grounds. Love is an earthquake of the soul that precedes our frail attempts at order, always threatening to destroy our illusions of control, always reminding us that we are the created, not the creator. Eros is born of black night, a dark-winged goddess for whom only nature's force, Wind, is a worthy lover. The forces of chaos and eros arise from transpsychic, transhuman realms, linking dark instinct and creative vision in a *tremendum* that we must try, and try again when we fail, to recognize as Other from us.

The nuance of this terror is already enfolded within the symbols of the myth. Our story links Eros with the theriomorphic forms of bull or lion, serpent, and ram. Of these, as Whitmont (1992) observes, the bull, serpent, and ram are among the animals associated with the god Dionysus (p. 6). The Orphic mysteries themselves were concerned with the essential expressions of the Dionysian. Indeed, the founder of these mysteries was considered to be the mythic figure of Orpheus, the human incarnation of Dionysus, who "with his lute, made trees and the mountain tops that freeze, bow themselves when he did play." Dionysus is known as the mad god, the god who dies and is ever reborn. Patron of music, drama, and intoxication, his rites abounded in wild ecstasy and dark terror, emotional excess and violent abandonment. These cathartic rituals and ceremonies were aimed at transforming mankind's bestial violence and needy sexual desirousness into harmonious and socially acceptable ways. Those who refused devotion to Dionysus' chthonic realms were torn to pieces like Pentheus of Thebes, or otherwise met with terrible and terrifying deaths.

In the name of order and rationality, our culture tends to repress and designate as evil these uncontrolled and chaotic realms of Dionysus, thus endangering our environment with expressions of hate and hostility, the numbing conventions of the status quo, and an incapacity to love. Our myth antici- pates patriarchal terror of the dark unknown when it admits that "even Zeus stands in awe" of the goddess Night, or, we might add, of the terrors of *nigredo,* or the unravelings of the night-sea-journey. The patriarchal ego prefers orderly progress and a predictable solar consciousness, an Apollo- nian understanding that can repress our instinctual excesses that signal a buried vitality that refuses to be silenced.

It must not be forgotten either, that Dionysus was prima- rily a god of women, and his rites were primarily women's rites. Our myth reconnects us to the lost Goddess and her Dionysian consort. In our Western tradition, chaos has played the role of the Other, and has often been depicted as female, and has even been connected specifically with women's experience. Chaos, as a system of nonlinear dynam- ics, draws our attention to this mostly marginalized feminine, especially in its cyclical, sensual, erotic, dark, rhythmic, and transformational dimensions. Such dynamics are eclipsed in the patriarchal ego's attachment to reasonable, linear, unchanging ideals that delude us into thinking that we are protected from the overpowering and unpredictable—other- wise known as Life.

If we could tend to the instinctual domains of desire and aggression with the devotion and awareness accorded to the god of transformation, as in ancient times, a god linked with the awesome presence of the divine feminine, these unset- tling archetypal energies could be ritually expressed, inhibit- ed, and contained, *and* be transformed into poetic and symbolic form, that is, into culture (Whitmont, 1992). Orpheus stands as that mythic symbolic image that translates raw instinct into consciousness, longing into sacred song. He is that transcendent bridge between the daimonic and human worlds that knows that chaotic violence is intimately connected with regeneration, creativity, and erotic love.

This enlightened gnosis of the dark chaos relationship with the sweet and formidable aromas of love is contained within the symbolic imagery of the golden-winged, androgynous Eros-Phanes-Aphrodite. The god(dess) comes before our visionary eye with glistening aura, a vast form containing the wisdom of earth secrets and instincts that long for rebirth into a radiant cosmos alive with Love. Until we find again appropriate religio-cultural channels for these transpersonal energies that move through our world and live in us as powerful affects seeking an individual ethical response, we will continue to destroy ourselves and dismember each other, like Pentheus, in ways—both individual and collective—that have become all too familiar today. And the great cosmic forces of chaos and eros will continue to degenerate into the shadowy depotentiated forms of impotent cherubs smiling mindlessly on Christmas cards.

The Goddess Vak and Her Visionaries

Ancient Indian mythological traditions include creation stories linking the richly fertile landscapes of chaos and eros. As Jenks (1992) elaborates, Vak, goddess of speech, is a feminine divine power whose name from the Sanskrit root—*vac* "to speak, announce, recite"—includes such clusters of meaning as voice, word, humming, the sound of a drum, the music of birds, an oracular utterance. English derivatives are found in such words as vocal, voice, evoke, vocabulary. The oracular nuance survives in our word vocation, which means to be addressed by a voice, the voice of God or some divine numen or sign. In evoking the presence of Vak, we must allow ourselves to be so addressed.

The goddess Vak is really related to the divine sound vibration before it becomes Word. Speech is conceived originally through the seven primordial visionaries (*rsis*), a group of both men and women who, by contacting a deeply hidden source within their hearts, translate "by the power of their love" cosmic secrets into namings and form. In this creation tale, undifferentiated energy vibrations are transformed into consciousness or patterns of meaning through love. That which arises from the nameless depths is a creative movement of love. The Word comes about through deeply felt cooperation, meditation, mediation, and love. There is no hint here of competition, or a drive for power, or of an order that is imposed arbitrarily.

The divine feminine Vak also arises out of the dark primordial waters identified with her yoni. She gives birth to the father of creation "from the brow of the world," that is, from an already conscious visible realm. Vak is the mistress of joy, the one who brings bliss to gods and men. She is later identified as Shakti. As the goddess of a sound-based creation, her throngs of singers inhabit a liminal, brooding place, where light is still immersed in darkness. These singers perform a cosmic rounddance in this realm of tumultous chaos, kicking up a thick dust cloud as they link hands vigorously, and whirl and spin vibration into form with their ecstatic love.

Vak is also present in the origin myth of ancient Indic theater, or *Natya* ("dance-drama"). It seems that there are resonances here that link Vak to the Orphic mysteries devoted to Dionysus, mysteries involving poetry, music, and drama as a container for primordial ecstatic and conflictual warring energies.

In the story, out of primordial dark waters, a hill arises which drifts, rootless, on the surface. This hill is a dark world of undifferentiated unity, containing all potentialities for life and light. This world, however, is unable to express this potential, because a strong force of resistance, in the form of a serpent, prevents its release.

The hill is viewed as nonexistence or chaos, or perhaps a state of dormancy (*asat*). Interestingly, in this undivided, pre-existent world exists a foreknowledge of the whole—and all possibilities—a gnosis that is lost when the material world comes into being. Similar to von Franz's story from the Chinese philosopher, once again, chaos loses something of what is most valuable about it when it becomes conscious. Here chaos is like a quantum field, and the serpent our resistance to daring renewal. Perhaps, though, when we descend into chaos with consciousness (a consciousness that inevitably unravels), or when we eventually bring consciousness to these chaotic states, we know that we have been in contact with a rich and vital realm at the source of our being, a realm that, of necessity, remains in an uncivilized state. Chaos can never be civilized without losing its essential nature, yet it conceals a hidden purpose. To mine its treasures, we have to visit *its* dark mysterious waters, descend to *its* realm to glean the wisdom that lies waiting for us there, ready to birth new levels of our being.[5] Perhaps this invites us to continually surrender our conscious thoughts and achievements to the unconscious realms of dream and reverie, those chaotic quantum fields that water us with unfolding possibility and further becoming.

In the Natya myth, the inhabitants of this primordial realm of *asat*, or chaos, are Prajapati and his mate Vak, though in this undifferentiated state, they are beyond male/female gender. Prajapati also remains in the dual manifest world, *sat*, as a representation of the totality of chaos. The phenomenal world comes into being when Prajapati first creates the *asur-*

---

5. M.-L. von Franz, *Number and Time* (Evanston, IL: Northwestern University Press, 1974), pp. 268–269. The West African divinity, Gba'adu, is considered even mightier than Fa (who is perhaps closer to the Sapientia Dei [Wisdom of God], or philanthropic side of the Self), and whom I mention in chaper 1. Gba'adu (see Prologue, page xxx) is a darker force, embracing all of existence, including its dark, deadly, and chaotic forces, and as such represents the ultimate mystery of existence.

as ("demons") and *devas* ("younger gods"). Suddenly Indra, "Mind," emerges out of the watery depths, and for reasons unclear, arrives as the protagonist for the devas. He hurls his spear at the floating hill, thereby splitting it open as well as anchoring it firmly in one place. In separating the hill into an upper part, Heaven, and a lower part, Earth, Jenks (1992) writes, "a cosmic tree (spindle, spine) arises from the primeval waters to support the sky" (p. 464). As the tree as *axis mundi* forms, four rivers gush forth. The roots of the world-tree lie in a great golden amrita-filled jar (*kumbha* or *patra*, also a term applied to an actor).

The movement into Creation, the eternal mystery of the passage from One to Two, involves a splitting or polarization—familiar from so many creation stories—a differentiation of unconscious chaos into life-giving waters. But the emergence of the world-tree rooted in amrita and stretching to the heavens keeps the Above connected and aligned with the Below—a differentiation therefore without a splitting off. Cosmos here keeps its connection to its instinctual depths; consciousness remains rooted in the underworld. The microcosmic reflection of this cosmic creation is seen in the Kundalini serpent energy rising from the base of the spine through all the chakras of the body to the crown, when activated either spontaneously or through meditation practice. Interestingly, the cosmic tree is related to spine, as Jenks indicates.

One of the deficits of the growth of consciousness as an independent power that we suffer in the West, is that consciousness loses its rootedness in the other seats of consciousness located along the spine in the chakras of the body. In this sundering of consciousness from its primordial roots, we split mind from heart, mind from sex, heart from sex, passion from inspiration, head from genitals, eros from chaos. The danger here is that we ruthlessly imperil ourselves and our world and lose our voices. Perhaps in our world the serpent is still encircled around a rootlessly drifting mound, and we remain on the surface of things, resisting the potential for life and light, resisting a grounding in the creative field of Vak's amrita juices. Surely, an unrealized erotic potential, situated around a central axis, lies hidden here, concealed yet ready to unfold.

Even in the myth, the cosmic serpent of resistance requires more than Indra (Mind) alone to defeat it. It requires his kin *agni* and *soma* (fire and Moon), lying hidden within the darkness of the hill. Surely fire and Moon evoke a passionate presence and vitality, a reflecting warm flame in touch with a central vision. This unification of passion and vision lies dormant and unrealized in our times, a sleeping potential ready now to awaken us from our ordered sleep.

Vak eventually decides to join the devas who are being attacked by the older asuras (on account of feeling betrayed by Indra's help from fire and Moon in slaying the serpent). Thus Vak ensures the gods' victory, for the battle cannot be won without her intervention. Only through Vakian voice, vision, and vitality is creation assured.

This speech is a joyous sounding, a consciousness rooted in the flowing rivers of erotic love, arising via the pathways of the heart into explosions of inspiration and opening up unimagined visionary possibilities. It is a way of being and knowing deeply connected with the chaotic origins of life, stretching open to the stars and back again to the eternal source, in a cyclical round of regeneration and rebirth.

In "The Churning of the Ocean" myth—literally, "the amrita-churning"—the warring asuras and devas, under the guidance of Brahma/Vak, agree to sacrifice their violent polar opposition to allow a cooperation that will free the amrita, the life elixir, from the bottom of the dark waters. The churning is achieved by pulling a cord—sometimes envisioned as a serpent—to and fro on two sides, making the churning stick rotate. The waters are churned so vigorously by this pulling motion back and forth that the elixir is dislodged and forced to the surface from the ocean depths. What also arises to the surface with this churning is amrita's dark twin, the deadly poison *kalakuta*.

One way that we might understand this story is to consider that consciousness is a crime against Nature, an act of violence against the instinctual realms, an assault on primordial chaos, an *opus contra naturam,* as the alchemists described their churnings. Edinger (1972) speaks of the birth of consciousness in a similar way, "as a crime which alienates man[kind] from God and from [an] original preconscious wholeness" (p. 18). The sense of guilt or shame, according to Edinger, that accompanies this Fall, expresses the feeling of estrangement between the individual and the animal or instinctual nature. Consciousness as a spiritual principle is the creation of another realm—"a counterpole to natural, instinctive animal function" (p. 20)—that endangers our instinctual ways of knowing and being, and therein lies its blessing and its curse. Psychology too often gets caught in this divorce of spirit and instinct.

Seeking the elixir of life is always dangerous because what always comes up in the search is duality, dissociation, repression, and the face of one's own dark twin. We have to confront the truth that destruction is the other side of creation; they belong inexorably together. Every incremental step in consciousness ruthlessly involves both forces. Perhaps another way to imagine this story is that life sought consciously always brings the reality and knowledge of death, loss, and dismemberment. Jung speaks of this darkness as containing the seeds of much gold, since the recovery of the wholeness that we lose in becoming conscious is achieved by the willingness to tread through the minefields of our experience and live such experience fully. Varuna, as the god of the dark primordial waters, will not allow his—of necessity—cosmic dismemberment to release the elixir to occur, until he himself is promised some amrita in exchange for his sacrifice. Love as an image of the Self is given, therefore, as that fabric of creation that will knit us back together, instincts and spirit in one undivided whole, if we submit fully to the challenges of earthly existence, and do not lose touch with our chaotic origins. Our Apollonic worldview is in dire need of re-immersion in its Dionysian depths.

It is Vak who carries the vessel of amrita's sweetness to the surface. Chaos and love belong together here as the inter-weaving of the shadows and mysteries of cosmic Eros, the one inevitably leading into the other and back again, richly informing each other's realms. Indeed, our myth explicitly indicates that the wetness of creation's ecstatic intoxicant lies buried in Varuna's ocean kingdom, lodged at the heart of the world. Vakian sounds come into being from emotions buried in watery depths, and arise in rapturous longing, bringing in their wake love songs richly textured by the soul's desire to sing the beauty of creation. This creation by the Word comes with the voice of the artist, the actor, the poet, the visionary—words with body and soul—the Orpheus figure who for each of us helps bend the primordial energies of the cosmos by churning them into the joyous strains of transmuted feeling and swollen image, and extends the offering with out-stretched hand and undefended heart back to the world.

But even today, chaos theory cannot fully mask our cul-ture's secret longing for the transformation that would reunite the range and complexity of feeling within its arche-typal matrix and mystery. This longing breaks through in terms such as "strange attractors" and "the butterfly effect." Eros and Psyche, having perhaps been disappointed with their inadequate treatment in depth psychology, have fallen out of Spirit into Matter where once again, from their cosmic, transpsychic spheres, they approach life in the human realm.

CHAOS AND EROS

Love, as we know, involves a fall, and as we have seen from the myths, chaos gives birth to this new creation, this fall into love. The word chaos itself attracts, attracts attention. "Chaos Theory," for example, is much more evocative than its prop-er scientific name, "nonlinear dynamics"! It lures us out of our safely distanced modes of being and invites us to let our hair down and abandon ourselves to unthinkable and unthought thoughts and wild, spontaneous acts. Chaos leads us into an unfamiliar, undomesticated world, one that precedes a more cultivated and civilized mode, a forgotten place where, leaving daylight consciousness and its neat and tidy theories behind, we enter the confusion and dark abyss of all we have both intentionally and unavoidably put aside. Now the chasm of a world opens up, a world unformed, unredeemed, yet somehow brimming with secret life and inchoate possibility. It is a world as yet unknown and completely unpredictable. In this place, we surrender to a destiny that we cannot imagine, much less impose. Being thus poised at the edge of the void is echoed in the first stirrings of Love. Sappho writes of it thus:

> like a wind
> crashing down
> among oak trees
> love shattered
> my mind[6]

Love takes us out of our mind with its neatly ordered arrangements, and our carefully constructed world comes completely unraveled. The daughter of Dione, goddess of the oak tree in which the amorous dove nests, takes us beyond the limits of what we think we know, and who we are, and fills us with a loving inspiration that charges the circuitry of our bodies with an imagination of worlds unseen and longing for recognition and incarnation; "the synthesis of wild emotion and high sophistication" (Friedrich, 1978, p. 123).

A cosmic shudder moves through our body, and we fall into the terrors and panic engendered by this sweetly bitter

---

6. Translated from the Greek by P. Friedrich, *The Meaning of Aphrodite* (Chicago: Chicago University Press, 1978), p. 119. Copyright © 1978. Reprinted by kind permission.

potion. Every new deep love undoes us so, loosens our limbs, sets us aflame. When we fall under the spell of this cosmic mystery, it is like falling through the cracks of a world into a new universe. A new birth occurs, and a new creation comes into being, one that is almost immediately attacked from within and without. We are virginal again, we lose our tongues, become like an awkward teenager, not knowing what to say: voice stuttering, face blushing, forgetting, distracted, sweating, lips trembling. We become so unsure of ourselves, humbled by the Visitation. In our total vulnerability to love's arrows, everything opposite to love emerges. Every shade, every secret, every doubt has a light shined upon it once more. All our most despised aspects—our jealousy, envy, hatred, and fears—parade themselves before love's eye. And the golden light of love around us attracts hatred and envy. The legions of disappointed ones, the unloved and the unlived in our environment, begin to try to undermine and spoil the bliss with poisonous tongue and venomous acts.[7]

Love is such a fateful factor in a life: we cannot make it happen, and our life is meaningless and very lonely if it never comes into being. Love brings us close to the deepest feelings of which we are capable. We are never more vulnerable than when we love. Love takes us to the heights of cosmic bliss and simultaneously to the depths of passion and suffering. In this sense, more than anything else, it has the power to release us from the limitations of what we are conscious of,

---

7. M.-L. von Franz, *Alchemy* (Toronto: Inner City Books, 1980), p. 123. In writing of the case of two people who fall in love, von Franz warns of the "poisonous mistake" that people make by infecting others with their own doubts about a *participation,* by calling it a projection. For the lover, the other is the beloved, not a projection of the *animus*. Strictly speaking, a projection is *only* such when doubt arises, causing a disturbance in the field. I emphasize this point because these days the word "projection" is used often carelessly, with the consequence of thoughtlessly hurting others. Along with von Franz, I believe we should exercise greater caution when we speak of projection.

and reveal to us glimpses of the heart of the soul of the world, the divine reality at the "Hunabku," the cosmic center, where god and goddess are entwined in the most profound and playful, ritual erotic dance. Love brings life, reimagines life beyond transience to a glowing *unus mundus* where spirit and matter are one, united in the *anima mundi*, where mere mortals become the microcosm of the universal, and stars dance in the fabric of our form. Love leads us to our goal; love is our goal. As von Franz (1980b) writes: "Whoever cannot surrender to this experience has never lived; whoever founders in it has understood nothing" (p. 142).

Chaos and Eros in Life and Dream

Not too long ago, I had the experience of the unleashing of a fierce range of affects that had a profoundly disturbing effect on me and poignantly commented on this relation between chaos and love. An early dream commented on the situation:

> *My daughter Sarah and I are together in midtown Manhattan. Snakes begin to come out. First one, then another, then they start teaming out. At first I try to get rid of them, or kill them, but then I realize it's a hopeless task because there are so many of them. I look at the patterns on the snakes' bodies to determine if they are benign or poisonous. Mostly they are benign, but I know that there is one snake amongst them that is poisonous. I must be able to protect Sarah from that one. I am filled with a kind of anxiety and vigilance that is almost overwhelming to me.*

Thrown out of the paradise of my daylight world, I am initiated into the Hadean realm with the promise of underworld knowledge, and a different kind of treasure, one where the poison is also potentially the cure. My soul and body were gripped by what seemed like alien powers and affects that dislodged the status quo and invaded my consciousness. "The old order has to die," a voice kept reiterating. I felt my world shattering; I no longer knew myself; I could not eat or sleep. *Assaulted on all sides by jealousy, envy, aggression, and despair, the descent into such a chaotic state felt as if it was destroying the fabric of my being. I felt profoundly unlovable, deeply unacceptable to myself and others; embarrassed by my feelings and their intensity. I began to withdraw.*

What was being cracked open was a self that felt it had to merit and achieve its welfare, one that could not trust that she could be loved for who she is, an exposed self who wants to be safe in the knowledge that she is loved "for better or worse," a self that wants to surrender in trust to the love offered, and to the Love bestowed as Gift. It was as if proving myself and pleasing others was a defense against annihilation and total despair. Now I was being invited into what I feared most, and did not know it until then, into the absence, the void, the nothingness. Terror seized me, and an excruciating kind of vulnerability. Giving up succeeding, giving up control, I felt displaced, unknown to myself, and a deep loss and melancholy overtook me. A sense of dependency and fragility such as I had never known began to melt still frozen rocks around my heart. It is only the power of Love that can reveal such tenderness, such terror, of feeling. Another dream ends as follows:

> *Then an unknown man passes through my house. He has got lost and is looking for a town by the ocean that is actually near where we live, but I have never heard of it before. It is called "Gweu" or "Ghent," and we are looking at it on a map that reminds me of France. The man is somewhat surprised that I haven't been there yet, because this coastal village is meant to be so beautiful: one of the seven wonders of the world!*

"Gweu" is the Indo-European root of the word "chaos"! So there is a spirit in the dream who is moving me in the direction of chaos, and supporting the dissolution of old ways of being. Ghent makes me think of Vermeer, and his paintings of women who are close both to light and darkness, and who evoke a quiet, strong presence. These two images are brought together in the landscape of France, a country that has always been associated for me with love.

HIDDEN GOLD: CHAOS AND EROS IN ALCHEMY

The collapse of the conscious attitude always feels like a death, the end of a world, and we feel abandoned to the wild elements and forces of nature, dissolved back into original chaos. Von Franz (1980a) writes: "The urge for individuation, as long as it is a natural inordinate urge, seeks impossible situations; it seeks conflict and defeat and suffering because it seeks its own transformation." She adds, "Sitting in Hell and roasting there is what brings forth the philosopher's stone" (p. 254).

Chaos is outlawed in cosmologies in the West, especially in the Judaeo-Christian tradition. The full impact of chaos's terrain tends to be marginalized as I have already noted, and in Western theologies it is devalued as the unknown realm of nothingness and nonbeing outside the divine order. In much the same way, evil has been marginalized and divested of its reality as the *privatio boni*, not embraced as a power and force in itself.

But anything excluded from the collective consciousness finds its way into underground and heretical movements. So in alchemy, chaos is the watery abyss, the loss of a familiar consciousness, the *prima materia*, the initial psychic and material situation where elements are separated and hostile to each other. It is an unredeemed leaden state that marks a hopeless loss of soul, a *solutio* in which our fixed attitudes begin their devastating dissolution. Yet this chaotic state is highly valued as containing divine but hidden sparks of cosmic love, and thus it is an essential stage in the opus. It is comparable to that moment in Gnosticism where an awareness of homesickness, strangeness, alienation, and secret longing is the birth of the moment of the sojourner's travels back to the Alien God and the divine realms of light, the stirrings of a deep knowing that was once known but has been forgotten (Jonas, 1963).

The alchemists recognized that in breakdown and desolation, a new birth takes place. The *coniunctio* first takes place in the underworld, in the New Moon, where there is no light, when we are in the deepest depression, and most alienated from ourselves, others, and life. It is only in these dark, vegetative, abysmal states that the *nigredo* can dissolve old structures that no longer accord with our soul's essence. Thus these states of deadness, withdrawal, and fragmentation are essential to the rhythm of transformation. But we must be willing to sacrifice what we know, what we know *about*, and sink into the unfathomable realms of unknown experience. The true meaning of "to suffer" suggests this ability to tolerate both intense affects and their absence, to undergo and be subjected to an original experience as in an initiation rite. Knowledge, method, and theory can shield us from such daring originality, and therein lies their danger and their protection. Alchemists, mystics, and poets—those pilgrims of direct experience—have always recognized that the link with the divine is through the transmutation of intense affect in the body, but we do need a body that is vital and strong enough to incarnate these subtle and piercing divine rays.

In a letter written in 1953, Jung (1975) writes: "The clinical practice of psychotherapy is a mere makeshift that does its utmost to prevent numinous experiences" (p. 118). Therapy is not a theory or a method; it is an initiatory rite, a harrowing process comparable to the death and rebirth mysteries of ancient times. The willingness to suffer intense emotion and the disorientation that accompanies it, *is* the *sine qua non* of the experience of the *numinosum,* and of new spiritual levels from the world soul or transcendent archetypal realms that have never before been made conscious. In the anonymous medieval text, *The Cloud of Unknowing,* von Franz (1980a) describes the fact that:

> the closer the soul of the mystic gets to the Godhead the darker and more confused [s]he becomes. Such texts say in effect that God lives in the cloud of unknowing and that one has to be stripped of every idea, every intellectual conception, before one can approach the light which is surrounded by the darkness of utter confusion (208).

Submitting ourselves to chaos, allowing ourselves to be worked on by such mysterious cosmic vibrations, we are led to the borders of a mystery, a revelation, a gnosis, that in its silence speaks more words than we ever imagined or dreamed.

But this Voice, which brings revelation as the experience of the numinous, is, as Neumann (1989) observes, "always new," and "cannot be other than anti-conventional, anti-collective, and anti-dogmatic," so the "ego affected by it comes into conflict with the dogma and agencies of the dominant consciousness" (p. 386). Heretics, mystics, and poets are ostracized by their societies as their seemingly new understandings threaten the status quo and the interests of controlling groups. It is dangerous to be original, and the inertia of large collective forces conspire to oppress authentic experience.

But we are already blinded by the light of our one-sided consciousness, and as in the story the ancient Orphites tell (in von Franz, 1980b), when the feminine spirit of God could no longer tolerate the light of God, she fell down into chaos, with sparks still clinging to her, from which place she tried to raise herself up again (p. 170). Surely we are at such a moment when the soul of the matter is in need of restoration, and the mysteries of Life and divine Eros seek our vision and our passion. Surely we are at a moment when we need to fall in love with the world again.

THE MYSTERIES AND SHADOWS OF LOVE

Could the chaos of our world, which is losing its way in breakdowns on all levels from the personal to the political, signal that moment of deadly peril where the consciousness we have achieved seeks its own destruction and dissolution? Perhaps this is to void a cultural false self and a deep disturbance felt at the heart of ourselves and our world. All our knowledge and differentiation, which at times are of inestimable value, border, too, on a congealment of awareness that is in danger of destroying and devouring the Thou of the Other, the Thou of the World.

At this crisis point, it is as if we must become a mystery to ourselves again, actually the mystery that we truly are; we must become again the One who I am not, the Stranger who I am, the Mystery that can never, and must not ever be understood. Rather to become again, in our vertical axis as it were, the Orphan, the Star, the one who has no human heritage but only a divine destiny, the one who must be protected, and can only be lived, the seeming impossibility of which being the very condition that rallies the latent forces of our spontaneous and creative natures. At this threshold landscape, we must allow ourselves to fall into "fateful detours and wrong turnings," and with no small terror become aware that our calling as humans has no models, no methods. We are addressed only by the secret promise and hints of the voices, images, dreams, and energies within, between ourselves and the Other, and without in a world that can never be wholly known. We must try, nevertheless, to embody such uncertainty, such chaos, such unknowns. We will do this inadequately, perhaps, but we can approach our tasks with a full heart, making the imponderables and the Invisibles known through our fragile frames, giving body to that which requires our participation, and our witness, our sacrifice, and especially our love. In this sense we are no longer hero or heroine, but rather the mystical adept ensouling the world through a translation of original experience into a human text for which there is no script.

Responding thus out of the wholeness of who we are, and not out of isolated elements that are always in doubt, invites us into a subtle attending to the "awe-inspiring guest who knocks at our door portentously" now that the dominants of our culture have disintegrated, and we are floating on a sea of collective and individual insecurity and exploration. And who is this coming guest? Who is this soul figure, at once so destructive and creative? This "sensing of a new dominant arising from the chaos of a world losing its way"[8] that Jung alludes to near the end of his life, is love, eros. Love, the incalculable, irrational, ungraspable, unanalyzable, impenetrable Mystery, the "creator and father-mother of all higher consciousness."

Freud (1930) too, considers this possibility for the future. At the end of *Civilization and Its Discontents,* and toward the end of his life, speaking of our instinct for aggression and self-destruction that "could now very easily exterminate one another to the last man," and which gives rise to "unrest, . . . dejection, . . . apprehension," he speaks to the importance of Eros for the future. "And now it may be expected[9] that the other of the two 'heavenly forces,' eternal Eros, will put forth his strength so as to maintain himself alongside of his equally immortal adversary" (p. 105).

Love's story is born out of a dark, windy night, with a sliver of a silver moon crowned with glistening golden stars, and the limitless watery abyss rising and falling to secret rhythms in deep harmony with the foamy cosmos.

Love, the source of every living thing, delivers us into the kairos, the meeting place of the worlds, the almost unbearable beauty of Presence, the place where spirit and matter transcend their differences and become One. This cosmic realm brings us into our full identity, embracing all of existence, including our dark and chaotic forces, and faces us with a fearsome, unapproachable mystery. Beyond a psychology of projections sustained by a world split in two, we enter the Temple of a cosmology of relations illumined by all of nature, and surrender into a devotional attitude that in rich simplicity inspires the artistry of a life. This landscape can

---

8. R. A. Lockhart, *Psyche Speaks* (Wilmett, IL: Chiron Publications, 1987), p. 51.

9. A better translation for the German word *erwarted* is "awaited," more hope than assurance. Personal communication, Dr. Christine Downing, Summer 1999.

never be understood or integrated, only deeply and playful-
ly related to by responding to its hints and gestures, and our
loving regard. Rumi writes in his poem, "What Hurts the
Soul?"

> We tremble, thinking we're about to dissolve
> into non-existence, but non-existence fears
> even more that it might be given human form!
>
> Loving God is the only Pleasure.
> Other delights turn bitter.
>
> What hurts the soul?
> To live without tasting
> the water of its own essence.
>
> People focus on death and this material earth.
> They have doubts about soul-water.
> Those doubts can be reduced!
>
> Use night to wake your clarity.
> Darkness and the living water are lovers.
> Let them stay up together.
>
> When merchants eat their big meals and sleep
> their dead sleep, we night-thieves go to work (p. 40).*

---

*Reprinted by kind permission from J. Rumi, *Say I Am You*, J. Moyne and C. Barks, trans. (Athens, GA: Maypop, 1994). Copyright © 1994.

Chapter 3

LOVE'S SUFFERING

The Orphan as Image of Abandonment

A collapse of the conscious attitude is no small matter. It always feels like the end of the world, as though everything had tumbled back into original chaos. One feels delivered up. . . . abandoned to the moods of the elements.

—C. G. Jung (1966c), §254

It is . . . only in the state of complete abandonment and loneliness that we experience the helpful powers of our own natures.

—C. G. Jung (1969a), §525

Love is on intimate terms with suffering. Suffering is the shadow side of love, its natural companion. Suffering, like love, is an earthquake of the soul; it exposes us to the elemental forces of our nature. Love always brings our keenest vulnerabilities to the surface. That may even be its purpose. Tenderness, vulnerability, and the deepest affections of the soul hold within the seeds of love's dark shadows: power, jealousy and envy with the attendant aggression, betrayal, destructiveness, and hate. Careful attending to love's woundings, those gaping psychic sores that link with love's origins in chaos, almost always opens us up to a larger field of love. Likewise, Jung wrote that the shadow is 90 percent gold. There is hidden treasure in our pathos.

In this chapter, I suggest that suffering first and foremost involves a surrender, a fall into the unknown. The Psyche and

Eros myth is particularly instructive in this regard. Psyche hurled herself off the cliff into unimaginable depths. It is a dark initiation that invites us to not know, to not see with daylight eyes, to not anticipate, and to not make premature meanings out of what pains and ails us. Suffering so often comes in the form of abandonment in one way or another—by a loved ones' death or betrayal; by attitudes and identities that no longer serve or contain who we are becoming; or by illness or depression, known as "soul loss" in other cultures. Or we ourselves abandon or betray, or become traitors to the self we once were, or to others around us. Suffering invites us to abandon ourselves to our life; it invites us to release ourselves to our fate.

Suffering, in whatever manner it comes, is often a wake-up call that heralds our vocation; it is the soul's way of jolting our memory to that thing once known and now forgotten but dimly recalled. To be able to adopt this attitude of not knowing, to treat abandonment with an attitude of abandonment is the essential ground of transformation and renewal—if it comes. It is a mood that requires patience. It is often the poet who captures this ground of patience, because poetry speaks in a language that hints at, or suggests, rather than defining the pathos of the human condition. It is as if the poet's language is already responding to those areas of ignorance that always shadow the heart of our knowledge. One such poet, who poignantly captures this need for patience is T. S. Eliot. In one of his (1943) *Four Quartets*, titled "East Coker," Eliot advises his readers, while instructing his own soul to wait for change—without expectation or hope. He says we must wait in stillness, for we would almost certainly impose the ego's desires rather than allowing the soul's wisdom to create genuine transformation in its own organic rhythm and timing (p. 15).

I would like to consider here, in particular relation to our suffering, the archetypal experience of abandonment. This archetype is symbolically imaged in the paradoxical figure of the Orphan, that numinous presence that holds the key to our uniqueness, that helps us remember who we are, and who stands by us when we fall to our knees, when we fall from our familiar attachments through the portal of the known into that rich but chaotic soil of the unknown.

Let's approach the experience of abandonment and the figure of the Orphan first by addressing the value of suffering as a darkening of our conscious attitudes, as an "unknowing" that brings us close to the Orphan's presence, that figure who guides us home, home as that origin place that resides in the heart of all of us and that lives in the heart of the soul of the world. Corbett (1990) recounts the following dream of a woman patient:

> I am in a boat at night, floating down a narrow stream. There are many stars in the sky. I see the eyes of jackals staring at me from the shore. Then I see a line in the water ahead of me. Beyond the line, the water is light. I see the figure of a huge black woman with six breasts standing knee deep in the water. She is about 20 feet tall. I cannot see her face—it is above the light. She is guarding the water. The water is lit with a beautiful white light and looks like daylight or starlight, having a mysterious quality. I dive out of the boat as it reaches the beginning of the light. I lose consciousness; it feels like the right thing to do [emphasis mine]—I belong in the light part; the water is inviting and warm and feels safe (p. 161).

Corbett writes that this dream belongs to a "severely borderline woman intensely dependent on a hostile mother" (p. 160) and uses the dream to illustrate the devastating effects for this woman of losing consciousness in the presence of this negative mother figure, "partly as a result of the cultural neglect of the archetypal feminine" (p. 161). I should also like to consider this dream from another perspective. Dreams with clearly archetypal contents may also be understood as belonging to the collective, so that what comes to us during the night is often also a cultural issue, of concern to many others also. With Jung (1961), then, in acknowledging his devotion to the psyche, we too can say, "I ceased to belong to myself alone" (p. 192). It is with this sensibility that I would like to regard this dream, a dream that on another level was perhaps given, dreamed, remembered, recorded, and made available for all of us.

The dream is situated within a cosmological setting bringing star and jackal, spirit and instinct, sky and earth together into a harmonious whole. The huge black goddess, that formidable Other of earth secrets that matter, who perhaps reminds us of the Egyptian goddess Nut, or the many-breasted Artemis of Ephesus, midwife to the embodied soul, yet whose identity remains veiled in accordance with her function as High Priestess of the Mysteries, is "guarding the water." Water, so richly resonant of the depths from which we emerge and to which we return for renewal and rebirth, is strangely lit with the qualities of both night and day, moonlight and sunlight, reflection and direction. Paradoxically, a dive into the dark cosmic waters of the unknown is also an invitation into "neither/nor" dreamy reverie, or perhaps difficult conflicts that bring the promise of a different kind of enlightenment. Could our suffering, both personal and collective, be the doorway into such a darkening of our conventional and fixed attitudes, a forgetting of what we have become so sure of? Could our suffering invite us into a ruthless reckoning with our shadow selves, and culture's dark underbelly, still not adequately achieved?

Sardello (1995) describes the Wisdom figure of Sophia, that subtle body presence that unites world, underworld, human reality, and divine substance together in a cosmic soul of love, in a similar vein:

> She is not known to our ordinary everyday consciousness; this consciousness must radically change if we are to enter into her depth. Entering the underworld refers to the transition from a materialistic point of view to a soul point of view. A darkening of ordinary consciousness is required. The Black Madonna, retrieved from beneath Chartres Cathedral and enthroned above, images this change of consciousness (p. 57).

The dream says that losing consciousness "feels like the right thing to do." Do we dare ourselves such unknowing? Perhaps such a dive would move us out of knowing about things, which is so gratifying to the ego, toward a deeper, revelatory gnosis—a kind of complex knowing that nurtures the soul, that responds to the wholeness of who we are, dark and light, known and forever a mystery. Such conscious sacrifice offers the possibility of what we might call a stellar consciousness, a warm and inviting place that resituates us within a psycho-cosmic whole, where we can at last feel safe because we feel truly home, home in a world where psyche and cosmos are one. In such a way, like Saul on the road to Damascus, all our breakdowns become breakthroughs to a more vast vision of reality, if we can tolerate not anticipating and not knowing what this might be in advance.

Culturally, do we elevate consciousness over unconsciousness? Or does this question already reflect that polarity that I am trying to avoid? Perhaps, more accurately, we might suggest that we are not adequately attuned to the subtle world soul that pervades and unifies all relations and yet requires a different vision from us than our daylight consciousness. Perhaps it requires our love rather than our rational modes of apprehending the world. Is this the imbalance that we are in? Does this dream seek to correct that imbalance? In the same way that, as Jung (1969a) writes in "Answer to Job" (CW 11, §553–758), Job had to revise his image of God to include God's dark side (and this in turn inspired God's desire to incarnate, for He perceived that man had something that He did not), so do we have to revise our image of what matters, of what is of ultimate concern today? Perhaps love is that mode of apprehending the world that is willing to risk losing itself in the unknown.

Has depth psychology succumbed to the hubris of the rational intellect and a singleness of meaning devoid of the darker complexities of the whole? Commenting on the fact that one dream alone never provides enough material to unlock its depth of meaning (and we would do well to remember this while commenting on a single dream!) and must always be situated within a series, Jung (1969a) comments:

> Since there is a continuity of consciousness despite the fact that it is regularly interrrupted by sleep, there is probably also a continuity of unconscious processes—*perhaps even more than with the events of consciousness*. In any case my experience is in favor of the probability that *dreams are the visible links in a chain of unconscious events* [emphasis mine] (CW 11, §53).

In the same way that consciousness is interrupted by sleep, unconsciousness (or sleep) is interrupted by dreams. The suggestion is of a world, a continuous reality unknown to us except when punctuated by dreams that reach awareness, that is perhaps more real than a rather precarious consciousness. Are we being invited into this underground stream, invited to take seriously the mysteries of its reality in a way that consciousness, with its attachment to the apparent certainties and meanings of its daylight world, has not yet been able to surrender into? Jung (1966a) writes that surrender into such experience "is a charisma which no human art can compel. . . . Not everybody is capable of this [unreserved] surrender. . . . The most healing, and psychologically the most necessary experiences are a 'treasure hard to attain,' and its acquisition demands something out of the common from the common man" (CW 16, §187).

As the woman patient's dream suggests, is the boat of ego consciousness drifting at night in the dark toward an inevitable limit, a line beyond which is the Black Woman, the Black Madonna, whose face we cannot see (perhaps because head knowledge only is not relevant here) yet who guards another reality, the mysterious light of dark waters? A white light that contains the colors of the rainbow, a new covenant between human beings and the Divine? A white light that "looks like daylight or starlight?" Surely two different kinds of light. What happens to us when we contemplate starlight, when we look up at the heavens at night and see the Full Moon rise up on the horizon toward the comet on its journey, hurtling away from us at unimaginable speeds, and perhaps wonder about our origins and destiny, and "are we alone in the universe?" and feel oh-so-small compared with such vast mysteries?

Or, what happens to us in dawnlight, early light, midday light, afternoon light, dusk light? Even our day is punctuated by many different moods and rhythms of light, the rising and falling of solar vibrations whose effects are mostly way beyond our ken. Or when, for example, is daylight like starlight, or vice versa, and when do such qualities of either never meet? What would happen to us if we could slow ourselves down adequately to drift into such uncertain reverie, or if we could adopt such a quality of being toward all that confronts and concerns us?

And yet this paradox of light reminds us of the Gnostic story "Pistis Sophia" (meaning, "Ever-faithful Wisdom") and Sophia's fall into matter. In Sardello's (1995) account of this story, a primal pair, Depth and Silence, bring forth 30 Aeons or levels of reality, or we might say archetypal forms. The thirtieth level is Sophia, who falls in love with the light of Depth and longs to unite with this light at her origins. Her desire, however, confuses her, and as she moves toward this light, she is in fact moving toward an equally brilliant light in the realm of Chaos. (Are there reminiscences here of our dream—the draw to the Dark Goddess guarding light that is of an uncertain origin or quality and the fall into this mysterious light-water?) Sophia is thrown into Chaos, where she encounters other beings and where she suffers fear, despair, passion, and sorrow. Out of this disintegration, this alchemical *solutio,* this painful dismemberment—the elements (earth, water, air, and fire) arise and the Earth is formed (p. 53). Our pathos gives us substance and forges our character.

From the pleroma, Depth and Silence see Sophia's plight. Jesus, united with Christ consciousness, enters Chaos to retrieve Sophia, but she is reluctant to depart, being filled with compassion for Earth. So she divides herself in two, the divine part returning to the pleroma, to Depth and Silence, while her earthly part remains as a reminder to the human soul—both of its fragmentation from unity and its potential to freely and consciously choose, through its own cocreating efforts, reunification in the World Soul.

There is a similar story from the East in the symbol of Quan Yin (or Kwannon), God or Goddess of Mercy or Kindness. Jung (1976) writes of her in *The Visions Seminars:*

> In most cases . . . [love] isn't concerned with kindness, it is just a hellish possession, but love should have to do with kindness—I am pleading for love.
>
> In the East, where they know as little about that kind of love as we do, they have a beautiful symbol for it in Kwannon, the Goddess of Kindness. She gives nourishment to all living things, even to the evil spirits in hell, and to do so she must go down to hell; but it would frighten the devils if she were to appear there in her heavenly form and, as the Goddess of Kindness, she cannot permit that to happen; so, having such an extraordinary regard for the feelings of the devils, she transforms herself into an evil spirit and takes the food down in that guise. There is a beautiful traditional painting where she is represented in hell as a devil among the devils, giving food to them; but there is a fine thread going up from her head to a heavenly being above, who is herself in all her splendid fury. That is the psychological attitude which real love suggests (p. 215).

Sophia's choice to remain in chaos's underworld domain while she simultaneously resides at her origins, or the beautiful image of Quan Yin's shape-shifting while remaining attached to Source, is comparable to love's immersion in its dark origins, to love seeking the chaotic starlight of the soul for growth and revivification. Chaos and love are inseparable for creation, and chaos and love are required for cocreation. The desire for unknowing, for darkening, is comparable to the yearning that arises out of the modern sick soul's suffering and its isolation from its cosmic heritage. That our woundings are so often woundings of separation and abandonment—bereft of love, or our love unwanted, lost, unrequited—brings us to the presence of the Orphan, the one who, reminiscent of Sophia and Quan Yin, in Jung's (1961) words, has "had to be fetched out of the deep like a fish, or fell like a white stone from heaven" (p. 227), the one who can lead us out of our alien context back home to the *unus mundus* of Eros' cosmic realm.

THE ORPHAN

When the often tormented Mexican painter Frida Kahlo (1995) was in Paris, Picasso taught her a song, which she often sang for her lover and two-time husband, the painter Diego Rivera, or for friends. It is called "El Huerfano" (The Orphan). The song portrays Frida's sense of loneliness, alienation, and despair. Her torment reaches deep into her soul, creating a void which was never healed and never filled. Her vivid, yet tormented paintings are perhaps her creative genius' response to this black hole in her soul.

On a stone tablet at Bollingen, Jung (1961) carved the following quotations from alchemical texts, although he actually writes that he "let the stone itself speak, as it were, in a Latin inscription" (p. 227):

> I am an orphan, alone; nevertheless I am found everywhere. I am one, but opposed to myself. I am youth and old man at one and the same time. I have known neither father nor mother, because I have had to be fetched out of the deep like a fish, or fell like a white stone from heaven. In woods and mountains I roam, but I am hidden in the innermost soul of man. I am mortal for everyone, yet I am not touched by the cycle of aeons (p. 227).

The acquisition of this stone is in itself rather an interesting and curious story. Jung had ordered, with specific measurements, stones from a local quarry to build a wall that was to enclose the garden by the Tower. When the stones arrived, the cornerstone was all wrong—it was a much larger square block than the triangular stone requested—and it was about to be returned. But when Jung saw the stone, he knew it belonged to him, and he made a carved monument out of it to express what the Tower meant to him.

Initially the stone was to him the *lapis*, the Philosopher's Stone (that is, an image of the Self), the substantive symbol that marks paradoxically both the beginning and goal of the work of alchemy, that which is both despised and rejected, yet valued above all things by the wise. According to some alchemical traditions (Jung, 1970b), this lapis is called "orphan" both on account of its uniqueness—"it was never seen elsewhere"—and because the "orphan" was the name of a precious stone or gem that was wine-colored and sometimes shone in the night, "but nowadays it does not shine (any more) in the darkness" (§13). Perhaps the wine-colored stone brings distant echoes of Orpheus' creative realm and Dionysus's underworld mysteries, no longer clearly heard.

There is also a reference to the homeless orphan who is slain at the beginning of the work for purposes of transformation (§13). Other associative images elucidated by Jung are "widow," "son of the widow," and "dropsical or paralyzed woman" (§14), images of parting, sorrow, and separation, both literal and symbolic, and a kind of ruthless rootedness to the spot, required for realizing the sources of support when it seems that we have none.

We might say that the cornerstone of our uniqueness and our fate is always that which tends to be despised and rejected, either by ourselves or our culture. Or, the realization of our being depends on precisely that which we might overlook, the thing that looks all wrong, that doesn't, as it were, measure up, or feel at home, the part that refuses to be domesticated. The cornerstone is perhaps that yearning, whether we know it or not, that takes us away from everything familiar and sets us on a search, that longs for us to differentiate from the collective values into which we are born, those forces that can threaten the gem of our uniqueness, our divine calling. It is hardly surprising, therefore, that Jung's treasured stone found him on the banks of the lake in the place where he was seeking material expression of his inner-most thoughts and knowledge, where he was building the home of his destiny, and spoke of the orphan.

The experience of being abandoned, of feeling ourselves lost, bereft, belonging to no one—not even ourselves, to fall into that place where nothing makes sense, and everything that we thought we could depend on has disintegrated or disappeared—be it person or belief system or collective insti-tution, is that necessary landscape that situates our fate and our destiny, not as the son or daughter of particular parents in a particular historical or cultural context, but as that crea-ture, both human and divine, yet neither mortal nor immor-tal—the orphan—that has chosen incarnation here, in this body, in response to the Call, the call being creation's longing to fulfill its own mystery—unknown even perhaps to itself, unknown to myself.

Until we become traitors to the self that we know, until we are betrayed by all that is familiar, we do not come across this destiny of ours, this orphan nature that has no authority outside itself to depend on and yet is held by the forces of Heaven and Earth. All good therapy brings us to this moment of betrayal. All good therapy brings us to this moment of being able to say *no* to the person we thought we were, to the idea of ourselves rather than who we actually are, to the pro-visional life we have led, to what we thought we were devot-ed to, including the therapy itself. All good therapy is a silent witness to a passionate engagement and vibrating presence with the "roasting in hell" (as von Franz [1980a, p. 254] describes analysis), and that inexorably burns off the dross and brings us to our origins—not the historical or chrono-logical origins of our most recent incarnational history (although that exploration and the fictions we construct about it is one of the ways we get there), but to the origins of soul in that dark landscape where the gem of our fate no longer shines in the night, where we *know* we are not living authentically, where we must let go of the illusion that our past is responsible for who we are, and where we are finally brought to our knees in complete surrender into our divine destiny, our calling from the stars, those vocational pulsations that reach us in dream, true meeting, synchronistic event, the extraordinary in the most ordinary, in the words of a song, in symptom, accident, all those hints of the everyday that invite us into the River of Life, supported by the amrita of cosmic remembering, and with what von Franz (1980a) calls "conscious spontaneity . . . with a slight retardation" (p. 238), the "truth without reflection," an awareness that is willing to not be perfect and daring enough to risk mistakes, to risk failure for the sake of enlivening and animating the world; to arrive at that place of unknowing and eccentricity that allows the jewel to shine again. Sardello (1995) writes of this darkening:

> Giving up our sense of the past means putting our ego into question, ceasing to live by what we receive from the past, and entering the unknown. If we can, but for a moment, put aside our accustomed ways of approaching the world, which have to do with what we have been given from the past, we will feel . . . a passionate longing, but for what? (p. 59).

The presence of the orphan assures us that those landscapes so easily overlooked and lost are the ones most valued by the soul, by the cosmos, by those vibrations that most call to us from the stars. Soul thrives on failure, failure of the ego's illusions about itself. Until we come to wobbly ground, until we are deprived of all the familiar sources of support, we will not find what truly sustains us. There comes a time when we must be willing to meet what we cannot be sure of, by anyone or anything, and still embrace it, wholly, while knowing that at any moment, it might betray us, or we might betray it. We have to be willing to fail, and fail completely, for the sake of soul. When we live from this more complete place, there are greater uncertainties because it includes all the unknowns, what we feel and intuit, the mystery of who we are that can never be fully known. This takes real courage; an attitude of risk and daring toward life, toward a darker uncertain whole. In this soulscape, the orphan greets us, is our guide, our psychopomp, the precious solitaire of our fate.

To welcome the presence of the orphan is to move from a world of projections, where we are still dispersed and divided, into a cosmic being, where there is no longer any separation between psyche and matter, soul and world, no longer any separation between who we are, how we live, what we do, who we love; that place where we enter life fully, without reservation. The orphan is such a cosmic being, such a cornerstone. The orphan is that being that allows for the necessary differentiation of consciousness that draws us into a unified field of awareness. The orphan inhabits a unified field of synchronicities—for example, the wrong stone finding Jung at Bollingen and speaking to him of its orphan nature. And the paradoxical and metaphorical language that the orphan speaks must of necessity befuddle the ego's longing to make sense, for the nature of the reality evoked is much larger than cause/effect, discriminating, linear, time-bound consciousness—as useful and necessary as this latter is in our four-dimensional space-time world.

We are a mystery to be revealed, not only something to be known; we participate in other dimensions and vibrations of reality. We are, and are not, bounded by the extremities of the physical body. Just think of the dreaming body, or moments of intuitive clarity or precognition, or the presence of the third in therapy, which is neither the analyst nor the patient, yet is dependent on the presence of both. It is really difficult for those of us who still live in a Cartesian universe to remember these other landscapes, these subtle body realms, these en-livened fields of experience where we are not separate, yet are differentiated beings within these landscapes.

Jung (1961) lamented how hard it is for most people to live on close terms with the reality of the psyche. This difficulty was something he had to learn repeatedly (p. 228). It is grievous and hard to live exposed to the unknown, that which we cannot understand, or capture with our meanings, that Power beyond us which presents itself to us as a mystery from anOther realm inviting our response and participation. Those delights and shades of Creation searching for a partner, a lover, a beloved, to dance with on the earth among the stars! The philosopher William James (1982) writes:

> Our normal waking consciousness . . . is but one special type of consciousness, whilst all about it, parted from it by the filmiest of screens, there lie potential forms of consciousness entirely different. We may go through life without suspecting their existence; but apply the requisite stimulus, and at a touch they are all there in all their completeness (p. 388).

The "requisite stimulus" may simply be an attentiveness, an attunement, a shifting of one's perspective, a sideways glance toward the unseen presences of the Invisible world, a small gesture that powerfully and poignantly enlivens the parallel universes that surround us.

The Indo-European root of the word "orphan" is *orbh*, meaning "to put asunder," to separate. I love the sound of this root word, for it also evokes a heavenly body, an orb, a vibration that calls to us from the distant cosmos, bridging worlds, bringing together cosmic and human reality in a unified pulsating field, the orphan as star traveler that whispers in my ear of secrets not yet disclosed. The presence of this orphan star is such a soulful paradox for only that which separates us, only that which betrays the family (the familiar), that which pulls the rug from under our feet, that which removes us from what we most depended on, only that which enables us to differentiate ego consciousness from the larger whole, is that which also allows us to surrender into the darker mystery surrounding us. It is a magnificent uncertainty that penetrates us on all sides. Recently I had a powerful encounter with this imaginal soulful figure that arises out of the crack between worlds—between reality and Reality.

The Orphan and the Knee

In mid-November (1996) on a Thursday night I was on the floor of my study taking great delight, with my daughter, in wrapping gifts for my husband's birthday. We were intent and focused on our task, which involved large framed pictures. But when I moved to get up from the floor I could not straighten my knee, and I was in pain. What turned out to be a tear in the medial meniscus, the cartilage, in my right knee joint, and which required surgery, also meant that for almost a month I was immobile and quite dependent on those around me. This is an excruciating surrender for one who prides herself on her athletic activity and independent spirit; but from the soul's point of view, it was a necessary humiliation. Rooted to the spot, as it were, by the gift that I was intending for my lover, I myself was being called into a larger destiny.

The damage to my knee recalled my earliest traumatic memory. As a child of 4 I had a growth on my left knee that required a lengthy hospitalization and large step-ladder stitches whose scar tissue is still visible. I have painful memories of a terrible kind of abandonment and homesickness, fueled by my parents either not showing up or being late for the limited visiting hours, and the deep sadness that would get stuck in my throat while I looked at other children in the ward surrounded by their loved ones. I felt isolated and very much alone, unable to speak up when the boy and girl in the beds on either side of me would take my things and, as it seemed to me, not return them. The worst thing of all was when I finally returned home to find that the only doll that ever meant anything to me was not among my belongings, the doll with the golden hair and royal blue velvet dress—gone forever, and never replaced. I remember the torture of being given the anesthetic, a huge red pill I didn't think I could swallow, and the numb terror as the nurse told me while I was being wheeled on a cold steely cart through the swinging doors into the surgical theater, that by the time I counted to ten I would be asleep!

I do not know if the chronic insomnia that has pursued me all my life began at this time. Nor do I remember if my preoccupation with the image of the orphan coincided precisely with this disturbing event. However, in soul time, they belong together in my memory as among the most formative elements of my young life. I was absolutely convinced that I was an orphan and that my parents were not my own. I believed that this was true because, first of all, I was the only one in the family with dark hair—everyone else was fair or blond—and secondly, I was the only one who was left-handed. In addition, I hated to leave home to visit friends or stay with cousins because of the homesickness engendered by such excursions and the psychosomatic symptoms, including stomachaches and nosebleeds, generated by such separation anxieties. Too, I was excessively shy, and as if frozen in an inner world of silence unable to escape into the outside world. So, I did not speak, but read instead. One of my favorite books was The Secret Garden, the story of an orphaned girl who goes to live with her grieving and widowed uncle.

It was not until twenty-five years later, in my first Jungian analysis, that I began to learn of the orphan image and its ancient alchemical resonance—that it is an image of one's uniqueness, of one's divine fate and incarnational destiny. But to reach this nuance of such a soulful figure, the "homeless orphan" of one's youth, in other words, the self that adapts defensively in response to a wounding too large to cope with then, like the alchemists knew, must be sacrificed in order to transform such a false persona into a radiantly alive being aware of its shadows and its vocation. When the reality of the orphan finds its way into consciousness, it is a lifelong process of continual refinement and deepening of octaves of experience to realize its implications, for the orphan, like Jung's (1959) description of the self, is so small and at odds with the prevailing values of the world that it is in constant danger of being lost, forgotten, and overlooked. Though it is "the smallest of the small," it is nonetheless "the secret spiritus rector of our fate" (§257). As a young child, that fate was already present, calling, but of course I was too little to bear it, and so I experienced it as imposed from without, as a "not belonging." In my analysis I painted this feeling state in tortured figures that suggested the artist Munch's power-

ful and excruciating depiction, "The Scream" (or Screach, as it is sometimes called).

The lack of safety and security that I felt in being in the world inwardly made me quite dependent, but outwardly I defended against a devouring neediness, and became a model of independence and exploration. This in itself was not all bad. I had rather an interesting life, and experienced many adventures and challenges. I left home at 18, traveled extensively whenever I could, and left my country of origin at 21. In the U.S.A., I was classified as a "permanent resident alien," which always rather amused me, for it seemed to be the bureaucratic version of the orphan! I became involved with the women's movement, and was determined not to have children, but to develop my career. Although I married, I achieved a way of making sure I made myself secure—in an outward and financial sense—and merited love and attention by all my "successes"— intelligence, graduate degree, beauty, successful private practice! Sometimes I sadly wonder if I became a therapist in order to be intimately close to people, but not really in life with them. In this way, I could have real but illusory relationships, and I would never be in danger of being hurt by love. In my private life, I never really let anyone touch me or reach me or love me. And I myself never really loved, or reached or touched, except with the births of my two children.

In terms of a mutually loving adult relationship, however, I was not able to be vulnerable enough for such experience until well into the midpoint of my life, when all these carefully constructed and well-walled adaptations began to crack and dissolve. First my marriage fell apart; then the life went out of my work; and finally the "ka" left the earth, the geographical landscape, I was living on. I left home, practice, and doctoral studies, and took my children to my native England, where in the north Devon hills, I roamed on an extensive walkabout and did nothing, became no one in particular, letting the beauty and wildness of the landscape exert its balm in the cells of my soul, allowing all identities to molt, as the I Ching (Wilhelm, 1977) says: "Times change, and with them their demands. Thus the seasons change in the course of the year" *(p. 190). The feeling is that one changes, only at the right moment, the moment of divine timing, the kairos, when there is no longer any choice, and decay and stagnation must now be done away with.*

During this period of letting go, it happened to me from the gods and goddesses to fall in love for the first time in my life. This wide field of love, anticipated in dream, brought about by signs and miracles, otherwise known today as synchronistic events, like all true love, began slowly to allow its shadows to emerge, all the woundings of heart and soul to surface, all the loss and grief to make its way from sealed off places into awareness and life. And so it came about that I began to lose all confidence in myself, finding it hard to believe that I could be loved, loved for who I am, loved as a fading rose, not as a flower in full bloom, and not because of what I achieved or what I did. But not trusting enough that new life could emerge from the allowing of such divine insecurity, indeed that one's vocation emerges precisely from the withdrawing of all such support and resources of soul, I allowed myself to be talked back into an old place of fear and mistrust, in a new analysis that I had recently begun, and to begin to shore myself up with notions false to mySelf.

Enter the dream and the symptom! The night before I tore my cartilage, I dreamt that my daughter and her daughter (a physical impossibility as she is only 11) were dying, and that the loss was so grievous and so profound that I was feeling it and was also so over-whelmed by sadness that I was in denial about it, too. In the same dream, my closest friends at Pacifica deserted me, and my husband completely abandoned me. As all these things were literally untrue, the force of the psychic reality was apparently so soulfully neces-sary, the threat of loss of soul with the inauthentic direction that I was beginning to move in, so acute, that in case I didn't get it, I was, so to speak, paralyzed: stopped in my tracks. Prevented in that place, the knee, that so long ago, unbeknownst to me, initiated me prematurely into my life's work, and now here the return of the repressed, the fateful invitation once again to take up the realization of the orphan nature. The initial reaction was utter defeat, literally and psychically. I fell into a place of utter loneliness, abandonment, isolation, and withdrawal. Angry, discouraged, unconsolable, and helpless, the 4- year-old child came back with powerful presence and reality.

But the child is also an imaginal presence, and as such is our becoming and our future, that creative force born from dark chaotic origins in the fertile ground of the soul, arising from deeper mysteries accompanied by a whole agenda, a whole fate. That alien, homesick child was for the Gnostics the constellation of the wakeup call, that moment of longing and yearning for our true home, home being that fulfillment of our vocation and destiny, that which returns us to the realms of light.

Jonas (1963) in *The Gnostic Religion* writes of the alien life as not only a predicate of God, but as an expression of an elemental human experience. What he says of the alien can easily be used to describe the orphan, and his description reminds us of Jung's own words on this theme. Jonas writes:

> The alien is that which stems from elsewhere and does not belong here. To those who do belong here it is thus the strange, the unfamiliar and incomprehensible; but their world on its part is just as incomprehensible to the alien that comes to dwell here, and like a foreign land where it is far from home. Then it suffers the lot of the stranger who is lonely, unprotected, uncomprehended, and uncomprehending in a situation full of danger. Anguish and homesickness are a part of the stranger's lot. The stranger who does not know the ways of the foreign land wanders about lost; if he learns its ways too well, he forgets that he is a stranger and gets lost in a different sense by succumbing to the lure of the alien world and becoming estranged from his own origin. Then he has become a "son of the house." This too is part of the alien's fate. In his alienation from himself the distress has gone, but this very fact is the culmination of the stranger's tragedy. The recollection of his own alienness, the recognition of his place of exile for what it is, is the first step back; the awakened homesickness is the beginning of the return. All this belongs to the "suffering" side of alienness. Yet with relation to its origin it is at the same time a mark of excellence, a source of power and of a secret life unknown to the environment and in the last

resort impregnable to it, as it is incomprehensible to the
creatures of this world (pp. 49–50).

The recollection, then, of our orphanic nature is a secret disclosure from the divine unknown realms that connects us
with our cosmic destiny. The orphan calls us to remember
that we are both immanently human and transcendently
divine; both homeless wanderers, easily lost, misunderstood
and anguished, and indestructible precious stones, marked
both by painful tragedy and glowing excellence. The wounding is our vocation. We might remember that the earliest
depth psychologists were called "alienists," a name we have
sadly given up. Have we become as therapists "sons of the
house," so adapted to the prevailing collective values of
rationality, order, meaning and what is already known—
divorced from a larger Whole—that we have dangerously
forgotten the true origins of our devotion to soul and that
part of us, as Jonas (1963) reminds us, "which stems from
elsewhere and does not belong here" (p. 49)?

But why the knees? What seat of consciousness speaks
from those flexible members that take us on different paths
and call us in a new direction? Onians (1989) writes that
according to the ancient Greek view, the knees have sanctity
and are symbolic of generative power, as the seed of new life
is to be found there. The knees were the source of vitality
and strength and, in addition to the head, were the other
home of psyche. The psyche was that on which the life of the
body depended, and it was thought of as being both interested in, and affecting, one's destiny. For Plato, the knees were
specifically connected with the alignment of soul, or fate,
with the constellation of the stars or, as we might say, the
alignment of our human and eternal or greater self; the resituation of our body in a more encompassing psycho-cosmic
field. When I engaged my knee in meditative dialogue, a
spirit figure called Fred (rather unromantic I thought!) spoke
up quite loudly about being trapped in there until I found
a way of speaking my truth, speaking what I know from

experience, and relying rather less on authorities outside myself.

The *medial meniscus* is the cartilage that cushions the knee joint or pivot. A tear here is a wounding to the "middle, little crescent moon" (the literal meaning of *medial meniscus*). Moon symbolism connects to all things of a feminine, nocturnal nature, including specifically at the midpoint in life, the shifts of the moon cycle into menopausal transformation, and the heating up of the body into wise woman knowing, a change from mothering primarily others, toward attending to instinct, vision, passion, erotic clitoral love, and the larger fate that calls through symptom and dream. It is the turning on the spiral of life, that pivot that ruthlessly insists that we give up the remaining vestiges of a persona-dominated existence, and move—now—into an eccentric, authentic, unpredictable, inconsistent, ethical, rooted, responsible life, deeply attuned to the multi-dimensional vibratory voices of Other, soul, world, and cosmos, voices that tell you that you must change your life. So, I gave up the pursuit of licensing or any remaining fantasies of training to become a Jungian analyst, and I fired my analyst. I radically let go of what was from the point of view of a larger fate, a wrong direction, and simultaneously surrendered into an insecure and unknown path.

About two months before these unfoldings, and after my first meeting with the new analyst, I had the following dream. In retrospect this dream—a calling from the stars—already imagined the course of events that in fact took place. Being rather slow, and not adequately hearing or trusting the message of the dream, it took a series of dramatic events for its disclosures to reach me!

Dream

I'm walking with a group of women. Suddenly in the distance, I see the most incredible sight: huge mythological birds—I've never seen anything like it before. They are crane or stork-like, but much larger and more fabulous than anything in reality. Their huge size is terrifying to me. Some seem to have the appearance of baboons with their young riding on their backs. I'm worried that these awesome birds are going to come near us, and that's what begins to happen; these creatures begin circling around, nearer and nearer.

Then I'm in an open field. Suddenly two more ordinary birds (one is like a woodpecker or kingfisher, but I'm not really sure) swoop down, and with their beaks, hold fast to my thumb and hand, as if to pin me to the ground. I gasp at their ability and strength to do this. It's as if they are insisting that I must have an encounter with these huge birds. Then one of the mythological birds—stork-like and pink in color—swoops down by my side. It is awesome; I am so afraid. But it does not harm me. It wants me to see something. I find that I cannot, dare not, look at it directly. From my averted gaze, out of the corner of my eye, I see that its belly is like a glistening, pinkish, huge round sphere, rather like a bubble catching the light and reflecting different colors, and I can see through and into it. In this belly are contained all the secrets of creation. It's as if there's a universe in there. I am so overcome; I cannot look directly at this; I keep my gaze averted. This is a very emotional, awesome, experience.

The group of women I'm with are both there, and not there, but somehow their presence is like a field of energy helping me tolerate or bear this transpersonal experience.

Next, I have to tell the community of my experience; it is my job. Somehow the news of the event is already out, and people are bickering about trivial things, like: "Did this really happen? Could it have happened? Such birds don't really exist." I start weeping: these details are not the point. I tell of my experience of the numinosum, an overwhelming experience confronting me with the Reality of the Divine. Then out of a feeling of grief for the impoverished state of psychology, I quote Jung on psychotherapy: it "is a mere makeshift that does its utmost to prevent numinous experiences." Then I continue saying something like: we have to get beyond psychoanalytic psychology's emphasis on technique, method, and interpretation, for these structures act too often as filters preventing real Presence and direct Experience. But direct Experience is often so original, and so terrifying (to the ego) we

erect dogmas to protect us from the "spirit blowing where it lis-
teth," and so fix our experience in systems that no longer matter.

The feeling in the dream is that the practice of therapy and pro-
fessional psychology has become crusty and decadent and is in decay.
There is a real need for new wine to be poured into new skins. There
is a feeling of urgency about this; this is really important. It is some-
how conveyed to me, or it becomes apparent, that my encounter
with the birds means that I am called to take a stand vis-à-vis the
importance of divine disclosures as leading to new knowledge, a
new kind of vibration and gnosis coming into the world from the
Beyond, at the ending of an aeon, and the beginning of another
aeon. New knowledge is often ostracized, but I must ally myself
with my vision, speak up on behalf of it, and not be afraid to make
a fool of myself! I can be assured that there is total support from
the other side for this. I must take my experiences (this, and other
visions) seriously. Cranes and stork-like birds are auspicious, pro-
pitious, and bring new life with them from the Divine to the human
realms.[1]

This dream came at a point when I was seriously struggling
with doubts about my vocation as a psychotherapist. What
strikes me about the dream is that while it addresses this personal issue, it is as if my own pain about my work mirrors the
suffering state of depth psychology itself; that psychology
itself, in its theory and practice, feels, as the dream mood
reflects, "crusty and decadent and in decay." It is as if my
own doubts about my work are in fact confirmed, and the
response to these uncertainties is to be encouraged to be a
witness to the importance of numinous disclosures as they
enter the human realm, for the dream suggests that new
knowledge is attempting to incarnate at this turn of the aeon.

The numinosity of the divine transpersonal realm
approaches me in the form of giant mythological birds that

---

1. Author's Dream Journal, October 11, 1996.

bring a sense of the *mysterium tremendum* with them. These birds, as image of the transpsychic Self, are, according to Corbett, "reminiscent of the occasions in the Tantric tradition in which a god (usually Krishna) shows himself to his followers in a way in which his body contains the universe."[2] In the belly of the bird, the secrets of creation are remarkably revealed, alluding to the cosmic nature of the Self. This is an awesome experience, glimpsing vast wonders way beyond the limitations of earthly life.

In many mythologies, birds represent a collaboration and connection between the human and spirit realms. Birds are often considered to be manifestations of the divine, and it is not unusual for a god or goddess to assume bird form. Different birds are associated with different divinities; for example, Athena's theriomorphic presence includes the owl, and Aphrodite is accompanied by a goose or a dove. Too, oracular utterances from the world-soul often were heard in the chirping of a bird's song—a "bird-telling"—or in the flight pattern of a group of birds, or in the appearance of particular kinds of birds. Shamans the world over relate to birds as manifestations of spirit and as companions that take them on their flights to the different planes of spirit and on their journeys of soul retrieval. A shaman's ritual dress may include feathered garments; they may carry an eagle feather as a symbol of the highly developed psychic, intuitive, and visionary powers of second sight. In all these instances the descent of spirit into matter is imaged, such as Jesus experienced at his baptism when the Holy Spirit in the form of a dove descended upon him.

Of particular importance in this dream is the stork/crane-like bird, and the curious appearance of the baboon-like bird, which made no sense to me at the time of the dream. Much

---

2. Personal communication, Dr. Lionel Corbett.

later, in researching Egyptian mythology for creation stories that might be relevant for the central theme of this book, I came across the image of the god Thoth, who is represented with either an ibis or a baboon head. This struck me like a thunderbolt. The ibis is very similar to the crane of the dream world. Thoth is also called Hermes and is the god of writing, numbers, measurement and time. He is also imaged as the baboon- or ibis-headed god who attends the weighing of the heart at death. He is the scribe who records the verdict of the weighing of the heart against the feather of Truth, the goddess Maat, who also symbolizes the principle of Integrity and Harmony as a cosmic law, and who, as cosmic consciousness, directs the refinement of all existence toward its treasured goal.

These revelations clarified for me that my vocation was leading me in the direction of writing, of writing not from the ego's point of view, but, in what I am attempting in this book, a writing that is willing to surrender into what wants to be written, a writing that brings the collective themes into the personal, a visionary writing that is undertaken in love as a union between a deeply felt experience and its articulation, a writing whose expression is also its content, a writing that tries to remain as close to the truth of what is attempting to incarnate through me. These disclosures felt like acts of profound love from the world-soul toward me. I can only say that the beauty and love of these revelations are among the most humbling and exciting experiences I have ever had. The only appropriate response to this numen is silence. After silence has been honored, then in fear and trembling, I pick up my pen.

The awesomeness of this dream points to the remarkable unity of Self and cosmos, and to an unknowable Reality that extends far beyond Itself. The vastness of the vision, too, has the effect of compensating for the isolated elements of the conscious self that, with its thoughts and feelings, and preoccupation with its conflicts, always remains in doubt. The dream reality responds out of a wholeness of being that includes knowing and not knowing, direct looking and averted gaze, and that emphasizes *experience* over understanding. As Jung (1969a) writes: this kind of paradox "does more justice to the *unknowable* than clarity can do, for uniformity of meaning robs the mystery of its darkness and sets it up as something that is known. That is a usurpation, and it leads the human intellect into hybris" (§417). Paradox, then, by allowing space for the unknowable, gives a more accurate picture of how things are.

In such numinous disclosures, the conscious ego is thrust out of its isolated illusion that *its* world is all there is, and which stance is, for Jung, the source of neurotic suffering. The ego no longer suffers alone, but with divine insecurity and wisdom it can now suffer consciously and ethically by taking on the invitation, perhaps even demands, of the other side to be witnessed. When the ego is so relativized, and united with a transpersonal authority beyond itself, it rests in a place beyond all involvements, and is comparable to the apocryphal mystical saying from the Acts of John (in Pulver, 1978): "If thou understoodest suffering thou wouldst have nonsuffering" (p. 180). Our self-knowledge and sense of identity are deepened, and a kind of empathic attitude toward suffering, toward our own and the pain of others, is realized.

Suffering transformed becomes the humbling act of responding to the call of the divine realms—freely given, freely acted upon. It is an experience that transforms life into glowing pools of richly textured complexity that beautifully compromise daylight consciousness, making it more like starlight. We stand on the edge of the abyss of the mysteries, brimming with a sensibility too large for ourselves alone, a visionary sight that includes everything, that forgets nothing, that encompasses all light and all shadows. Suffering tranformed, like love, is that difficult work for which the patient attending to our wounding is but preparation. Suffering tranformed is that shattering that eventuates in a disclosure of the cosmos as fueled by love. The mystical gnosis above (in Pulver, 1978) continues: "See through suffering and thou wilt have nonsuffering. . . . Understand the Word of Wisdom in me" (p. 180).

The numina of the psyche, those divine images from a transpsychic source, seem to require what Jung (1969a) suggests in "Answer to Job" as mankind's edge over God, his "slight moral superiority over the more unconscious God" (§575). This is the ego's capacity for self-reflection within its own limited and bounded scope. Mankind provides the awareness that the *phenomenon* (§600) of the deity sorely lacks. As with Job, keeping one's suffering in awareness and standing one's ground—in Job's case, he sees Yahweh's inner antimony without doubting His unity—without succumbing to the temptation of making it about this or that, and thus falling victim to the more powerful Other, finally leads to the reward of a glimpse into the nature of the transpersonal psyche.

The word "pathos" is from the Greek *pathein* meaning "a spiritual experience," and the revealed knowledge, or "gnosis" (not rational, scientific knowledge) that comes from successive stages of suffering, of experiencing the divine. Jung (1975) writes in a letter: "But the fact is that the approach to the numinous is the real therapy, and inasmuch as you attain to the numinous experiences you are released from the curse of pathology. Even the very disease takes on a numinous character" (p. 377). The wounding is the vocation.

The knee then, for me, was that agent of change, that landscape of body and soul that from earliest times was the place of constitutional weakness, or incarnational vulnerability, the site of a wounding that recoiled in on itself in protection and terror, and yet held within itself an opening, a vocation and a destiny that opened me to the stars, the habitat of the orphan, the homeless, parentless stranger, who paradoxically takes us home. At the moment when I was about to be estranged from my true origins in a comfortable but, from the soul's point of view, tragic life, the collapse of the knee, that other home of psyche, brought me back to that necessary place of exile, that place of homesickness and longing that is the beginning of the return.

THE ORPHAN AND THE STONE: RETURN

The Australian author David Malouf (1996), in his novel *An Imaginary Life,* writes of the protagonist's relation to the child, the wild uncivilized child, nourished in a place of exile in which he—the protagonist—is then increasingly enabled to take on his true destiny:

> We barely recognize the annunciation when it comes, declaring: Here is the life you have tried to throw away. Here is your second chance. Here is the destiny you have tried to shake off by inventing a hundred false roles, a hundred false identities for yourself. It will look at first like disaster, but is really good fortune in disguise, since fate too knows how to follow your evasions through a hundred forms of its own. Now you will become at last the one you intended to be (p. 94).

The orphan, then, like Orpheus, next to whom he stands in the dictionary and who is likewise of parentage both human and divine, is that star-traveler, that shamanic figure, who knows how to travel between the worlds, who has mastered consciousness such that he speaks the language of neither mortal nor God, who is as much at home in the underworld as in nature, who hears the voices of the Invisibles and translates their sound into song, who, divorced from the familiar attitudes is willing to risk—and fail—for the sake of the transformation of the human into the divine, the divine into the human. The orphan is that figure who straddles both the transcendent and the immanent, life and death, work and love. The orphan is that liminal presence who stands at the threshold of the therapy room, calling us out of the collective into our destiny and vocation, into the larger world where spirit and matter dissolve into a unified field of radiant mysteries, into a vibrant cacaphony of multidimensional resonance, that landscape where we are not only humans on Earth, but citizens of the cosmos.[3]

---

3. Robert Romanyshyn has also written—though in a different way—on the figure of the orphan and its link with the angel in his (1999) book, *The Soul in Grief: Love, Death, and Transformation.*

"Evening" Rilke's (1989, p. 13) poem, suggests this nei-ther/nor orphan resonance when he talks of watching the sky, and that life inside each of us is bounded and also immeasurable—stone and star. The link the orphan figure provides between stone and star, between our destiny here and our soul's origins, between what we remember and what we have forgotten, became particularly clear to me one day while roaming through an old stone circle in England.

Ancient Stones

It is a cold, blue, March day, and I am visiting the massive stones at Avebury Circle in Wiltshire, England. Even the name, Ave-bury—as if the name itself is a dream—calls to me: Ave! Hail! Greetings! It has always been my favorite stone circle haunt. I pre-fer it to the more popular and stunning Stonehenge, which griev-ously, due to pollution, wear and tear, you can now only look at from afar. Avebury is a site whose hoary whisperings sing ancient songs of faraway memories and mist-shrouded roots. These sounds echo here as if by nature this place still reverberates with memories of times long ago that still call out to us.

Wandering among these stony beasts, I was struck this time by how these ancient standing stones seemed to be at once both alive beings frozen in gestures of speech, song, and celebration, and at the same time enduring a terrible kind of agony, as if they still remember something that we have sadly now long forgotten. Could it be that these faithful guardians remain as keepers of a knowledge through the vicissitudes of our less enduring human pursuits, and stand as sentinels for the cosmos, gate keepers of the mysteries to which we are ever invited to return?

Could it be that this ending of a century, ending of a millenium, ending of an Aeon also marks the ending of a massive cosmic con-traction and the turn toward a longed for cosmological anamnesis? Could it be that we are recollecting what was once known, and per-haps still remembered somewhere in the cells of our souls, before the hubris of knowing about, separated as it is from the unknown and dark visionary gnosis of the Whole, set in? Could it be that our suf-fering and our woundedness—both ours and the planet's—are invi-

tations to let go of what we have come to know so well and to darken what has become both so illuminated and so devastated?

Like a piece of music that penetrates the heart by its beauty and its pathos with an immediacy before words arise, these huge stones sang out to me their harmonies and disharmonies of dim remembrances and of vistas not yet seen, horizons which in their longing reach out to me from the future.

We are in danger of betraying the original vision and call of depth psychology that is possible with the transformation of consciousness with our all too limited perspectives ensconced in personalistic psychological theories. Affective complexes are woundings of the soul and body, vulnerable openings through which, in a vertical rather than a linear fashion, so to speak, the transpersonal center of the psyche (the divine realm) tries to get our attention and incarnate in the human body. When bearing the abandonments that suffering brings, by allowing our wounds to reveal our vocation, the human realm completes God's creation by singing back to the Divine the grievous state of his losses, the poignancy of his failures, and the wondrous beauty of his attempts at love, creative work, and the artistry of a life.

Jung (1969a) speaks of the necessity of conscious suffering as a precursor for the constellation of the healing activity of the psyche that comes from the transpersonal levels of the unconscious, and is experienced as grace and revelation, rewarding the individual by reconnecting her with "the sources of psychic life [which mark] the beginning of the cure" (§534). The regaining of such a religious outlook on life (which has nothing to do with institution or creed) is for Jung the only *experience*—because by nature, *transformative*—that truly brings about a healing, a restoration of the whole (§509).

Such an approach holds that an "anamnesis of the origins"[4] is not only of a personal kind, but of a cultural, histor-

---

4. C. G. Jung, CW 9ii, §279.

ical, and even cosmic nature, anamnesis being a recollection, a remembering of what has gone before, a recovery of a lost and forgotten wholeness, a re-connection to the foundation of existence, and the re-situation of a differentiated, but in our times often sadly alienated, ego consciousness within its psycho-cosmic home.

Could our willingness to descend into unknown chaos, to make that journey to the underworld once more that inevitably accompanies our suffering, also constellate that numinous longing of the soul, voiced by that devotee of Aphrodite, Sappho, when she says, "I want. I yearn"? A longing perhaps for the rebirth of the soul, a rebirth of the soul into life and into love, and into a rich texture of creative daring and eccentricity? This cosmic fullness is guarded without ceasing by the challenges of our suffering, the hints of our dreams, and by the stones at Avebury.

Chapter 4

THE OTHER WOMAN
Chaos and Clitoral Consciousness

It is striking that in the case of the goddess many more dark, even
quite sinister, unfathomable aspects are emphasised along with
the light aspects. . . . Consequently, this feminine goddess all-
Nature also possesses cunning, cruelty, wickedness, unfathomable depths of passion and the uncanny gloom of death . . . in
equal measure with the potentiality of new life and rebirth. . . .
[N]o woman can become conscious of her larger, greater self
without having lived *these* aspects of the goddess within herself.
—M.-L. von Franz (1980b), pp. 155–156

"I'd rather die than be fat."
—Quote from a young girl
in K. Gilday (1990)

This chapter explores chaos and the marginalized Feminine.
In our Western tradition, chaos has played the role of the
Other, has often been depicted as female, and has even been
connected specifically with women's experience. Chaos is a
system of nonlinear dynamics, and this chapter emphasizes
how the feminine, especially in its cyclical, sensual, erotic,
dark, rhythmic, and transformative dimensions, has been
eclipsed in patriarchal consciousness. Because of our attachment to order, reason, and progress, of the wide range of feminine qualities only the virginal-as-chaste and motherly
aspects have been acceptable to the patriarchal ego. We have
even lost the original meaning of the word "virgin," who is a
"free woman," with her own integrity and life unrelated to
anyone else and certainly unrelated to her sexual choices.

The alienation of the chthonic and chaotic depths of feminine instinctuality in the West has often led to the irruption of the devalued feminine in our culture, in forms terrifying to ego consciousness: maenad, witch, mystic, hysteric, and now borderline and multiple personality disorder. But you are also this Other woman, and this essay seeks to explore the often treacherous yet inspirational shift from domestic fidelity to the center of gravity rooted in the law of your own feminine being. This Other woman, neglected and abused through- out history, will not be silenced. She is here to stay, to find her voice, to voice her wounds, to find her creative work, to be met—not infantilized, disregarded, or acting as caretaker for her partner—and to live her life with love, with integrity, and in truth.

THE MARGINALIZED FEMININE
AND SUPPRESSION OF LIFE

In 1993, Katherine Gilday's film *The Famine Within* (1990) was widely broadcast on public television in the United States. When I first glanced at the title, my eyes deceived me and I read, "The Feminine Within." Actually, the film is an accomplished and painful documentary on the continuing oppression of the feminine and the goddess in our culture, via a penetrating analysis of eating disorders and other disorders of the body that continue to haunt women. It made me weep, such was the depth of sorrow, longing, and grief touched by an awareness of the absence of an embodied, sacred, feminine presence in contemporary life. Abundant, voluptuous, regenerative archetypal images of the ancient goddesses were interspersed with emaciated, pre-adolescent bodies of young women exercising excessively to control their appetites, sensuality, and sexuality. For these young women, the scales are the evaluator and regulator of self-esteem, feeling, and mood.

The idealization of this specialized body type among the beauty and fashion industries bears no relation to the reality of women's bodies, bodies that need substance to menstruate, procreate, and be the carriers of a wise, vital, and dark consciousness. Yet the media can override our everyday experience, which is now manipulated and determined by the preponderant eye of the camera. It struck me as the embodiment of evil, a modern version of Nazi Germany, for this socially sanctioned starvation continues to encourage the psyche/matter split prevalent in the West and promotes a myth that deludes women about the radiance of their vitality, strength, and creativity, exalting the ideals of abstract thought and civilization at the expense of physical earthiness and the organic rhythms of nature. It is the embodiment of the patriarchal myth that splits male and female, within and between.

Why do we allow ourselves to be so deluded by the values of the status quo, values that promise equality as long as we remain thin? How can young girls become women if culture conspires to keep us children? It seems that as long as men and women are unconscious of the power-driven, goal-oriented, bottom line, materialistic focus of our modern belief system, with its willful demands to be best, perfect, rational, and distanced, we will all suffer the ravages of a lack of attunement to process, presence, surrendering, receiving, and trusting, and to what the shadows of the psyche want with us in a more complete way. Until we can once again value the mystery of who we are, the mystery of reality, we will continue to please and be unconsciously devoted to the dominant cultural values. As long as we remain blind, the unique vision of life that our bodies hold continues to remain obscured, our vision of life continues to be separated from living, and the Spirit of Truth continues to be divorced from an authentic relationship to matter.

As I watched the film on television, I was moved into an altered state of consciousness, emotional and participatory, into a Homeric dreamscape of poetic performance and maenad possession, watching the symptomatic shadow presence of the goddess as writhing anorexics sought their ecstatic highs on treadmills and in collective workouts to MTV music. The obsessive attempts to perfect the body and strip Her of any signs of softness portrayed a quite out-of-control cult of body in a manic attempt to control the fat. The apparent distrust of body and nature—viewed by anorexics as a *massa confusa* of chaotic and dangerous impulses—rests in a need to achieve immortality and control decay. True suffering and pleasure seem eclipsed in instincts run amok.

All at once, I felt I was experiencing the shadow body of recorded history, the oppression of the goddess in her many shadow incarnations as maenad, witch, mystic, *soror mystica*, hysteric, borderline, and nowadays women who yield to the knife in unnecessary medical operations. What is it that women carry that historically is so dangerous to culture and must be gotten rid of? Skafte (1992) suggests that women's bodies symbolize dark beginnings and cyclical tides; they are rhythms and reminders of life and death, the incarnate limitation of flesh, the expansive wisdom of second sight. Women's bodies bleed, birth, gestate, swell, desire and love, like the pulsating rhythms of the ocean, or the unpredictable vicissitudes of the moon. Women's bodies are strong, needy, moody, eruptive, feeling. Women embody a multidimensional, "antennae" consciousness, a telepathic awareness borne of millenia of engaging many activities simultaneously: working while gossiping while cooking while knowing while creating while attending to children while tracking the emotional atmosphere! Women's consciousness is closer to the shadows of psyche.

Patriarchal societies wish not to be reminded of these values that emerge from the wisdom of the instinctual soul/ body, rather than from the control of an ego split off from what matters. Patriarchal societies hate change, and resist surrender to the chaos of the unknown and the dangers of the overpowering and unpredictable, otherwise known as Life! The patriarchal ego prefers progress and predictable, solar consciousness, the external regulation of behavior and impersonal collective attitudes—often seen, for example, in the role of mother—and above all, the fantasy of its own immutable and orderly continuity, without too many displays of emotion—especially dark emotion—thank you! Perhaps the development of left brain activity required the suppression of the feminine mode in both men and women. Perhaps the acceleration of knowledge required the liberation of the developing ego from its entanglement with the things of nature and of the world.

But what recurring pattern of human experience is this shadow body attempting to incarnate and ensoul through time and refusing to silence? Could it be, as Gimbutas (1989) writes, "the renewal of life, not only human but all life on earth and indeed in the whole cosmos" (p. xix), a renewal on an altogether different plane of reality, a transformed embodiment of psyche, not seen since the pre-Homeric age of the goddess? Could it be that we are not just going through a cultural transition, but a major Earth-shift of unprecedented proportions, a transmutation with radical implications in Earth/Human body consciousness? Is this a time when left and right brains, male and female, must be brought into a new synthesis within the individual, between persons, or within society and culture as a whole? Is this a time when our endangered life cycle once again requires divine containment?

During Gilday's film, I was struck by the collective consciousness of those who suffer so-called disorders of the body, the nonparticularity of a possession gripping thousands. My point is not to focus on the diagnostic categories, but to try to see how our symptoms address us, how they call out to us to listen and give voice to what would otherwise remain silenced. What are we being called to remember by this demonstration of the shadow body of our culture? Is an *appetite for life* being culturally oppressed and in desperate need of vital conscious integration?

Perhaps, unless we are willing to be original, to embody the face we had before we were born, to initiate ourselves individually and collectively into the vision that each of our bodies holds, the shift will abort itself and we will lose the opportunity again. We live at a point in history when we have the tools to become more aware of the darkness that each of us houses and the light that each of us radiates, and to be ethically responsible for, and responsive to, that darkness and that light, so we can stop having others carry it for us—either our neighbors, those we alienate and condemn in our societies, or foreign nations that become designated as the enemy.

This process involves an awakening of our passion, longing, and depth; it is a journey, often terrifying, of conscious suffering to bring to awareness the love, vitality, and ecstasy that resides in the human heart; it is an attitude that values abysmal, chaotic states of vegetative decay as much as uncontrolled ecstatic experience; it is an attitude that values the ordinariness of mundane existence. This journey requires conscious knowledge of the destruction and evil of which we are all capable, and a soulful ethic willing to sacrifice the demons for the good. This journey invites us to affirm consciously and live out our gifts and resources; to be conscious and clear of the "I want" in the psyche that arises out of *who I am*, not *who I think* I am, that arises, that is, out of an awareness in touch with its shadows; and to become deeply grounded in our instincts and the natural wisdom waiting to be born in the secrets of the flesh.

The initiation requires both psychological knowledge and an appreciation of the energetic nature of humankind. This necessitates the full, simultaneous functioning of the chakras of tantric yoga, housing a range of vibratory parallel universes of body/consciousness, and the alignment of human, astrological, and cosmic rhythms, for which the chakras—those spirit/matter transformers—provide the connecting link. And lest this sounds like a lot, let us remember that in all likelihood the ancient Mystery Schools, of which our own institutes of psychological training are but an impoverished echo, required at least 30 years of initiatory devotion and education. In reality, this transition from an adaptive patriarchal mode to one that includes a relationship to the archetyp-al feminine is a move of unprecedented proportions. It is no easy task, and can take years, or a lifetime, or more than a lifetime.

The oppression of passion, vitality, and vision, carica-tured by obsessive "working out" and fads of every kind, and by a culture on the verge of collective and individual chaos, seems to lie at the root of our contemporary malaise. We live in an age of breakdown, breakdown of the order that we have constructed in the West. We live at a time in which institu-tional and geopolitical boundaries are collapsing; in which the hierarchical structure of the family is dissolving and peo-ple are finding where and to whom they spiritually belong; when individuals are being visited by beings from other dimensions; and when the scientific worldview has already moved in the direction of an a-causal, a-rational, universe comprised mostly of an unknown dark matter. This moment of deadly peril and unparalleled potential at the turn of a mil-lenium and at the shift of an astrological Aeon (from Pisces to Aquarius) invites us to a radical revisioning of life, to an expansion of our worldview beyond the fringes of our knowledge, to a much more vast vision of reality. This moment invites us to remember the mythological origins of the cosmic forces of chaos, those forces that birth eros, not order.

MARGINALIZED MYTHS

If we survey the archetypal images and patterns that are most oppressed in our culture, they are images most associ-ated with an irrepressible expression and celebration of life, but devalued in patriarchy as dangerously unboundaried and chaotic: the beauty, sensuality, and sexuality of Aphrodite; the creativity that would emerge from our woundedness, from those gaping sores that make us vulner-able to cosmic vibrations seeking human embodiment such as we find in Hephaistos, husband of Aphrodite; and uncontrolled, ecstatic experience, a Dionysian revelry that values the wet instinctual planes of body and nature as being infused with soul and celebrates the feminine as all those matters exiled by our Apollonic modes.

Most profoundly oppressed is Eros, who requires connection to the depths of Psyche and who, still disowned, re-emerges as the coming guest. Eros is that primordial deity linked with the mysteries of Earth and the Underworld, that mighty-winged daimon arising out of the foam-born Goddess Aphrodite who, collapsing boundaries and shattering our outmoded and split collective beliefs, invites us down the other road, that path less taken, that might make all the difference. Often the individuation process of women in our culture signifies this unification of instinct, underworld, awareness, creativity, and love in our attempts to contain our experience within an archetypal feminine ground.

In my own life, the power of the neglected goddess addressed me quite forcefully in a dream. In a way, it is a miracle to me that such ancient and lost knowledge can reach us in this manner. In spite of collective forces, both in the culture and in our consciousness, keeping us in our place, we are visited by a Teacher from another realm, who indicates a gnosis completely at odds with everything we have been taught. For Her, the dream teacher, a woman's body is holy. The center of women's ways is not the head but the genitals, not the womb but the clitoris—clitoris not only as sexually pleasurable, but as birthing a whole new consciousness for women; clitoris then as body, metaphor, and symbol. Woman become virgin again, woman-unto-herself, woman birthing herself.

The Breakthrough of Clitoral Consciousness

I am with a woman who is instructing me about my body, specifically about my genitals. The focus is on my clitoris. The woman is conveying to me that my clitoris is a seed and needs to be planted, the point being that woman gives birth to woman; woman gives birth to herself/Herself. In the dream my clitoris has become quite large (not like reality) and it is throbbing with life, a mixture of pleasure and pain unlike anything I've ever experienced. The power of the feeling wakes me up, and I realize in coming to reality that few human orgasms can compare with the feminine energy—raw, original Shakti energy—of the superhuman, goddess clitoris of the dream world. The feeling in the dream was that if that energy was released, you would burst through into a different universe, or a different order, or create a completely new world.[1]

The dream is a celebration of the feminine Self, a new world in which I am given the gift of my true essence, a fierce, instinctual, primordial love of being female, a compelling introduction to my lower sexual chakra that will create new realms of feeling, creativity, and vision, rooted in the body of a full, untapped range of goddess power and imagination longing for recognition and incarnation, lost to the world for centuries. Stripped of false personas, I am laid bare to She who initiates me to the deep and dark chthonic powers of the underworld, to the Earth and her fertilizing, decaying, and regenerative possibilities. What would it really be like to live, work, and love from a clitoral consciousness, from that seed-bed of imagination? The work of uncivilizing myself from those upper-world-cultivated adaptations that no longer worked, but that had served me well for almost half my life, seemed daunting and dangerous—the work of the next half of my life, and beyond.

The dream, coming early on in a lengthy and devastating divorce process, initiates me into a birthing or manifestation of my own vital feminine Self, a movement away from mothering primarily others (perhaps more appropriately imaged by the womb), to an erotic relationship to life, creativity, work, and self, centered in the symbolic image of the clitoris. That this sacred sexuality could be traced back thirty thousand years to cultures in which the goddess was the matrix for valuing life and death was a numinous revelation and endowed profound meaning to my life. It made the loneliness of going my own way possible. An inner female authority, with

---

1. Author's Dream Journal, May 9, 1990.

her joyous juicy ways, was in the process of rooting and sprouting! This was a profoundly different experience from the distorted and impoverished feminine image of the TV movie described at the beginning of this chapter. This embodiment of jouissance separate from birthing literal children is generally denied women in our culture who, because of the patriarchal myth, are denied life's vitality in the production of nurturing others, to the detriment of their own organic, emotional, spiritual, and creative needs.

Marilyn Gimbutas, in *The Language of the Goddess* (1989) writes: "The vulva is portrayed either as a supernatural triangle associated with aquatic symbolism, as a seed and sprout, or as an oval vulva swollen as in preparation for birth. Each category has its own meaning: the first is the cosmic womb of the Goddess, the source of the waters of life; the second is the sprouting of life; the third is the giving of birth" (p. 99). I wonder, too, if the seed marks the clitoris, and the swollen vulva marks a heightened state of arousal, symbolic of a sacred sexuality, "indicative of the profound relationship which exists between sexual energies, and 'religare,' religion, and unity with the God(dess)" (Men, 1990, p. 138). Humbatz Men even adds that human orgasms move the Galactic Center, from which all creation emerges. The human is imaged as erotically involved in all events in the cosmos. Certainly, the feminine sexual organs relate to the root chakra of tantric yoga and is the red or orange center of rooted vitality that maintains our lives, physically and symbolically. The dot, like the seed, in Maya esoterism, also symbolizes *Hun,* the manifestation of everything.

FEMININE IMAGES OF CHAOS/EROS

The worship of Shakti is an Eastern Indian tradition. Both men and woman worship Shakti and her image is the yantra, or the sacred triangle, which represents the threshold through which life emerges. Shakti is the Shining One, a powerful feminine force who energizes every manifestation in the universe. Shakti is also Kali/Durga in images that suggest to our minds a terrific, devouring, and coldly unfeeling aspect. These images of creation and destruction—too easily polarized into good and evil in patriarchal consciousness—are held together in Hindu thought as differentiated aspects of the same divine, feminine, vitality. In fact, Kali arose from the Great Goddess Durga in order to annihilate demonic male power and restore harmony in the universe. Kali resurges into life again today as an unstoppable, creative force, that will not tolerate the travesties of destruction and disharmony—and the consciousness that perpetuates it—in her universe. Shakti/Kali is the Goddess that disrupts the order erected by the male spirit. She is concrete, related to matter, sexuality, creativity, procreation, and attraction. She is the One who not only preserves life but destroys it. She is able to refuse, to say "no," and to let old structures that no longer serve life die. She enables women to remember and reclaim ourselves as sacred and powerful, earth-centered, body affirming, irrational, chaotic, holistic, connected, responsible. She is not only wife and mother, but consort and virgin, in the true sense of that word meaning "a woman who belongs to herself." Rilke (1989) captures this sensibility in woman when describing Eurydice coming back from the underworld, in his well-known poem "Orpheus, Eurydice, Hermes" for people who are looking to read about a Western image.

When a woman makes a descent to the underworld and reclaims her lost instinctual powers, retrieves those chaotic and erotic qualities stolen from her by patriarchal order and reason, she returns to daily life as virgin, belonging to no man as *his* property, no longer an extension of *his* way of seeing things. The marriage that once promised safety has become a source of irritation. She is no longer contained by the image of *anima* woman for her man, no longer the *femme inspiratrice* for *his* creations, but returns now as an earthy being—hair, root, and rain—who can no longer even recognize the world she left behind, much less the man who imprisoned her by his poetry, suffocating her with his need for her to be *his* soul-carrier. Husband Orpheus, in Rilke's poem, is unable to grant the integrity of the eerie space needed for his transformed beloved's slow return, already wanting to impose himself into it with his anxious eye, unable to let her make her journey alone. Eurydice is changed though. She cannot see with the same eyes, feel with the same body. Her former world has fractured; it is unrecognizable to her. She returns already knowing she was never really regarded as herself before. *"Who?"*

Shakti/Kali images a wide range of feminine possibility for our all-too-limited cultural vision. She is the manifestation of spirit that mobilizes a woman's imperfections and limitations until they become allies and helpers—a salve for the perfectionists among us! She is the energy of Shiva who, without her, would be a corpse. When the old structures crumble, Shakti/Kali enables a woman to go to the foundations of her feminine being, and in the grievous and difficult descent, to remember the death and renewal mysteries of the ancient Goddess.

Shakti/Kali is Chaos and Eros combined!

Betty de Shong Meador (1994) has written powerfully about this initiation to the depths that many women in our culture are called to undergo. Meador enlists the help of the stirring and beautiful stories of around 3500 B.C. or before, surrounding the ancient Sumerian goddess Inanna, Queen of Heaven and Earth, and her dark descent to her underworld sister, Ereshkigal, as a containing myth for those of us called to find our authentic feminine voice. Here are parts of poems translated by Meador, of the goddess erotically celebrating her body, and longing for sexual fulfillment. From "Vulva Song":

> I am the Queen of Heaven
> let chanters recite this chant
> let singers sing this song
> let my bridegroom rejoice with me

let wild bull Dumuzi rejoice . . .
I Inanna sing to praise him
I give him my vulva song

peg my vulva
my star sketched horn of the Dipper
moor my slender boat of heaven
my new moon crescent cunt beauty
I wait an unplowed desert . . .

my high mound longs for the floodlands
my vulva hill is open . . .

vulva moist in the floodlands . . . (p. 59)*

And from "Holy Song":

this song is holy
let me tell you where I'm coming from
my vulva is
the power place
a royal sign
I rule with cunt power
I see with cunt eyes
this is where
I'm coming from . . .

I live right here
in this soft slit
I live right here
my field wants hoeing
this is my holy word . . .

I want you Dumuzi
your bough raised to my cunt . . . (p. 60)*

---

* This and the quote on the following page are from Betty de Shong Meador, *Uncursing the Dark: Treasures from the Underworld* (Wilmette: Chiron, 1994). Reprinted by kind permission.

Meador (1994) writes that womens' center of gravity is located in these moist, dark, underground regions, alienated by patriarchal cultures, the cunt wetlands, richly textured terrains holding mysteries that need to be restored and uncursed:

> Women in our culture are separated from the pathways of their natural growth. Adapted to a religion of light and a culture that upholds light and reason, women are cut off from their roots and from their creative transformative energies which lie in the chaos and mystery of the dark (p. 116).

Often the first step toward a retrieval of our buried feminine soul and imagination is a stripping of sorts, a sensing of a loss, the recognition that in spite of successful achievements of one kind or another, there is something deeply missing. Here we are, in our mid-40s, married, two children, graduate degree, a profession that provides income and a certain status and freedom, and, my god! we've escaped from the deadly fate suffered by our own mother who hated our attempts to free ourselves, and who watched in a denial of pain and envy as we said the "no" and the "yes" that she, hopeless, was too depressed to utter. Yet there is a gnawing dark hole in this substantial self, shaped to civilization's demands, and in that dark cave lurks instinct's primordial claim. Sometimes the only way back to this forgotten fertile soil is through a shattering of the upper-world adaptation, a leaving behind of the collective fathers, a divesting of those hard won gains. Then we become aligned with those outcasts again, and descend into our orphan natures, often in the face of unkind, "for-your-own-good" opposition from the outside, and with great anguish, despair, and doubt on the inside.

Descent to the Other Woman

In my own case, this divesting of everything I had achieved came first through the body, in a kind of somatic alchemy. The divorce process was completed. I was now a single parent with two young children, and had begun a doctoral program in addition to my pri-

vate practice. This was undertaken with the intention not only of developing my thinking, about which, like many women, I felt inadequate and insecure, but also creating a certain unpredictable chaos in my life, as once a month I had to travel to the West Coast from Connecticut in pursuit of my studies. I also hoped to meet people with similar interests and forge new friendships, as for a few years I had been considering moving to California, away from the excessively cold winters of New England. This clear and honorable purpose had its underworld schemes, however.

During one afternoon in October (1993) I am reading Jung's essay, "Archetypes of the Collective Unconscious" (CW 9i, §1–86) when I slowly become aware of the fact that the words are no longer making any sense to me, and my body is transforming itself into a leaden weight. I can hardly move. It is almost as if I am turning into stone, into hard inorganic matter. I somehow get myself to my bed and lie down, whereupon I fall into a combination of a dreamlike sleep, and hypnagogic state. I am transported to a temple-like structure, which has a round dome with lights situated all around a high gallery about two thirds up. At first I am in the center of the dome, standing on the floor looking up.

But simultaneously it is as if I am entering the dream Jung records in his autobiography that foreshadowed his wrestling with the problem of Job.[2] I enter the dream at the point where Jung's father is leading him to a high chamber where Uriah, King David's general, lived. Uriah was abandoned on the battlefield under orders from David so that he, David, could steal Uriah's wife, Bathsheba, for himself. For Jung, Uriah was the prefiguration of Christ, the god-man abandoned by God. This story was influential for Jung in tackling the dark side of God, His unconciousness, that Jung claimed—controversially—required mankind to be conscious for him. This "edge over God" placed tremendous responsibility on human consciousness as the second creation; indeed it suggests that abandonment is the necessary condition for realizing our cocreative natures, even the heretical notion that humans are divine.

---

2. C. G. Jung, *Memories, Dreams, Reflections* (New York: Vintage, 1961), pp. 217–220. See also Jung's "Answer to Job" in CW 11, 1962, §553–758.

What was relevant for me was the experience of abandonment, the withdrawal of a prevailing conscious attitude, and the feelings of sadness, betrayal, loss, lack of interest in life, heaviness, and inertia that I was thrust into by this descent into the neglected dark shadows of psyche. Jung (1970b) writes in Mysterium Coniunctionis:

> Life wants not only the clear but also the muddy, not only the bright but also the dark; it wants all days to be followed by nights, and wisdom herself to celebrate her carnival, of which indeed there are not a few traces in alchemy. For these reasons, too, the king constantly needs the renewal that begins with a descent into his own darkness, an immersion in his own depths, and with a reminder that he is related by blood to his adversary (§471).

The experience engendered a terribly painful hiatus with the external world, and invited a profound metanoia that reached low into the foundation of my being in the world. It felt as if I were thrown into depression and doubt by a force quite beyond me. All my convictions, ideals, and values became like empty shells, and I found myself walking about as if in a dream. A veil descended, and life was hardly real any more; I was merely going through the motions. I felt as if I had died, that a part of me had departed, and that my body would somehow keep going through the motions during this painful, numbing experience, until it suffered its own transformation. I went to a Chinese doctor who diagnosed a deficiency of Yin energy. She prescribed "Twin Immortals," Goddess food.

When the familiar sources of support are withdrawn in this way, when the collective values of human life fall into decay, when the water of life slips away, psyche wants to produce new dominants, new wine in new skins. Falling into the shadows threatens our very life and identity, and the descent puts us in the wilderness, in the underworld, where we slowly dissolve and decay, where we betray the self we thought we were so attached to, where all our identifications are dislodged. Rejecting traditional solutions, we seek immediate personal experience and direct knowledge of the eternal roots. In the breakdown that becomes the breakthrough, in the depths of the heights, in the evil of the good, in the blackness of the whiteness, the soul of the matter can be restored. We become like Inanna, who as Meador (1994) translates:

> turned her ear
> to great earth
> left heaven
> abandoned earth
> went down below (p. 19)*

In this landscape, depression or melancholy, far from being a symptom to be cured, is the call that first attempts to restore us to the dark chaotic depths, to soul. This soul-call restores us to a state, not of archaic identity, but eventually to a differentiated consciousness that does not separate above from below, and in which the mystery of life can once again be embraced and lived on a renewed level.

Living the Other Woman

In my case, the call was so strong, so insistent were the dreams, that within a period of two months, I had decided to close my therapy practice of fifteen years, rent my house, and return with my children to my roots in my native England, that I had left some twenty-odd years previously in search of myself. Allowing a further three months to make the necessary preparations, to respect the inevitable separations and endings, the three of us, taking all my savings, flew to London at the beginning of the Spring.

For almost a year, while my children attended the local school, and thrived on Celtic soil bathed in the gleam and magic aura of the grandparental eye, I did nothing except read novels, take extensive aromatherapy baths, surrender into dreams, and roam (for hours at

---

* Betty de Shong Meador, *Uncursing the Dark* (Wilmette: Chiron, 1994). Reprinted by kind permission.

a time) the hills surrounding my parents' old farmhouse in the wild and remote west of England.

On this extended solitary walkabout, I tried to let all identities dissolve, becoming nothing and no one in particular. It was as if the personas and roles of my life receded in their definitions in such a way that I became a human being—a woman—first, and in a sense, only that. Like Inanna—who in the wisdom of her descent to her dark sister (the word for ear in Sumerian also means wisdom), was gradually stripped bare, and at every gateway was divested of one more trapping of the upper-world identity behind which her full nature is concealed—I, too, needed to see what my life depended on when there was nothing left to hold me. In what great mystery was I held, if any at all? Could I really let go? Could I surrender, and fall into Life? Fall into the Great Below?

Like Eurydice in the underworld, I felt myself pouring out into hair, root, and rain. The intense connection with the raw, natural world acted like a balm on my dissolving identity. Nature became so alive for me. The world was always changing, the landscape shifting with the vicissitudes of the weather. At one moment it was a sunny spring day with soft, gentle winds, clear azure skies, fields shimmering with golden gorse and silvery grass, the sea a calm lapis blue, and the body alive with an erotic sensuousness and optimism. At another moment, it was penetrating drizzle, while gale-force winds churned ferocious seas at the almost-full moon spring tide, battering and devouring the land. This wild and awesome beauty suggested a chaotic and abandoning frame of mind.

My soul, too, is a force of nature moving among the realms of wonder and sensuousness, touched at times by pure delight and the beauty of the world; tossed at others, by oceans of disintegration, doubt, and a sense of inexpressible loss; penetrated at still other moments by a wild desire to run and sing in the fields at the top of the cliffs that look out to sea.

But the inconstant and mutable landscape never ceases to disclose its great wonder whenever my eyes see with an open heart, and my body stands present to the experience. When I allow myself to be infused by nature's great gift to us, her balm penetrates my otherwise hardened and self-indulgent preoccupations. Learning to slow down, to stand still, rather than anxiously moving on as if the world depended on my actions seems unbearable to my human form that in some ways has not yet borne itself. Neither acting nor retreating, I bear tension and paradox, in an in-between state—the place between God's and Adam's fingers in Michelangelo's depiction of Creation—the simultaneous touching and not touching between the divine and human realms. In this place, in an epiphany of image-filled shared affect, the transpersonal as god or goddess reveals itself, and I am invited to bear witness and embody the moment, stand it if I dare. This silent "making present" that speaks worlds (and in which we may or may not literally speak) is that moment when love is born and love is borne, heralded by the world's beauty, sustained by possibility, birthed in suffering, yielding to ecstasy. This ability, in this moment, to withstand, tolerate, the whole of who we are, dark and light, consciously, seems to relieve God and substantiate us, and the soul of each radiates with life.

THE COMPLEX RANGE OF CLITORAL CONSCIOUSNESS

Among the many blessings of this choice that felt so dangerous and filled with terror—a journey made probably as much out of blind recklessness as conscious courage—was a completion of family karma, especially with my parents, and the dissolving of those relationships into the eternal sphere where they properly belong. Also, during this fateful year, I met the lover of my soul, an earthy, instinctual man, with a big heart, and a feeling, creative mind. The meeting was also a recollection, but that, as they say, is another story —a beautiful story that by soulful necessity and gentle design released many of my vulnerabilities and silent, shy shadows.

I do not want to suggest that something was finalized by these experiences, and of course, much more could be said, especially in regard to the releasing of earthquakes of emotion that such transformations generate, and that need to be fully felt in the body before they can be channeled into new containers of creativity. Much more, too, could be said of the hardship of facing limitation, mortality, constriction, and the difficulty of exposing those last vestiges of hidden hopes for some idealized way, that come paradoxically with such a stretching of awareness. Marie-Louise von Franz (1980b) speaks of this kind of exposure to the dark feminine energies when a woman, abandoned in one way or another (through loss of her children, death of a loved one, or erotic betrayal), has to fight her own way alone through life. She writes that the fierce, rageful, and whining surfaces at these dangerous crossings, and these aspects of a woman need to be lived and embodied to complete her larger reality (p. 156).

In my own case, the necessity to abandon and disrupt my life came about, I believe, because, once again, I was too identified with values not my own. (The danger this time was that in pursuing academic work I was also endangering connection to my feminine instincts.) The Goddess who initiated me into the secrets of the sacred yoni would not let me go so easily. Once the psyche has introduced a new content, she makes it harder if you betray those new values. Falling back into old ways signified the inevitability of another descent. The necessity to reconnect, beyond the familiar, cultural roles, to those realms where the dark and the light wish to be embraced is aimed at helping us women become once again carriers of refined culture and raw instinct. Betrayal of the upper world conceals the invitation to trust in a more complete gnosis. This is a difficult journey, for the trick is always: how to bring this gnosis practically into life, into work, and into love? In my experience, a cycle of many such descents needs to be endured to incarnate the new knowledge. We need lots of practice!

It is Inanna/Shakti who restores our divine gift—the embodiment of these opposites of dark and light, and their myriad reflections, the complexities between two poles—to resituate woman's experience within the birthright of this royal role of soul. It is Inanna/Shakti who urges us to take fearless action with what needs to be done in awakening our-selves and the world to the secret center in the pelvic chakra that is seeking new expressions of life. As my dream indi-cates, the Goddess clitoris is the seed that is a doorway to a new world, one in which true feminine imagination is highly valued.

It is not only women who are called. Both men and women are being initiated to this profoundly difficult task, this awareness and action of making way for repressed arche-typal feminine energies to come again into our culture, and into individuals' lives, creating unimaginable disruptions, losses, deaths, and the invitation to change, transform, and love in a different way, that comes in the wake of such chaos. The need to approach the dark, to revere life as an impersonal force larger than the merely human, to reconnect to a deep instinctual base, that also seeks new creative forms, is a com-pelling vocation demanded of these times in which we live, times of tremendous cultural upheaval and transition.

From Early Lack to Continuing Loss

The world of the archetypal feminine surging into conscious-ness via dream, imagination, and event in the lives of men and women, synchronistically in a century that has seen the rise of women's rights, women's studies, feminist scholar-ship, and archaeological digs uncovering ancient prehistoric goddess cultures, deeply challenges the Freudian view that a woman's identity is based on lack and envy of the male mem-ber,[3] a view that surely marks Freud as a man of his time.

---

3. Freud's theory of feminine development is outlined in his paper, "Femininity" (1933), in *New Introductory Lectures on Psychoanalysis* (New York: Norton, 1965), and is based on two earlier papers written in 1925 and 1931.

Actually, Freud himself recognized the oppressive social climate that forced women into passive situations and roles and, of course, his conflictual and ambivalent theory that would reduce the psyche of women from the psyche of men was contained within a cultural context that had marginalized the feminine for centuries—feminine being material, physical, mystical, natural, erotic, wet, wounded, weak, dark, reveling.

Nevertheless, I wish to linger here awhile, for we still live in a time that has inherited this lack, this sense of something missing, this yawning gap at the heart of chaos's realm. Though feminine psychology has been revisioned, we still continue to marginalize psyche herself and the imaginal domains in the souls of both men and women.

There were of course significant women analysts writing early on in this century who deeply challenged Freud's initial attempts to grapple with the nature of women's psychology. Karen Horney's essays of the 1920s and early 1930s were lost to the light of day till 1967 when her *Feminine Psychology* was finally published. The Jungian analyst Esther Harding, too, was writing as early as the 1930s. The central theme in her (1990) now classic text, *Women's Mysteries*, is "initiation to Eros" (p. xiii), which she claims is a neglected realm leading to the sinister, feminine depths of "the dark Eros of the feelings" (p. 33).

Freud's early formulations have continued to be refined, and reimagined to our advantage by feminist psychoanalytic writers, and also by Jungians going beyond Jung. In recent years, for example, as Toril Moi (1985) writes, citing other feminist critics, the narcissistic woman can be viewed as a representation of female power, or, penis envy is the girl child's first attempt to differentiate from the mother, an act that is crucial for her future creativity (p. 28). Many have

---

4. For example, see Miller, 1986; Rose, 1986; Kristeva, 1987; Irigaray, 1992; Downing, 1996.

redefined women's development in terms of a patterning related to the girl's pre-oedipal attachment to the mother.[4]

Similarly, Jungians have resituated women's psychology beyond the confines of overly personalistic and cultural definitions, within the matrix of the archetypal Self as female.[5] Within this frame, as my dream suggests, the clitoris also contains an ancient sacred symbology, representative of a whole creative approach to life beyond mothering in a literal sense. More than this, the dream is like a vulva creation myth, reminiscent of the goddess Vak arising out of her primeval watery yoni, presenting the hint of a feminine consciousness and its numinous instinctual energy just beginning to birth itself. As Meador (1994) suggests, the "lack the woman experiences is not the missing penis. The lack is the absence of the vital symbols of the feminine and its sacred vulva" (p. 134).

In spite of all these gains, there is, however, still a feeling of loss that many women experience in some form of inferiority related to our social status. In analysis, the deprivation often first, or eventually, reveals itself in relationship to felt hatred and disappointment toward the inadequate personal mother who failed us. But our mothers were perhaps just as deprived. The social influences on their generation, however, belonged more to surviving the traumas of war in England and Europe, or the Depression of the 1930s in the U.S.A.—or to surviving at all. Perhaps they didn't talk about their feelings and experience then, or only in hushed, private tones, or perhaps in small, women-to-women groups (and to their daughters sometimes). Certainly they did not speak up with the kind of psychological introversion, interiority, openness, and intensity that we have done since the early 1970s.

Even so, the true aim of the rage at parental failure and shortcomings—a normal part of the individuation process—is not to put them down, but to separate us from those fig-

---

5. For example, see Perera, 1981; Woodman, 1982; Bolen, 1984; Downing, 1981, 1992; Meador, 1994.

ures, to dislodge our identifications and introjects, to see how those patternings continue to operate favorably or not, so that we can take responsibility for ourselves, and for changes that we may, or may not, elect to make. In this way we can make ourselves carriers of consciousness into the next generation. This is the work of individuation that costs, the costs that rally together our resources.

It is essential that we women continue to unearth our buried voices, to reclaim our passions and our visions, and to find authentic expression that is faithful to what we know, for this sense of loss to be overcome. Only then will we be able to find authentic modes of action, action that is not an imitation of men's ways. The patriarchal way has kept women involved in the domestic sphere, saying that we are both dangerous and unreliable, emotional and untrustworthy, and also lacking in creative talent! Fortunately, because women's psychological development has received its own study and attention, many gains have been made in "uncursing the dark." As I know from experience, it's the archetypal experience that has the power to make real change possible. A visitation from She-who-desires-to-be-related-to, may only be experienced within the context of a lengthy therapy devoted, patiently and lovingly, year after year, to the hope for this kind of transformation.

I want to make sure, however, that I do not omit the observation that behind the missing link, the deprivation and loss characterizing the early psychoanalytic views of women—and wherever these views continue to prevail either overtly or covertly—is the presence of a much larger loss. This loss is that other country of soul—psyche—that is found everywhere about us, penetrating our dreams, our symptoms, our landscapes, and our relationships. The hate, lack, and envy of Freud's early theory sounds more like the ways the neglected goddess first appears in everyone's dreams and experiences as that Other, that "Other than patriarchal" consciousness, the image of feminine psyche that, like

Ereshkigal, comes at us demented and deformed on account of Her neglect in the culture for so many millenia. Or, She reveals herself in the appearance of unknown natural forces in the psyche due to the neglect of instinctual energies of a lifetime, or at least a period of time in a lifetime. Or She arrives as overwhelming forces in Nature—hurricanes, floods, earthquakes, fires—on account of our disregard of Earth herself.

The hate, lack, and envy are also reminiscent of the psychopathology of the borderline patient, who is most often assumed to be female—a patient (residing somewhere in all of us) who, more than any other, challenges us to face the dark underbelly of a culture devoted to reason and light. The borderline also challenges the analyst, for psychology increasingly seems to value order and meaning, rather than dark, chthonic chaos.

Borderlines are also those liminoid patients that therapists joke about, saying that the only appropriate treatment is to refer out these patients. The truth behind the joke is perhaps the realization that borderlines, more than any other patients, in their struggles with the opposites of dark and light, good and bad, bring to us a unique combination of archetypal en-ergies that emerge in all their primitive chaotic strength from the unconscious, the collective and cultural issue of needing to relate more consciously to the reality of the psyche, and the individual expression of this necessity in the life of one person at a time. It is an overwhelming task that we would understandably rather refer elsewhere. The strong so-called countertransference reactions commonly spoken of in relation to borderlines have much to do with the darkness and chaos we would rather not look at in our own souls, not to mention the untold suffering that is brought forth in working with such patients. But we must not turn away from our calling, from our cultural and individual responsibility to face the darkness and the chaos that always discloses more love.

Is it that girls' maturational process is based on a sense of failed masculinity? Or is it that our culture continues to fail the signs of the times with a bankrupt patriarchal attitude that insists on holding on to old outmoded gods and refuses to bow low to the split-off dark instinctual realms and their images that desperately need our attention? Neither is it only women who can feel impoverished, impotent, and uncreative and whose individuation requires a peeling away of attitudes not truly their own, a movement from father's daughter and *anima* woman, from negative *animus* identifications to Woman's woman. Men who remain identified with culture's expectation for them to provide and keep the family firm heroically going (that is, the inherited life) also fall apart in midlife and are forced to face the dark unconscious, or be overwhelmed by it, or keep the *anima* split between family values and a mistress on the side, in whatever form that takes: unrecognized depression, alcoholism, affairs. But the irruption of this *anima* disturbance is the dark potential carrier of the primordial feminine psyche that seeks a more conscious (less hidden) relationship.

That women are the object of all kinds of projections on the part of men, from idealization to devaluation and from glorification to dread, may have to do with the effect of the power of the unconscious psyche that first mediates itself through women, and from which men need to distance themselves from by attempting to control its terror. This also happens the other way round, and men suffer the same distortions from women. Often we women fall in love before we can realize our unlived creative potential. We live at a time when there are few socially sanctioned containers for transpersonal energies, and that leaves us humans open, exposed, vulnerable to, and overburdened by the chaotic forces of nature. Those of us who can stand it must do our part to embody that portion of the world soul that comes our way, as Rilke suggested, to create new realities out of the masculine and feminine (not only gender, but symbolic reality) within each of us.

Visitation: The Lioness Goddess

While I was working on this chapter, I had an uneasy feeling that something was not quite complete about it, but I didn't know exactly what it was. Then I had a dream.

In the first part of the dream I was the "myth teller" for a community. We are in another time and space, long ago. This dream "I" was both me and not me, a kind of androgynous figure that felt as if it was a combination of male and female characteristics.

Next, my husband and I are in a bedroom that is in a cave-like place with a dirt floor in a mountainous area, both protected from and exposed to nature. I know there are a lion and lioness nearby. These lions are intimately connected with the functioning of our community. Sometimes the lions are tethered; at others they run free and wild. My husband is sleeping in our bed, but I am uncertain of the whereabouts of these large beasts and anxious that if they are not chained, they could easily attack and devour us.

Then I see one of the lions, the female, come plodding around the corner. I am terrified. She sees me, stops, alerts her ears, then comes immediately toward me. I rush into the bathroom which is separated from the bedroom by a wall that is too makeshift to protect me from the power of this animal. I start screaming to my husband Robert to wake up and call for help, but he doesn't hear me. I become frantic with fear. I know the wall won't hold.

Then suddenly the lioness thrusts her huge paw through the door. Her paw is dripping with blood (which cannot be only from this thrust I think illogically to myself). I am horrified and fascinated simultaneously, and, still staring at her paw, remain fixed to the spot. The matriarch's claws clutch at my right hand and she drags them back toward her (her body is still on the other side of the door) making deep cuts in my (non-dominant) right hand. These etched markings begin to bleed. "She has marked me," I say to myself. Strangely I know now she won't harm me.

*My husband has finally woken and is calling for help.
What he is doing is also necessary, but we are in two different worlds at that moment.
I wake up with an intensity of feeling and awe.*[6]

On the morning of this dream my husband and I flew to a mid-Western city together, and while he attended a workshop I decided that I would take the day for myself and continue to work on the edits for this chapter that was troubling me so much. We were staying at a beautiful old hotel on the banks of a river on the other side of which was the city Art Museum, which at that time was housing The Egyptian Mysteries as a special exhibit. I wondered if my dream had brought me to Sekhmet, the lioness-headed goddess of Ancient Egypt.

After working on my text, the lion dream kept intruding itself into my awareness, and I found increasingly that I could not concentrate on the task of editing. So, putting my work aside, I wrote out my dream and associations, and then bundled myself up in my old winter coat, and walked over the bridge in the freezing snow to the Egyptian exhibit.

Standing guard at the entrance to these ancient and all but forgotten mysteries were statues of the major deities of the Egyptian pantheon, the first of which was Sekhmet, lioness goddess, "Beloved of Ptah." Her name means, "She Who Is Powerful." I became still and fell into a reverie, overcome by a deep emotion that began to travel through my blood. She stood upright, huge, regal, intimidating, alive, with staff in hand, and what appeared to be either a solar or lunar disc above her head. Golden, dark, primordial, powerful, she radiated a still presence protecting secrets lost for centuries. She recalled the stones at Avebury that likewise hold a vibration of knowledge lost for millenia, waiting to reawaken.

---

6. Author's Dream Journal, February 17, 2000.

The dream lioness made her appearance, inserting herself between me and the statue of Sekhmet, as if for moments the two became one, the statue enlivened by the presence of the dream matriarch. Simultaneously, I remembered the lions we had seen in the African bush several years previously. Their nights were active with hunting, led by the females, and our nights were filled with the sounds of the grunts of their distant roars. Their days were spent in sleepy communion with each other, bound by animal loyalty, but not by sentimentality. I remember seeing lionesses swiping their paws at their cubs as much as letting them feed and licking their fur. Here was a mixture of pure instinct and devotion.

I wandered through the exhibit in my dreamy state. There were several more statues or parts of figures of Sekhmet, some tiny, others larger, but She was notably contrasted with the more domestic, and perhaps more familiar, cat goddess Bastet, symbol of motherly devotion and care. Sekhmet is a more powerful and ruthless goddess who represents a more fearsome and aggressive agency, and who holds the forces of creation and destruction in her being. She represents both a less than, and more than, human reality in her theriomorphic and divine manifestation, a trans-psychic force, further from human consciousness than the benign Bastet, of whom, interestingly, there were many more examples in the exhibit.

In her posthumous publication, The Cat, von Franz (1999) links Sekhmet and her more domesticated image, the cat goddess Bastet, with the fearsome Isis, Egyptian goddess of the highest, divine spirituality, but whose power extends to the underworld, to an earthy, embodied instinctuality, a black goddess who ruled darkness, the dead, the night, and evil, marginalized aspects of the divine feminine long fallen into oblivion by our enlightened world.

I felt strangely addressed by this numinous feminine power and its claim on me. I wondered if my unease about my text had to do with a danger I was in of falling into old, cautious, and overly domesticated patterns, as if I might be losing my voice, or the voice of my topic. The dream lioness appears as a visitation of Sekhmet-Isis, symbol of the power of the union of instinct and spirit, matter and the divine, reminding me of the presence of a living myth such as ancient Egypt once enjoyed, and of the range and depth of the vital chaos/eros landscapes of experience—my living myth. Be bold! Don't hold back! Keep a riotous, outrageous tone! Don't be too careful! Be full! This was the sacred injunction of the dream.

The crowds of people flocking to this beautiful portrayal of an ancient culture and gnosis seemed more or less intuitively aware of the hunger and thirst in their souls that drew them to such lost vitality, depth, and beauty, and to a way of living deeply immersed in transpersonal, cosmic realities.

New Ways of Loving

We live at a time when male and female (at least potentially) have been adequately differentiated, so that we can come together in new syntheses, and new kinds of relationship, honoring our differences and our own soul's integrity, joined as humans, with a common goal of fulfilling our own life's calling. In this way, we can go along with Horney (1967) in her more optimistic approach to relationship, when she wrote much earlier in this century of the need for "an inner renunciation of claims on the partner. . . . I mean claims in the sense of demands and not wishes" (p. 121). We need to hold on by letting go.

Perhaps in this way we will move in the direction of soul-engendering relations based no longer on hierarchies but rather on the equality of the brother/sister pair; no longer on power but on the coniunctio of adept and *soror mystica;* no longer on mutual suspicion but on Eros as the dance that takes place between partners. In this way, perhaps we will become the shapers and weavers of a new kind of culture, one that honors not only gender, not only individual difference—you as wondrously *not-me*—but one that honors the timeless depths of psyche, and her time-bound rhythms of soul. The following is a story of how those timeless depths appeared spontaneously in the landscape of the mother-daughter mysteries.

A Modern Day Arretophoria

Because my husband was to be on sabbatical the following January, and he and I would be out of the country for seven months, there was much discussion during the summer about what would be the best way for my 12-year-old daughter and 10-year-old son to spend the school year. Different options were presented among the four of us, and feelings were explored and expressed, while we also waited for dreams to comment on our decisions and changes of mind and heart.

I was having the most difficulty with the decision, and my source of anguish mostly had to do with separating from my children for such a lengthy period. It seemed that the wisest course of action was for the children to be with their biological father on the East Coast for the duration. This would allow them to make a significant connection with him, something often denied children of divorce. We had moved to California two years previously, and the year before that was spent in England. So the children's connection with their father was sporadic and often limited. In any case, he really wanted to have them, and they welcomed the opportunity to be with him for an extended time, and to get to know him in ways that would only happen with the daily round of school and homework, sports and other activities. It made such good sense all the way around.

When I allowed myself to penetrate my hesitations and my pain at the thought of letting the children go, I realized that what was most disturbing me was the feeling that I might be inflicting on them the very abandonment that I had suffered in my own family, especially in relation to my mother. Nothing could be worse than that. And I knew better! In addition, my daughter was just 12, and had not yet started menstruating, so the likelihood of this major life transition occuring while we were apart from each other was very real. I found that very difficult to imagine into. She herself was determined not to grow up, and revealed to me that she was "holding it in!" But I knew that the impersonal forces of nature would visit my daughter when they chose, not when we mere mortals would find it convenient. So I paid attention to the echoes of old lin-

gering wounds, and realized that far from abandoning my children, I was releasing them into their lives, into Life itself. I could do so, not without the pain of separation and loss, but with a fearlessness and trust that came upon me as I worked my old wounds.

When the decision was finally settled upon, it came to me to do a special ritual with my daughter that would honor the beautiful young woman she was becoming, even if she had not yet been visited by her moon. She liked the idea very much of doing this something together, although nothing was specified about what would happen, mainly because I didn't yet know! There was, however, already an aura of this being a secret kind of unusual event; something that, following some ancient code deep in the cells of our bodies, only mother and daughter could participate in; an atmosphere of mystery and the unknown; something from which the men in our lives were definitely excluded. We set aside a warm afternoon, giggling softly and knowingly between the two of us, my husband and son, in full regard, agreeing to stay away till evening. They would do their own thing together! down in the town with the men!

Not thinking particularly, but just acting, following the movements of what our bodies seemed to want to do, we first dressed in shorts, tee-shirts, and hiking boots, and went on a long walk from our house, to the base of a mountain trail, up the mountain and back down a different path, returning home some three hours later, completely wet from sweating and exhausted! On the journey we talked girl talk, mother-daughter talk, gossiped, laughed, made fun of, joked, had serious talk, talked feeling talk, meaning talk, deep soul talk, silent talk, talked out! Then while I made tea, my daughter prepared the hot tub, and we got in, soaking our weary muscles, and relaxing and growing increasingly more silent, in the hot waters into which I had put several different kinds of aromatherapy oils, ones specially chosen to honor feminine energies.

When we had enough, I invited my daughter to be wrapped up in bath towels and to lie down, releasing her body into further perspiration, into meditation and dream, into whatever place she wanted to go, or was led, even to fall asleep if that's what happened. She seemed, silently, to welcome this; by now, we were in a rhythm that *was beyond daylight consciousness, in a flow beneath the surface of things, moving in a land half forgotten, once known, beckoning to us, slipping through the cracks, honoring the old ways, in an altered state of awareness, drawn aside through the veil by the physical exertion, and the heat of a summer day, and the sweet tea, and the hot waters, and the sweating that detoxified and freed us, cleansing the field, relaxing, surrendering, into dream, into other worlds, into someone else, enlivening another country that longed to reach us, too.*

Now, no longer mother and daughter, but Mother and Daughter, I made a sacred space around my girl, wrapping her in prayers, welcoming the presence of her guardians, angels, spirit helpers, animal powers, honoring all those Invisibles who accompany us here, stones, gems, sounds, flowers, birds. I lit a candle, and put quiet flute music on. With her permission, massaging her back with lavender-scented oil, and speaking softly in a language I hardly knew, I drew down the energies of the mother-father divines, the earth energies from deep below, and wove them through the multi-dimensional levels of my daughter's chakras, between the cells of her form, around her Temple body, protecting her, holding her, connecting her with an ancient past, linking her with her future becoming, placing her within a tradition of all those women who, deeply honoring the ways of Woman knowing, were there present with us in the ethers of our devotion. When it was completed, I asked my daughter to speak whatever she wanted to of her experience, or not, or to make whatever silent requests or gestures that seemed right for her. Then I told her that I would leave her alone, for however long she needed to remain there, to complete this part of the ritual. Then she was to dress, and we would eat together.

While she rested, I prepared dinner for the two of us. When she was ready, I brought her to the dining-room table, and we celebrated with food and drink—joyful, calm, and tired. We came back into space and time, and back into our local selves. We came back, but we were different people. My husband and son returned, and we completed the day together, talking of our different adventures, but remained silent about the rich tapestry of experience that lay between mother and daughter, not because it was secret, but because it was not communicable in words. Before my daughter fell asleep, she asked if we could "do that again," before she left! Of course it would be impossible to repeat what had happened, but I knew that she had changed, had moved one step further into her new body.

It came as a complete but delightful surprise to me two months later, while reading Meador's (1994) book, that there was a separate rite celebrated in Greece for young girls who had not yet started to menstruate. It was called the Arretophoria, in which girls enact parts of the ritual drama of the Thesmophoria (a yearly three-day event for mature women) but the mystery is carefully hidden. Meador describes it thus:

> *Four girls of noble birth lodge during the festival in the temple of the goddess. On one of the nights, the girls carry sacred objects which cannot be named and cannot be seen. Women place the objects in baskets which the four girls carry on their heads. They walk down a natural underground passage [from Athene's temple to Aphrodite's[7]]. At the bottom of the descent, they exchange the sacred objects for something else that is wrapped and hidden. This they bring back to the temple. Thus the young girls begin their preparation for the central mystery of their lives which they will later celebrate in the festival of the Thesmophoria (p. 94).**

These ancient earth ways linger, tidal rhythms of nature, moonbeams flowing toward us, deep feminine knowing, the temple of the goddess, waiting to be found again.

In this chapter we have witnessed the chaotic neglected Feminine in her shadowy distortions of body and soul. We have also reclaimed this Otherness of the Goddess and cele-

---

7. Personal communication, Dr. Christine Downing. "From Athene's Temple to Aphrodite's" is not in Meador's text.

* Betty de Shong Meador, *Uncursing the Dark* (Wilmette: Chiron, 1994). Reprinted by kind permission.

brated her clitoral fullness and visionary daring. We moved from archetypal realms punctuated by personal experience toward the consideration that Freud's early theory of the feminine remains as a threatening lack of soul in our times. This missing link is order's collapse into chaos, such that love's origins can be redeemed into a celebration of soul, that other country of absence and longing, that brings vision and passion back into the embodied landscape of our cellular and vital forms.

The shadow body of the feminine in our culture conceals the breakdown of an order seeking regeneration in its chthonic origins offering the potential for a bold appetite for life with its instincts and its dreams, its mystery and its eros to emerge glowingly intact.

The willingness to suffer the path of self-knowledge, cycling through doorways of illusion to ever-increasing attunement to our originality, passion, vision, and an ethical commitment to living what we know, is one way of bringing the tidal rhythms of the cosmos into the cells of our bodies, strengthening our form as a chalice for the rebirth of the Goddess in present time and space. Ensouling our bodies in this way will redeem the oppressed voice and body of the Feminine Presence, liberating her shadowy and distorted forms into a joyful resonance of transmuted reality, and singing back to the cosmos a darker, mysterious Whole.

Chapter 5

DIVINE AND CHTHONIC LOVE
The Chaotic and Numinous
in Depth Psychotherapy

The practice of psychotherapy is a mere makeshift that does its utmost to prevent numinous experiences.
—C. G. Jung (1975), p. 118

Between doctor and patient, therefore, there are imponderable factors which bring about a mutual transformation. . . . The doctor is as much "in the analysis" as the patient. He is equally a part of the psychic process of treatment and therefore equally exposed to the transforming influences.
—C. G. Jung (1966a), §164, 166

The alchemists thought that the *opus* demanded not only laboratory work, the reading of books, meditation, and patience, but also love.
—C. G. Jung (l966a), §490

In this chapter, which intends to make some reflections on psychotherapy, I wish to linger in a landscape of those "imponderable factors." I wish to linger in those places where we doubt our work, where we hurt and suffer not knowing, where we experience difficulties, where in an attempt to remain with those unthought thoughts and feelings at the edge of our consciousness in the spaces where we diverge from collective values—including what have become in my view the dogmas of depth psychology—we might give voice to those unseen and hidden worlds that seek expression through us and that everywhere penetrate and surround us with their veils of mystery and invisibility. In this way I wish to indulge a desire to look about the world in wonder and contemplation and reflection, the original meaning of the Greek word *theoria*. The willingness to enter the chaos and confusion of our doubts can make way for acts of grace that bring greater depth and a numinous sensibility to our work. It is perhaps this sensibility—which Jung emphasized—that is important for our time.

In speaking of a therapeutic attitude appropriate to the treatment of depression, Fierz (1991) affirms Jung's idea that a philosophical or religious point of view is important that requires "extensive *knowledge,* knowledge that encompasses the world and life, history and the present time" (p. 328). Such a broad encompassing of knowledge is comparable to ancient mystery school or esoteric traditions in which the training of initiates was known to be extensive and took place over decades. Even Jesus' whereabouts until he was over 30 are veiled in obscurity and have led scholars and others to postulate that he studied extensively in the mystery traditions of Egypt and India and even perhaps England. Perhaps one's vocation spanned a lifetime, and as Jung stresses about analysts, one is constantly learning or should be so educating oneself. He (1966a) writes:

> No analysis is capable of banishing all unconsciousness for ever. The analyst must go on learning endlessly, and never forget that each new case brings new problems to light and thus gives rise to unconscious assumptions that have never before been constellated (§239).

Such a liberal education as Fierz (1991) alludes to includes what the ancients called *philosophia,* which was not book knowledge but always "personal knowledge of what is essential" (p. 328). How do we individually arrive at this sense of what really matters? I wonder if, in the training of analysts, too much book knowledge (important as it is) has replaced an attitude born of the union of *theoria* and *philosophia,* of contemplation and the essential? Even among Jungians, the polarization of two different schools of thought has already occurred: what Henderson (1984) describes as "the clinical-personal and cultural-anthropological" (p. 17). We hear much talk of those Jungians who have remained faithful to Jung's original, unstructured, symbolic approach, and those who have become more clinical, which usually implies a devotion to pre-oedipal psychologies and their techniques and methods.

Perhaps in practice these demarcations are not so rigidly maintained, but nevertheless I think there is still a tendency toward what the French author Camus, writes: "Quand il n'y a pas de caractère, il faut la methode." To have character, you have to be a little eccentric, out of the circle, and to trust your own quirkiness. This is difficult in cultures such as ours that, because of the marked separation between ego consciousness and the shadows of psyche, tend to condone conformity, professionalism, and the status quo to extremes. Education has become a consumer affair, and knowledge is now generally divorced from gnosis, that is, revealed, visionary knowing. In this way it has become another example to me of the spirit/matter split that characterizes our times. But there are experiences that suggest to me that these split worlds yearn to reside together again, long perhaps for a new synthesis, differentiated yet interpenetrating, so that a certain kind of unity can be restored, an integrity once known but forgotten, perhaps now on another level.

In this chapter I will consider two case examples, one from my practice and one from the culture, that for me suggest that the whole project of depth psychology is primarily for the purposes of a cultural re-education (*e-ducare* in Latin means to lead out), an invitation to re-member our galactic origins, to resituate ourselves within a larger whole, a dark and beautiful unknown Mystery, requiring a more subtle knowing or gnosis. This is the true anamnesis, the anamnesis of the origins, origins that reach beyond our families of origin to clan, culture, and to the stars. Stars, those constellations of ancestors and souls that have gone before, and that are already ahead of us, are those dream-weavers that nightly call us home to our place in the galactic community.

Comparable to ancient mystery traditions, only an initiation into love and its sacred mysteries and dark shadows that the ritual container of psychotherapy can offer allows such a fall into self-knowledge, the prerequisite of the restoration of the Whole. In such experiences of Otherness, one's humanity is forever humbled and relativized, and soul, that in-between, neither-nor space, becomes the orienting star of one's life. In this paradoxical, bounded link to the infinite, Jung (1961) writes that we experience ourselves simultaneously as both limited and eternal, and as both one and the other (p. 325).

It was clearly Jung's view that psychotherapy could offer this link to the sacred, and that the whole analytic process was not so much about curing symptoms and enabling adaptation, but discovering through one's pain a link to the infinite. Jung (1966a) writes: "One cannot treat the psyche without touching on [humankind] and life as a whole, including the ultimate and deepest issues" (§175). Indeed, the suffering symptomatic body appearing at the turn of the last century through the particular lens of Jung's vision, became humanity's wake-up call that the time for relinking to a larger Whole was perhaps the thread upon which the very survival of our species depended. And still depends!

In fact, one could argue that the symptomatic body of the hysteric and neurasthenic one hundred years ago has worsened into the predominant diagnostic categories of borderline and multiple personality disorder, whose primary features involve various kinds of splitting mechanisms, and pathological deficits in linking, as a result of the cultural failure to recognize and respond to the necessity of placing ourselves once more within a viable and larger mythological context. Perhaps as long as some psychology continues to restrict itself to the cure of symptoms within a personalistic frame, we unavoidably continue to perpetuate the split between spirit and matter, body and world, that has increasingly hastened our drive toward human and environmental destruction.

Certainly individuals had suffered before the end of the 19th century. And in many cultures, there were, and still are, elaborate rituals and customs for responding to the many variations of soul loss and physical ailment. Such cultures also begin with an undivided world view, and are embedded within it, as constituting what is most real. Consider, for example, the Aesculapian healing sanctuaries in Ancient Greece, with their elaborate preparatory rituals for aromatic and sensuous cleansing, catharsis via passionate engagement with theater, and the meditative incubation period that culminated in the visionary healing dream. The whole body/psyche was intensively activated and attended to, from the physical to the emotional, intellectual, and spiritual, to rally the latent healing forces of the cosmic soul within a community and sacred context. Surely the purpose of such elaborate ritual was not only the healing of individual pathology (whether of physical and/or spiritual nature) but the knowledge that true healing can only be achieved by the human/divine alignment, "As Above, So Below."

Or another favorite ritual, recounted by Ellenberger (1970) is the "festival of dreams" (p. 26) among the Huron and Iroquois Indians in northeast America, in the 17th century. In these healing ceremonies, a sick individual is provided with everything his or her heart desires, and unfulfilled wishes are satisfied either literally or symbolically within a collective celebration of dining and dancing. This idea would most likely seem unthinkable to us. In fact, to the modern psychological mind, such wishes belong to the regressive longing of childhood primary processes and need to be made conscious so that psychic energy can be made available for a respectable adaptation to the demands of adult reality. The fact that these wishes could belong to the drive toward self-realization, not to mention the ceremonial factor as a healing element in itself, whose purpose on a larger scale might be the restoration of a cosmic homecoming, is mostly completely alien to our way of thinking and being in the world. Jung is perhaps singular in his understanding that regressive longing is a return, beyond biography, to the waters of the collective unconscious, and therefore inevitably a longing that eventuates in the rebirth of the personality, the second birth in which one becomes the son or daughter of one's unique destiny, one's inheritance, not from the biological parents, but from the stars.

The Hummingbird

It was extremely painful and difficult work, for my patient—a dancer in her mid-30s—was remembering horrific and unspeakable acts of abuse and terror in her childhood and youth. It was a confrontation with evil of a magnitude that I had not previously witnessed. The suffering of her ravaged and war-torn soul and body was almost unendurable. I was aware of a deep grief and despair overtaking me that I knew was hers also, but I was helplessly contaminated by the material, and I began to feel inadequate and hopeless, not yet conscious of an inchoate rage, too, in the field between us, aimed at these transgressions of humanity, that in time would birth the sorely missing, rarely present self-respect. I began to lose faith. How could any kind of healing, restoration, or transformation come from such horror? It was as if in one frail human being, the demonic ravages of the dissociated shadowy consciousness of Western Christian culture were being lived out before my eyes. I thought of the frescoes on medieval European churches that depict the evils of this split between the light and dark face of God. I knew that only in relationship, in love, in reconnecting the broken fragments, could there be any hope for change, but I was not optimistic.

And then—a miracle!

Suddenly outside the window—a hummingbird—hovering just to the right of my patient's head (I can see it; she can't).

I was struck by the visitation, first, because I had never seen a hummingbird in our garden before. I wondered whether to say anything, but its lingering position above her head reminded me of paintings depicting the Baptism scene, or the Annunciation of the angel to Mary, and I decided (if I can put it that way, for it was not so logically formulated, more an intuition of the dynamics of the shared field) that I must speak, trying to find the "right" moment. I said, "There is a hummingbird hovering above your head outside the window."

Her face began to melt from its contorted pain and broke out into smiles. Now I'm wondering what the connection is, for surely there is one.

She told me that her non-American name means "hummingbird" and that she had, in fact, been considering changing her adopted English name back into her original name.

At that moment, the whole atmosphere in my study changed. Were we being addressed by the angel? The room became charged with an unseen Presence, this tiny bird baptizing my patient, naming her, calling her into the realization of her being and her destiny, for a baptism initiates one into one's unique relation to the divine, what alchemy (in Jung, 1970b) symbolically refers to as one's "orphan" or "widow" nature, beyond the influences of family and history (§13–14). These images of abandonment are paradoxically both characteristic of the black chaos of the *nigredo* stage of the work, and simultaneously symbols of the Philosopher's Stone sown invisibly into the beginning *massa confusa* like a grain of wheat pregnant with hidden growth.

The experience of the complete withdrawal of the sources of support in both patient and therapist alike seemed to be the necessary condition, the fertile ground for the constellation of the helpful and healing powers of the archetypal psyche. It was as if surrendering into the field of intense suffering and even evil itself engendered the creation of new structures that had never incarnated or been made conscious before. Schwartz-Salant (1995) writes:

> If we engage the field, we can become aware of a deep organizing process. . . . Through faith in a larger process, one often discovers that the particular form of the field is

actually far more archaic and powerful than anything one had imagined. . . . This can have a transformative effect (p. 10).

In baptism, too, originally a dangerous crossing from one vehicle of consciousness to another, you are not only recognized as the daughter of your parents; you are ritually recognized and named, often renamed, as a child of God. It is the ceremony that acknowledges the second birth, or rebirth, or spiritual birth of the individual.

Into the chaotic disorder, grief, and fragmentation of her world, a visitation from the spirit realm bestowed dignity, wholeness, and numinous sensibility to what until then had only seemed brokenness without hope or meaning. Not only evil, but beneficence revealed its face, perhaps as parallel universes seeking a meeting ground for mutual transformation. We could both surrender into the arms of life herself, and be carried by a river larger than either of us. Some confidence—a trusting loyalty—was restored. No matter what the outcome, we were both resituated within a larger field.

This event struck me profoundly. My own association to the hummingbird was what I knew from certain shamanic cultures, where it is the bird at the center of the Medicine Wheel that takes the prayers of the day to the Great Spirit once an integration of the four directions has taken place. It was a reminder that this therapy process was more like an act of prayer than anything else. Interestingly, the hummingbird is also "the first curing shaman, summoned by Coyote to heal his daughter, who is ill because of being impregnated by her father. Hummingbird sings over Coyote's daughter, and Coyote pays him with awls [sharp, pointed implements], which become Hummingbird's bill."[1]

---

1. Sam D. Gill and Irene F. Sullivan, *Dictionary of Native American Mythology* (Santa Barbara, CA: ABC-CLIO, Inc. 1992), p. 130.

In Jungian terms, we would say that with the appearance and acknowledgment of the hummingbird and its particular relevance to my patient, the archetype of the Self was positively constellated, that this woman had been initiated into her journey of individuation, of becoming herself, of realizing consciously the union of her eternal spirit in her human body, and of uniting herself in relationship to the sacred circle of nature as a whole and thus ensouling the world. This was her vocation, expressed too in her love of dance and in her love for her husband.

For me also, what seemed like the irruption of another order into the therapy room, was a calling. I experienced it as an act of grace that moved me deeply. Marie-Louise von Franz (1992) writes that "synchronistic events constitute moments in which a 'cosmic' or 'greater' meaning becomes gradually conscious in an individual; generally it is a shaking experience" (p. 272).

I wasn't certain I wanted to continue working as a therapist and had been struggling with that question, and more generally the question of my vocation, about which I had terrible doubts for some time. But after this experience with my patient and the hummingbird, I felt called back into my work—not precisely in any specific way, but called nonetheless. I did realize that I should complete my unfinished PhD, and this epiphany from the spirit realm was instrumental in my reapplying to the program I had withdrawn from two years earlier. But there was a deeper sensibility at work than the completion of a degree. It was more that the process of finishing the doctorate would open to other vistas that I could not then either articulate or yet see.

It had to do with finding my own way in the work and penetrating more deeply into the kinds of questions that were plaguing and irritating me at the edges of my consciousness. More specifically, the quality of world, or level of reality with its infinite ripples, that had disclosed itself with the visit of the hummingbird seemed to require particular attention. The more so, because these kinds of mystical or numinous experiences have been among the most formative for me since early childhood. It began to feel as if I had been keeping, and was continuing to keep, at the periphery something which needed to become more central for me. This became compelling. In a way, I might say that the Visitation shocked me into taking myself more seriously, and it imposed, in spite of myself, a more devotional attitude.

Jung (1959) speaks of the self requiring this kind of care and devotion, because although it is older than the ego and "the secret spiritus rector of our fate" (p. 167), it is also "the smallest of the small" and can be easily pushed aside. He writes:

> Since [the self] stands for the essence of individuation, and individuation is impossible without a relationship to one's environment, it is found among those of like mind with whom individual relations can be established. The self, moreover, is an archetype that invariably expresses a situation within which the ego is contained. Therefore, like every archetype, the self cannot be localized in an individual ego-consciousness, but acts like a circumambient atmosphere to which no definite limits can be set, either in space or in time. (Hence the synchronistic phenomena so often associated with activated archetypes) (§257).

There is no suggestion here that psyche or soul is only inside. On the contrary, the Larger Presence is more like an atmosphere or field that extends from an unknowable transpsychic realm and reaches into the environment, including those of like mind, as if, like a magnet, we as individuals draw and are inexorably and imperceptibly drawn to the landscapes (including birds and animals) and people to whom we belong—possibly, and probably even, through the ages. Thus we are part of a stream that extends backward into the mists of time and forward into the Great Unknown—and then again, circling, circling, the themes of our incarnational destinies in an eternal *kairos*.

In what has become our normal rational state of consciousness, we are oblivious to this universal energy field and act as if—and in fact can depend on—space-time causality is real. Moments of synchronicity then are exceptional events, fragments of a cosmo-psychic world that draw our attention to this glowing Presence and speak to us out of its veil of Things pregnant with meaning. It is as if when we are cut off from this Greater Reality that we are embedded in and dependent on and feel blocked or thwarted or hopeless (as I did with my patient), a synchronistic event explosively effects the reconnection. Once back in the flow of Life, we are guided to a creative discovery, a new idea, or a healing insight. That is why von Franz (1980b) writes, "Jung also called synchronistic events *acts of creation in time;* they indicate that the experiencing subject should realize something" (pp. 198–199).

The shadow side of attending to this field might then be envisioned as inflation, that is, not self-aggrandizement, but rather, in the sense of the hubris of the isolated ego, an alienation from self, a presupposition that there is no such thing as either an autonomous psyche beyond consciousness, or this larger cosmic field that embraces psyche/matter while simultaneously transcending it. Symptoms of such inflation might then include, as Jung (1959) notes, "our growing disinclination to take note of the reactions of the environment and pay heed to them" (§44). In a synchronistic worldview we are called to pay as much attention to events happening around us in nature and in the world and people's reactions to us, as we are to our nightly dreams. It is perhaps this art and act of paying attention that in these times we have too often sadly forgotten in our practice of psychotherapy.

The *coniunctio* experience with my patient close to the beginning of the work allowed for the unfolding of the traumatic memories of her chronic childhood ritual sexual abuse (experienced as intrusions and sensations) to take place over the course of the following year. This powerfully dark and disordering cathartic process, primarily witnessed by me as an empathic, believing presence, seemed to allow her to come more and more into her body, and the memories gradually subsided. The work shifted—she became more empowered; I became less idealized—and we were able to begin to focus more directly on her present life, relationships, and work. The dreams changed, too, reflecting this greening of rebirth and healing as it was imaged. Paradoxically, getting better was initially suffered as a feeling of loss, much in the same way that the fall into matter is initially experienced as a shock, or wounding, for the spirit.

After fifteen months of work with my patient, I presented her case at a clinical colloquium. In speaking out loud to a group of other therapists about her, I became intensely aware of how much suffering I had endured in working with her. The suffering was my own experience of the dark Hadean realm that lived in and through my patient, that shadow landscape of the Christian Aeon, that torturous, chaotic, destructive world whose torments are unendurable, and that my patient suffered to the point of shattering. Evil requires a response, but we cannot integrate it beyond the contents that have personal meaning for us, that is, beyond the personal shadow elements. We can only do our part to witness and accept its reality. As von Franz (1980b) warns, there are definite limits—as with any archetypal structure—to the integration of archetypal Evil. "To this structure one can only relate, ever and again, 'religiously,' by taking it carefully into account as long as one lives and awarding it respectful attention" (p.121).

The question often arises in such circumstances whether these events "really" happened. Certainly the phenomenon of satanic ritual abuse is widely documented, even if the difficulty of locating such phenomena is as widely acknowledged. All I know for certain is that the details of the horrors are compelling, so that whether they really happened or whether they are the experiences of a split-off domain of collective consciousness, finding its way into individuals' psyches, makes no difference. Phenomenologically the material has entered therapy, so I approached it "as if" real.

The day after my presentation, the following vision was disclosed to me that I recount here for reasons that will become clear. During the afternoon, an unaccountable sudden exhaustion pulled me into a hypnagogic sleep. This is what I saw:

Cosmic Eye

The Eye of the Divine, its gentle vision penetrating into the heart of my soul, seeing me, seeing through me, embracing me in its Sight— this Eye at once so benign, compassionate, and in its opening and closing, bringing worlds into being and allowing others to pass away. This Eye, in its slowly pulsating emanations of creating and destroying, is both infinitely merciful, intimately connected, and utterly indifferent to the presence and fate of the cosmos in its multitudinous levels of material, subtle body, and potential manifestations. It is as if the Divine both grievously cares for, with a constant tear in its Eye, and has no attachment whatsoever to, the world. Paradoxically, in this attitude there lies the utmost freedom for the cosmic destiny to play itself out. But even these words are far too human for what I saw.

The Eye then becomes the Eye of a Cat, a royal feline creature that both is, and is not, the Egyptian Lioness-Headed Sekhmet and/or the Cat Goddess Bastet. This vast creature seems to be the cosmic blueprint for what we know here as the cat family. In lion, panther, and kitten here on Earth there resides that faint reminiscence of complete independence, instinctual wisdom, superior insight, and affectionate presence when It chooses.

Then the Eye transforms again into the Eye of the most powerfully and exquisitely beautiful gentle woman, a radiant female priestess, a goddess-like figure, of such poise, sophistication, royalty, humility, compassion, fierceness. She is a woman deeply centered, slowly moving, a sweet smile on her lips, but barely. She is a woman of passionate loyalty, revealed knowledge, deep wisdom. She is a priestess of the heart, the Illumined and Discriminating One, who with sensuous beauty against a backdrop of unapproachable darkness, is robed in stars, the sun and moon in her hands, bathed in the faint white glow of the origins of the universe, a feather in her third eye, a sword down the length of her body, its hilt placed over her heart.

"Now is the time," she says, "And the time now is," meaning for the shift of the Aeons, for a World is passing away and another cosmos is painfully birthing Itself. "This is the time," meaning the favorable moment when the "hub" of the timeless Aeons is synchronized with the unfolding of that emanation of the eternal "whole" Timeless-Time into temporal linear day-night-day chronological time.

These images of the Eye of the Divine, the Lioness-Cat, and the Cosmic Woman, come into full view, then recede out of vision, in pulsating waves of energy.

Then I'm alone in a barely furnished room—the ambience of the light, even though it is night, is suggestive of Greece or Israel—looking up at a rectangular-shaped window located high above my head. Am I in prison? Or in a monastic order? Or in the holy room of an ancient Mystery School? Through this rather narrow aperture, I see the night sky full of mysterious constellations. My eye is then drawn to a particularly bright star that is pulsing, sending waves of its stellar light into my body. As my gaze fixes on this star, I'm either drawn up to it out of the window into the cosmos, or looking at it dissolves the room I'm in, and I can now only see the star. It moves to the right, pulling me with it as if taking me somewhere. Then it stops, and the stellar pulsations are again beamed at me, altering my field and cellular form, filling me with a new kind of sensitivity and consciousness, preparing my body for what it is about to see.

Then a veil is drawn back so I am looking in on a scene as if from above, through a circular opening like a big eye. It is as if some cosmic secrets are being disclosed to me. Far below is the most extraordinary vision. A Council of Advanced Beings is assembled. This is the "Galactic Federation," a kind of cosmic United Nations! Its meeting point is the "Hunabku" or Center of the Universe. The Council is gathered around a central point or platform called the "Squaring of the Circle." This focal point is surrounded—like a moat around a castle or cathedral—by a void, or empty space, called "Sacred Space." It is essential that the gap between the center and the rest of the activity be ritually and devotedly maintained, as the Sacred Empty Space is also the Chaotic Void full of the potential of all Being.

First, though, I see men and women in pairs, situated at consoles (comparable to computer consoles) intently focused on their task. These male/female pairs are in a circular arrangement around the central point and spiral out into several rows, radiating back as far as I can see. Their task and religious intention have to do with keeping certain energies in the cosmos (both material, etheric, and potential) in a certain kind of alignment.

Encircled around the outermost pairings, at the edge of what I can see, are statues that emanate energy vibrations to support the work of the advanced beings at their diamond crystal consoles. These statues, like huge ancient standing stone circles, have the appearance of golden, Hebrew letters. (I don't know if that's what they are, but that's what they look like.) They are symbols, really real realities, in huge statuesque symbolic form that send their rays toward the center.

Behind these golden entities are even greater mysteries that are hidden from my view, and that cannot be disclosed to my sight. No matter how hard I try, I am not allowed to see. It would be too shattering for my human self.

Then my eye is taken back to the central force, the so-called "Squaring of the Circle." On the platform are two figures: I think of the Indian God/Goddess pair, Shiva and Shakti (but I do not know for sure if this is who they are). They are each adorned in richly colored and elaborately embroidered ritual dress threaded with gold and silver, and wearing bejeweled pointed hats or crowns. They "hold the field" in the center by making love in the most delicate and passionate embrace, a sacred ritual whose intertwining energies participate in ordering and sustaining the beingness of the cosmos.[2]

---

2. Author's Dream Journal, July 15, 1997.

When I awake from this vision (which according to clock time, lasted about 45 minutes), I feel deeply rested, in a blissful mystical state, totally relaxed, and full of renewed vital energy. It was as if I had died in my exhaustion and been reborn again into Life.

Could this vision reflect a symbolic image of the union of Divine and Chthonic Love, a healing vision restoring wholeness to the dark underworld of the ravages of evil and its effects in splitting the world of spirit so dangerously from the world of matter? Could this contemporary manifestation of the cosmic forces of Chaos and Eros combined hold out the possibility that these are the foundational energies on which the new Aeon is resting? I do not know. It is a very different reality than that of the image of Christ suffering on the Cross, however, that has marked the Aeon of the last two thousand years.

This is a female vision of a high order, at once both deeply personal and archetypal, mirroring an independent, compassionate, feminine consciousness. Could it be another reality attempting to emerge out of the chaos and shadows of the Christian underbelly as embodied by my suffering patient and many others like her? Is that the connection between my work with her and its presentation, and this vision taking hold of me on the following day—for surely there is a relationship between these events? Could the vision reflect a level of transformation for me comparable to that experienced by her, on account of our work together? Or perhaps it is a gift bestowed because of the trauma of working with her, and keeping faith, and being so deeply in the muck of life with her. I do not really know why it was given to me to see such remarkable realities.

One clue is offered by something I read a couple of months after this experience, in Edinger's (1996) then newly released book, *The New God-Image*. In chapter 5, titled "The Paradoxical God" (pp. 51–62), Edinger is writing of the possibility, spoken about by Jung, of the Christian myth evolving into the time of the Holy Spirit in which, increasingly, individuals will become carriers of consciousness, holding the opposites, especially the shadow, and making the God-image conscious in history. He notes, quoting a letter of Jung's, that Joachim of Flora (d. 1202 A.D.) was the first to receive such intimations of these developments—called the *evangelium aeternum*—"'in a time when the great tearing apart had just begun'" (p. 60). Jung (1975) adds:

> Such vision seems to be granted by divine grace as a sort of *consolamentum*, so that man is not left in a completely hope-less state during the time of darkness. . . . We are actually living in the time of the splitting of the world and of the invalidation of Christ. But an anticipation of a faraway future is no way out of the actual situation. It is a mere *con-solamentum* for those despairing at the atrocious possibili-ties of the present time (pp. 136–138).

Edinger (1996), in discussing this text, says, "The modern world is in a state of desperate darkness," and adds:

> What Jung is saying here is that, for a few anyway, there is a vision of what the next aeon will bring. It will be the age of the Holy Spirit, when the warring opposites will be rec-onciled in the *coniunctio*. It is this vision of the future that Jung calls a *consolamentum* (p. 61).

In its origins the *consolamentum* was the central rite of the heretical Cathars in the 11th and 12th centuries. It was a bap-tismal rite of passage, performed amid fasting and lengthy solitude to stimulate the psyche and to produce a visionary and revelatory gnosis, comparable to a vision quest. The experience was considered a baptism by the Holy Spirit or Paraclete, sometimes also called the Comforter. The word *consolamentum* itself means, according to Edinger (1996) "a substance, an entity that conveys comfort or consolation" (p. 61). The Cathars split the god-image into two: the good God, and the evil God. This latter, Satan, was thought to have created the world. So the Cathars were struggling with the paradoxical God that Jung takes on in a more differentiated fashion in his psychology.

My patient's experience of the dark side of God, my own experience of this shadow reality (especially as the daughter of an Anglican Bishop), and our work together to bring this into consciousness—blessed by the baptismal Annunciation of the hummingbird near the beginning of the therapy and graced by the consoling vision of the *coniunctio*—may be an example of how the Otherness of the chaotic chthonic under-world and the numinous love of the divine exist together as two faces of the god-image, two faces of cosmic reality that we are called to witness. It could be—and it was our (my patient's and mine) experience—that these two realms of chthonic chaos and divine eros, increasingly split over two thousand years and more in the West, long for acknowledg-ment and differentiation, so that a conscious reconciliation can dissolve into a mystical revelation of a world held togeth-er in love, and surrounded by a sacred void full of the poten-tial of all being. Perhaps the male/female pairs at their con-soles reflect the possibility of this reconciliation, and are aligning the world within the context of a *consolation* that is arranged by love.

Perhaps it is this world that is presided over by the cos-mic Sophia, the radiant Priestess of the vision, that Goddess described in the book of Revelation (chapter 12) in the fol-lowing way: "And there appeared a great wonder in heaven; a woman clothed with the sun, and the moon under her feet, and upon her head a crown of twelve stars." This is, as Sardello (1995) writes, an image of Sophia as "the formation of the new world of the unity of the cosmic soul, the earthly soul, and the individual soul, now in full consciousness" (p. 55). Or, guided by the image of Sekhmet, this cosmic fem-inine presence and awesome, gentle power reunites the high-est spirituality and love with the lost chaotic, instinctual realms.

The guardian of the vision is the Eye, the eye of the Self, soul, or the Divine, from a centering position in the back-ground of ego consciousness, bestowing sight or insight from

God(dess). Marie-Louise von Franz (1980b) writes that "at first this eye from the Beyond sees us; then through this eye we see ourselves and God or the unfalsified reality" (p. 166). It is as if the eye of consciousness is looking into its own background in the soul, while at the same time we are being looked at, as it were, by the Self from within. This seems to be achieved in a compassionate, but dispassionate manner in the dream. M.-L. von Franz continues:

> When this eye opens up in a mortal being, that being has a share in the light of God. When a man [or woman] closes his [or her] outer, physical eyes in sleep, his soul "sees" the truth in his dreams . . . Jacob Bohme even says: "The soul is an Eye in the Eternal Abyss, a similitude of Eternity" (pp. 166–167).

According to the Tantric text, *The Lalita Sahasranamam* (in Walker, 1983) "The series of universes appear and disappear with the opening and shutting of Shakti's eyes" (p. 930). And we have also seen this bringing of worlds into being and their passing away with the opening and closing of Re/Ra's eyes in Egyptian mythology. M.-L. von Franz (1978) mentions the Indian Brahman (the Universal Spirit) or the Supreme God Vishnu, who "transcends Time but reveals himself also as 'Time which in progressing destroys the world.' In his sleep on the surface of the primordial ocean Vishnu 'dreams' the world; when he awakes it disappears" (p. 70). Jung (1961) also records a dream in which he enters a small chapel to discover—not Christian symbols—but an altar with a flower arrangement on it. Then he sees a yogi in deep meditation on the floor in front of the altar. On looking more closely, Jung is shocked to see that the holy man has his face! He awakens with the thought that this yogi is dreaming him, and with a certainty that when the yogi comes out of his meditation, Jung would cease to exist (p. 323).

Jung comments that the self—here in the figure of the yogi—is an image of unconscious prenatal wholeness who, when it gives up life in the eternal realms, assumes a religious posture while it enters earthly life and passes through the experiences of the three-dimensional world on its journey toward greater realization.

Shakti is Cosmic Energy and the animating principle of human and god, including Shiva, Lord of the Dance. Together their union of world and self guard the central image. Through the rhythm of their dance, it is said (in Walker, 1983), they direct and control "the constant movement in time and space of all material things" and this dance is performed in a place called "Chidambaram, the 'Center of the Universe'" (p. 936), also located within the human heart. Too, it is said that Shiva joined to the Goddess and became the Bindu or spark of creation. Every human orgasm was believed to share in this creative experience as "an infinitesimally small fragment and faint reflection of the creative act in which Shiva and Shakti join to produce the Bindu which is the seed of the universe" (p. 936). Maya mythology shares this dream of human orgasm, as we have already expressed. In their religion, as von Franz (1974) notes, "the transcendental primal god, hovering over all creation, is Hunabku, the 'Single One' (from hun, 'one')" (p. 144).

Shiva is the God who rules over the destructive phase of the ending of the world before a new creation begins. Perhaps we are in such a phase of the ending of an Aeon.[3] This vision then puts in divine context ways in which for me personally, as a couple, and professionally, a stage of life is ending, and another level on the spiral is simultaneously constellating. It is perhaps true for many at this time when constructs are dying and dissolving that no longer serve Life.

---

3. See also Jung's primeval boar dream recounted in a letter of 2 November 1960, in C. G. Jung, *Letters II* (Princeton: Princeton University Press, 1975), pp. 606–607.

The golden Hebrew letters, like all symbols, remain pregnant with meaning.[4] M.-L. von Franz (1974) writes: "Symbols can propagate in our thoughts an unlimited series of further intuitions and insights" (p. 73). The letter is symbolic of divine sound vibration as creative breath becoming Word. The creative word, as the goddess Vak has imaged, is a means of translating archetypal mysteries into human texts that communicate through what is understood that which can only be hinted at and never fully comprehended.

The star pulsates with quantums of image and energy that imagine into realms as yet undiscovered, landscapes seeking disclosures not yet revealed; it is a guide that pulls me forward into new vistas of life.

THE NUMINOUS VERTICALITY
OF CHAOS AND EROS IN PSYCHOTHERAPY

We live in an age that has produced the demonic outpourings of the radical split between spirit and matter. Like two galaxies hurtling away from each other over the last two thousand years, spirit and matter, having forgotten their origins in a unified whole, have degenerated into rampant materialism and rational intellectualism. Although this separation allowed an extraordinary acceleration of knowledge, and the differentiation of an ego consciousness disentangled from the things of nature and the world, the cost to the soul is inestimable. We need only mention the release of the atom bomb,

---

4. In the foreword to Judith Cornell, *Mandala: Luminous Symbols for Healing* (Wheaton, IL: Quest, 1994), p. xvii, Joan and Miron Borysenko write: "In Judeo-Christian terminology, it is said that the world was created through the word—through sound. Rabbi Lawrence Kushner writes of the Hebrew alphabet, 'They are more than just the signs for sounds, they are the symbols whose shape and name, placement in the alphabet, and words they begin put each at the center of a unique spiritual contellation. They are themselves holy. They are vessels carrying the light of the Boundless One.'"

the extermination of millions of people in two world wars, and the continuing atrocities that mark our present times. We live in an age of breakdown, a breakdown of a rationally ordered consciousness that was marked at the turn of this century by the entrance of the hysteric and the neurasthenic into the therapy room and onto the stage of history; marked by the casualties of war veterans and their so-called "post traumatic stress" disorders, otherwise and more brutally known as shell shock; marked by abuse victims and all the many other kinds of violence and abuses of power that mark our current times, including our devastation of the environment. And when our two-thousand-year-old attempts at order break down, chaos is released, offering us another chance to dance with creation and celebrate the world.

The practice of psychotherapy has all but lost its original vision—the stirring *massa confusa* of the transformation of consciousness—and broken down into an orderly time-limited system, reduced to methods of problem solving and adaptation, via an overweening attitude of devouring empathy and understanding. Our practice has all but lost its soul. Even the therapist's much-needed reality and character is often obscured behind a veil of theory not her own. In this regard, our practice has fallen into the shadow of its original intent, fallen into a neglect of the proper attitude on the part of the ego toward the transpersonal Mystery that surrounds us, and extends to us our being. "Neglect," which means "not to take into careful account," comes from the same etymological root as the more ancient origin of the word "religion," *religere,* which Jung (1969a) describes as:

> A careful consideration and observation of certain dynamic factors that are conceived as 'powers': spirits, daemons, gods, laws, ideas, ideals, or whatever name given to such factors . . . [we have] found powerful, dangerous, or helpful enough to be taken into careful consideration, or grand, beautiful, and meaningful enough to be devoutly worshipped and loved (§8).

Jung considered the essential nature of the human psyche to be religious, and individuation or self-realization, therefore, to be an act of religious devotion, scrupulous observation of, and loyalty toward what Edinger (1996) describes as "a living experience of the psyche and its transpersonal center" (p. 39). Jung (1969a) clarifies that "the term 'religion' designates the attitude peculiar to a consciousness which has been changed by experience of the *numinosum*," and carefully distinguishes the term "religion" from the word "creed," which is a "codified and dogmatized form of original religious experience" (§9, 10).

The fantasy in psychology—of growth and development and concern for origins and their effects and meanings—can be seen as a misplaced "religion," from the later Latin etymology of *religare* (as distinguished from *religere*) meaning to tie or bind back, in the sense of, as Edinger (1996) writes, "to tie oneself back to some prior state of existence, to an earlier source of being" (p. 35). This linear and chronological approach (which might explain how my childhood might have caused this adult pain), while participating in a preexistent archetypal patterning of human experience dominated by meaning, and satisfying our need for causality, is what I call the "credal" version of psychology. The patterning may indeed reflect our need for guidance and authority from without. It is, however, a psychology that in its theoretical constructs, methodological formulations, and interpretive measures, is unwilling to withstand an encounter with the living psyche, those numinous powers-that-be, in Jung's (1975) words, "all things which cross my wilful path violently and recklessly, all things which upset my subjective views, plans, and intentions and change the course of my life for better or worse" (p. 525). In its place, such a psychology situates a dogma, an already fixed and congealed set of usually rigid ideas, in the field between therapist and patient. In such a setting, the patient does not usually feel seen, or is only seen through the filter of the particular theory, which is the same as not being seen. This can generate enormous frustration in the patient, who is then told she is resisting treatment.

The truth in such a case is usually that the libido is not being followed, or in religious terms, the Spirit is not being allowed to bloweth where it listeth—psychology, the word on the soul, reduced to a creed. The therapeutic process may thus create another false self, adaptive to the needs of the psychotherapeutic institutions and professionals. Clow (1991) adds: "Intense consciousness of self . . . may also cause us to limit our potential to past experience and to three-dimensionality, and cause us to misjudge the opportunities to transmute that are now before us" (p. 153). Guggenbuhl-Craig (1995), in an article titled "Reality and Mythology of Child Sexual Abuse," puts it most emphatically:

> We live in a scientific age and science sails under the flag of cause and effect. This is adequate for the natural sciences, but not adequate for psychology. According to the psychology of C. G. Jung the psyche is acausal: it is not ruled by causes, and does not follow the law of cause and effect. What makes our psyche, what characterizes our soul, is the fact that this is a part of us which cannot be explained by causality. The psychic reality can only be expressed and approached through symbols, through images and through mythological, symbolical stories. To put it in extreme terms: all psychology is mythology, or: psychology is modern mythology (p. 65).

If we allow the illusion—perhaps more accurately, the mythology—that our destinies are linearly and chronologically determined to prevail, the essential unique life force of the individual lies in danger of remaining unlived. The practice of therapy is thus in danger of contributing to the continuing oppression of our authenticity and passion in much the same way that the Church with its emphasis on power over, impersonal authority, and codification of what is acceptable, has often failed to help the individual realize his or her own transformation through the major life transitions in the maturational cycle.

Most heinously, these causal psychological theories are usually unable to appreciate the many individual natures who resist collective solutions. Jung (1966a) comments:

> The question then arises whether the therapist is prepared to risk having his convictions dashed and shattered against the truth of the patient. If he wants to go on treating the patient he must abandon all preconceived notions and, for better or worse, go with him in search of the religious and philosophical ideas that best correspond to the patient's emotional states. These ideas present themselves in archetypal form, freshly sprung from the maternal soil whence all religious and philosophical systems originally came (§184).

These reflections resituate our neurotic suffering within the context of symptoms searching for a much more vast vision of reality. The suffering individual is the one who has lost connection to the numinous sources of life, who has not been touched by the Mystery that surrounds us. In other words, we might say, we are sick, individually and collectively, if we do not know God. Or, the secondary phenomenon of ego consciousness is impoverished to the point of death or extinction if it does not find its way back to a relationship with a transpersonal source. It is only an experience of the Divine, of "the Power beyond us"—call it what we will—that touches the soul, that vast region, without beginning or end, in which we all reside.

This was Jung's unique vision, his contribution to suffering humanity: that the psyche is unknown and unknowable; that it extends beyond the human sphere into nonhuman, mineral, animal, mythological, archetypal, imaginal, and divine dimensions; that it is really real; and that it is by nature, and essentially religious. Only by dipping into the sacred stream of Life, do we ever really get healed, meaning a transformation of consciousness that makes us, in Bachelard's (1969) fine phrase, "cosmically happy" (p. 157).

Any other form of therapy may relieve symptoms, may improve our relationships, may make life a bit more tolerable. But we will not have been initiated into a secret, into the secrets of creation. As Jung (1961) comments, "There is no better means of intensifying the treasured feeling of individuality than the possession of a secret which the individual is pledged to guard" (p. 342). I mean individuality in its true sense, meaning undivided, that is, connected to the wholeness of being, in a differentiated yet unified manner. And we will not have realized our divine natures, the eternal and the finite. Neither will we be engaged in living vital, excessive, eccentric, daring, creative, juicy lives, no matter how outwardly simple. We will probably remain slightly depressed, and somewhere remain slaves to the collective spirit of our times. In all likelihood, we will not realize our destinies, or become true to "the face we had before we were born."

We need to be attuned to how and in what ways spirit becomes once again trapped in matter and remains unredeemed. The overinstitutionalization of psyche is in danger of preventing the spirit blowing where it listeth, and our originality is in danger of remaining dormant beneath the surface.

Hillman (1996) writes that wounds and scars are the stuff of character. The word character means, at root, "a marking instrument that cuts indelible lines and leaves traces" (p. 260), like initiation cuts. In his "acorn theory"—that is, "the calling of fate, of character . . . which holds that each person bears a uniqueness that asks to be lived and that is already present before it can be lived" (p. 6)—Hillman contends that the nubs and acorns of our pathology mark our destiny and essence, what we are growing into and becoming, the changing and the changeless of our human natures. We need not so much to cure or overcome these chaotic eccentricities of being, but to move ever more deeply through these doorways into the mystery of who we are, and how we can find ways creatively to express our uniqueness as responsible social creatures, in respect and wonder with the rest of the created order.

Psychotherapy can provide ritual space for our initiation and transformation, which allows for the successive stages of suffering the chaotic waters of the abyss to unfold into unimagined vistas of a world held together in love. In some of my own experiences in analysis, and with patients—such as the story I tell in this chapter of my patient and the hummingbird—I was struck by how these deep levels of experiencing were comparable to mystical states of consciousness. It was as if in these moments what was most palpable was a kind of field effect in which analyst and analysand dissolved, becoming participants in a larger story in which there was an intimacy that protected solitude and separateness, and a disclosure of beauty that was both compelling and almost unbearable.

It seems to me that in these moments we transcend the dimensions of ordinary reality and penetrate into what Jung eventually described as the psychoid aspect of the archetype. Paranormal experiences, and especially the phenomenon of synchronicity, led to this reformulation of the archetype. Observations of these kinds of anomalous events suggested that the distinctions between the psychological or spiritual, and the instinctual or material, could not in all instances be so clearly upheld. The appearance of figures such as ghosts (Philemon, for example), or alternatively, the fact that neurotic disturbances could embody as physical symptoms, led to the conclusion that the spiritual and material worlds must be intertwined and mutually influencing each other, perhaps all the time, and in ways that we cannot fully understand. In other words, spirit and matter seem to be held together in an *a priori* unified field—a field that Jung called the *unus mundus* (borrowing from medieval alchemy)—and "blip" into existence, as it were, sometimes as a psychological fact, sometimes as a material event, and sometimes as both, as in a synchronicity.

Our felt experience of the intersection of the material and the spiritual seems to have varying degrees of intensity, from our sense of ordinary, consensual reality (inner thoughts and feelings/outer events and people), to synchronicities that begin to feel more intense as the *unus mundus* field breaks through into ordinary life (and discrete boundaries begin to blur), to a level of reality that so transcends the ordinary that we feel that we have stepped through a veil into another world, another outside. While the hummingbird visit was a profound experience of a synchronicity, my visit to the being of love, recounted in the Prologue, was a stepping through to another place, but clearly not an ordinary place (as I was also asleep on an airplane, but not having a dream).

While the notion of the psychoid archetype refers to the *a priori* union of spirit and matter before any kind of consciousness arises, including the collective unconscious, Jung also used the psychoid in a specific sense to refer to the extension of archetypes into matter and the natural world. Psychoidal experiences themselves refer to profound levels of union that the mystics (and Jung following them) called the *unio mystica*. Jung does not elaborate on these deep levels of mystical experience, but we need to try to because they are increasing in number in our time (in NDEs, shamanic journeying, or extraterrestrial encounters, for example) as individuals struggle with new paradigms of reality. The psychoidal, mystical domain is a kind of fourth or fifth dimension perhaps, a realm that is experienced as particularly powerful in a feeling way, a realm that has its own figures and landscapes, a realm that is often experienced as healing, and a realm in which qualities such as beauty, ecstasy, and divine love, move into us and—momentarily—remind us spiritual pilgrims, of whence we come and whither we go.[5]

---

5. See Jeffrey Raff, *Jung and the Alchemical Imagination* (York Beach, ME: Nicolas-Hays, 2000).

This third body of the world is also described by Henri Corbin (1972) as the *mundus imaginalis,* following the Sufi mystics, who claimed that visionary and mystical states *really* took place in non-ordinary landscapes. In other words, these deeper experiences occurred in an objectively existing real world (or level of reality), an in-between dimension not seen by the physical senses but apprehended by the creative imagination, and located somewhere between the senses and the spirit in a subtle, psychocosmic geography. Visits to this subtle world transform our ordinary ways of knowing and being into a world glowing with abundant possibilities, and a fullness of meaning beyond our personal realm. We fleetingly experience what it is like for body and soul to be one. This is perhaps why everything is experienced in the subtle world in such a heightened way: colors more intensely bright, affects more deeply and viscerally felt, sounds more clear, cosmic meanings telepathically disclosed.

In the field of psychotherapy, attention to these subtle domains needs further elaboration. This is increasingly important as Jung's psychology and quantum physics converge toward the mutual study of consciousness, itself, and as actual people find themselves having all kinds of experiences that no longer fit our consensual views of reality. Psychological theory needs to pay attention to these developments and make much needed revisions. This work has already begun.

For example, deep levels of the transferential relationship have been connected with the acausal, nonlocal, invisible, potential nature of quantum fields identified by physics. In these experiences, synchronistic events, subtle body manifestations, and a mutually experienced active imagination become a combined psycho-physical organ of symbolic perception in the constellated archetypal field. This field appears to structure the interaction of both parties and implies a deep acausal interconnectedness. In this intimate and multi-textured numinous quantum field, Eros as the strange attractor

and invisible presence of the dark matter of the soul, is working his magic to dissolve fixed attitudes so that a deepening
of the personality can occur to yield to a rich resonance of
creative possibilities.[6]

These mystical rapturous states, when they occur in the
therapy relationship or in our lives, are closely related to profound levels of erotic union, too, where boundaries blur and
there is a seamless connection between body and soul, interpersonal relationship, intrapsychic image, and cosmic
Presence. Surely we need more of this felt depth here on our
fragmented Earth? Don't our souls long for these disclosures
of divine love? Are we not hungry for a mystery beyond
words, beyond arguments, beyond divisions? And these
experiences are *not* necessarily defenses against the complexities of life, are not escapes from the intolerability of conflict,
are not longings for inertia or death (although we have those
kinds of experiences, too). Actually, they often appear unbid-
den, and they do not rob us of our destiny, of our conflicts, or
of our difficulties. On the contrary, they often present us with
a keener sense of our vocation (which can be very difficult!),
and they remind us that such difficulties and conflicts are
faces of cosmic love, and are part of the chaos of creation that
forges character and gives way to new revelation.

In fact, such experiences of relationship in therapy often
come about when the patient has suffered consciously their
personal complexes or traumas, and are blessed, as it were,
by these new transforming energies that seek to dissolve rep-
etitions of early patterns and mutual distorting projections into a new third body or presence. This new field arises
from a transpersonal source yet requires human participation, perhaps even longs for it, as much as we desire contact

---

6. See J. M. Spiegelman and V. Mansfield, in *Journal of Analytical Psychology* (41.2,
1966, pp. 179–202), and Nathan Schwartz-Salant, *The Borderline Personality*
(Wilmette, IL: Chiron, 1989).

with the divine. It brings with it the numinous power of the golden god Eros.

This sensitivity to the field of the therapy relationship may be opening the door to deepening the therapeutic process as initiatic. Maybe one function of the therapist is to be the mystic, shaman, or visionary, for a culture or group. In other words, to be able to hold energetically, and with awareness, in the body, multiple levels of consciousness simultaneously: instinctual rootedness in physical form (Chaucer's Wife of Bath image), through emotional awareness (the gazelle in the heart), to ecstatic or visionary states (Bernini's St. Theresa of Avila). Meador (1994) writes about this in a slightly different way, as follows:

> With a woman client, I open myself as far as I can to the entire continuum of cultures, from the most fully developed woman-centered cultures to the most extreme male-centered cultures. Very soon the woman will tell me, through her dreams and her story, where she now sits on this continuum. When dreams of the feminine come . . . I see them not only as a needed compensation to a masculine-adapted woman, but also as a beckoning . . . to begin the long journey back into the matrix of ancestral female orientation (pp.147–148).

Here dreams are not only presented as compensatory to an over-determined consciousness, but as opening a door that leads to a profound transformation of consciousness, that is, here dreams are presented as initiatory. Henderson (1967) has fully articulated the archetype of Initiation and its expression in contemporary individual human experience of that liminal landscape—continually forgotten and rediscovered throughout history—that awakens to a sense of wonder and numinosity comparable to the ancient religious rites and Mysteries.

The idea of therapist as mystic or visionary connects with initiatory processes, for a mystic is one who has walked through all the stages that eventually lead to a revelation of the Divine, an experience of union known as a *complexio oppositorum* that dissolves all projection, liberating the soul into the world, and transforming life into meaningful depth. Mystery schools taught initiates about the seven chakras, each center of energy being a door, way, and truth, having its own integrity, imagery, body parts, and level of consciousness. Enlightenment, or union with the God(dess), depended on training related to the opening of these vortices that linked individuals to cosmic rhythms. Therapy could benefit from integrating the mystical and energetic perspectives into practice with more awareness than its orthodoxy demonstrates, for I feel that these traditions encourage direct, original experience (which often includes anomalous experience) with preparation and timing, and most effectively help reveal to us the face we had before we were born.

It could be that when Jung (1969a) comments that "the attitude of the therapist is infinitely more important than the theories and methods of psychotherapy" (§537), it is not so much that the theories are unimportant, but rather, as he says, that the therapist's words have power or a healing effect only insofar as they reflect the actual spiritual/psychic state of the therapist. In the same way that *who* a parent really is, is infinitely more important and influential finally than what a parent *says* to a child, a therapist conveys meaning or has significance to a patient in a kind of inductive way related to the embodied state of his or her consciousness, and how refined, energetically so to speak, he or she is. In this sense, only as words match the reality of the therapist are they effective. In the same way, patients can be most forgiving of analysts' so-called mistakes, because telepathically they read the truth of the therapist in a more whole way, as it were. Conversely the patient leaves treatment when there is a dissonance between what is being said, and who the therapist really is. Often the aborted therapy is blamed on the patient's resistances, but equally, the therapist may have misread the situation (technically, a misreading of the countertransference). In families, of course, this dissonance is crazy making.

Too, we all know that it is not only spoken language that defines the character of the analyst. Healers have an atmosphere about them, they sit within a whole ambience, a field, an energetic resonance that can be felt or sensed, often immediately, but certainly separately from the exchange of words. People who have spoken of their experience of Jung, for example, have often remarked on this "mana" aspect of him. John Haule (1997, May) has searched to differentiate the theoretical process of individuation in therapy, and the actual experience of individuals undergoing the procedure. It seems that there is a marked difference. I think this difference has to do with the field phenomena between the two apparent individuals in the room, and the field's powerful influence in healing, or in what happens in the room, in spite of what is said, or not. Jung tried to document this in his description of the unconscious to unconscious relationship in the transference, but the full aspect of this has not been adequately explored.

Mystical and shamanic traditions know more about the mastery of energy and its different expressions. It may be one reason why the rituals involve the participation of the whole village or community among traditional or indigenous healers. Healing energy available to any one person may exponentially increase with the number of people present. The inductive effect can be used destructively, too, as many fundamentalist religious groups demonstrate. Maintaining free will demands a differentiated consciousness, already a high achievement.

But the mystical and shamanic traditions remain marginalized for many depth psychologists, and their traditions are hidden in culture's shadow. This may be slowly changing as psychology begins to confront its limitations and its increasing insistence on the necessity for spirituality, or as a kind of orthodoxy becomes the prevailing status quo no longer affording opportunities to honor one's individuality. A truly individuated person is a presence to be reckoned with, a

powerful human who is not easily be swayed or manipulated, and the collective strains in society do not want too many
of those. It is dangerous to be original, to be a *heretic*, "to be
able to choose" (the root meaning of the word "heretic").
There are places on Earth where women are still burned at
the stake, covered, shamed, and given clitorectomies, not to
mention where political dissidents are routinely imprisoned.
Authentic experience continues to be oppressed in a myriad
of ways.

Is there any hope that as we slowly differentiate consciousness from the psyche as a whole and begin to move in
the direction of situating ourselves once again in a psycho-
cosmic whole, we will move toward a time when heretics will
be increasingly accepted into society? If we are to survive, we
must become authentic.

Our symptom of order breaking down releasing chaos into
the world and offering the possibility of birthing eros again
does not only happen in the therapy room, but in the culture
as well. The tragic death of Diana, Princess of Wales, in
August 1997 brings the shadows of our culture's continuing
driven insistence on body without soul, on matter that is
uninspired, on consciousness without feeling and ethics dev-
astatingly into view. We live at a time that is, on the one hand,
striving to achieve a unified worldview—particularly as science moves toward the ineffable, and psychology attempts to
incarnate its gnosis—yet grievously the transformation of our
worldview remains constricted by our inadequate and unrealized transformation of the view of the feminine. This
change is not only about women's issues; it deeply concerns
our relation to body, matter, and instinctual life and to all
those things considered weak and inferior by our culture and
thus relegated to a chthonic underworld. In our continuing
disregard for what really matters, we hover ever on annihila-

tion's edge—and this underworld realm and its ignored gods wreak their revenge.

It is my view that Diana—both ignored and disregarded within her own private realm, yet carrying so public a role—embodied so fully this weakness, this sense of lack and inferiority and her beginning attempts to come to terms with its pathos, that she has become a mystic for our culture and its attempts yet to redeem itself. In her visibility, she has drawn attention to what we need to reclaim so we can move forward into the fullness and radiance of what we can become. Diana's much-publicized suffering made her a figure with whom, somewhere, we could all identify. As much in her life as in her death, she became a living myth whose tragic outcome released universal grief and a cosmic outpouring of love into the world.

DEATH OF A PRINCESS—GRIEF OF A WORLD

The untimely death under very tragic circumstances of a major public figure, a woman, a commoner (albeit from the aristocracy) who became a princess, who had captured the heart and imagination of not only her native England but of people around the world, is worthy of some deep reflection. Such an event has sent shockwaves throughout the globe, unsettling the very fabric of our being, of what we feel we can trust and depend on. Such an outpouring of public grief and universal mourning has somehow stopped the world in its tracks, halted business as usual, as we hover precariously on the borders of an event that simply does not make sense, that is not acceptable.

My mother called from England on Sunday morning, August 31, 1997, to tell us the sad news. Her voice was shaking and she was audibly upset. She related to us the events of the accident as they had come to her over the BBC. She said the whole country had gone into shock and that almost immediately people started arriving at Buckingham Palace and Kensington Palace (Diana's London home) from all over England with notes and flowers and tears, as expressions of grief and outrage began to take form. The whole rest of our day, too, became draped in a gray pall, as we moved from a state of shocking disbelief to a feeling of sadness and loss.

We don't have television, but as we met with people, read newspaper accounts, and listened to public radio news and interviews on Sunday and Monday and throughout the following week, I found myself beginning to be amazed and curious that the death of Diana, a woman whom none of us knew personally, could unleash such a world shattering expression of collective grief and depth of feeling. It was as if each one of us had in some way lost someone very close to us. And yet that didn't make any rational sense at all.

What was particularly interesting to me after the first wave of confusing emotions began to subside was how, in the public eye, Diana had been perceived and appreciated. The *leit motif* of these views was that she was extraordinarily beautiful, not only in her physical appearance, strikingly good taste in clothes, and zest for life, but also in her inner beauty: her compassionate attitude toward patients with AIDS, leprosy, cancer, and heart disease; her visits with prostitutes, drug addicts, and homeless people whose names she knew and remembered; and most recently her attempts to ban the use of land mines—all reflections of this inner beauty. Personal accounts of her relationships with people and their families who were suffering, until now protected in confidentiality, also filled the news. Her contact with people less fortunate than herself was by no means always a media event; many of these contacts remained private and anonymous.

Beyond her beauty, Diana also seemed to radiate a deep sense of integrity in spite of her feelings of insecurity. Her willingness to break the bonds of royal respectability and discretion in not keeping secret her suffering in her marriage, especially her struggle with eating disorders, her suicidal despair, and her affair, together with her openness about seeking therapy, and help from advisors, made her a visible witness and spokesperson for women's issues, particularly in areas that have until recently been shrouded in unspeakable secrecy. This kind of honesty and openness, though it drew criticism from some quarters, mostly won her the respect of millions around the world.

The Shy Di of the 80s became an icon of what it means for a woman to find her own dignity, autonomy, and self-respect in the excruciating face of what turns out to have been rejection in her marriage from the beginning. Any illusions we might still have had about the privilege of royalty protecting one from the ruthlessness of some of life's most painful issues were sadly yet mercifully dashed as we saw the then wife of the future King of England struggling as hard to find herself—if not more so—as the more anonymous among us do. Too, in spite of a very painful public and publicized divorce process, she emerged as someone who seemed determined to make a go of her life, post-Palace. She neither portrayed herself nor was seen as a victim of circumstances beyond her. She emerged, as one public radio program described it, as a woman not of the 20th, but of the 21st century.

Embodying as she did in her life a range of those women's issues that have increasingly gained attention since the 70s, that is, the movement from daughter of the father, to wife and mother, and then to single parent—a princess who no longer needed her prince—made her, on account of her royal role, goddess-like and gave her mythic proportions. Occuring at a time in history when women have no culturally sanctioned transpersonal feminine vessel that represents and contains the complexity of our experience, when the controlling, orderly, power-driven, impersonal aspects of patriarchy, increasingly criticized, debunked, and replaced, nevertheless remain in control, and when a woman with an integrity beyond her identity defined in relationship to father, lover, spouse, and child, is still regarded with suspicion and criticized and devalued, Diana's life took on larger-than-human dimensions.

But there are deep cultural shadows in both taking on, and in burdening one fragile human being with so large a destiny, so public a life, so collective a role, as that of Diana's in England's monarchy. American movie stars suffer from a similar fate. Think of Marilyn Monroe, for example, and the discrepancy between how people imagined the beautiful, sexy, movie star and her actual lived life, and the terrible circumstances of her death. In carrying a transpersonal, archetypal, goddess fate, you become larger than life, and people imagine you to be all sorts of things that you may or may not be, according perhaps to absences in their own lives, or lacunae in the life of a nation, or collective trends of what the psyche of a particular generation requires, what it needs to idealize, or alternatively, denigrate, or what perhaps it is seeking to become. A royal, or a movie star, becomes the unwitting target of enormous amounts of collective energy, and being only one individual after all, this kind of onslaught is almost insufferable, and perhaps too much to bear. We should keep this in mind, too, when thinking of Prince Charles, and the two children, Prince William and Prince Harry.

Diana became a very visible princess in today's media-focused culture, not only on account of her striking beauty and the unpopular charities she chose to support, but also because every detail of her fairy tale turned every-modern-woman's-tale was writ large on the public's consciousness. Her acts of compassion, her public expressions of all too human feelings that any one of us can identify with, brought her out from behind a wall of impersonal duty and made her accessible to ordinary people. This was part of her tremendous appeal, that she gave the cold face of monarchy a very human presence. So, too, it comes as no surprise that Diana was increasingly angry and saddened by the *paparazzi*, those agents of collective opinion and image that exist because we the people fund their efforts. Is it really, then, a surprise that those collective forces against which she struggled, hounded her to her death? Her brother, Earl Spencer, living in Cape

Town, seemed to know this. He is reported to have said that he was deeply concerned that they would eventually kill her. Sadly, he was right.

Diana, a princess who attempted to combine her public trust with the needs of an individual woman striving for an authentic life of her own, died in a head-on collision with those insensitive, driven, and out-of-control forces of our contemporary culture, that managed, quite literally, to divest her of her own private identity. That perhaps is what fuels our outrage, and our grief: that collective interests won out in the end. A greatly loved princess was sacrificed to our basest needs, our most superficial, image-is-all, high speed, addictive, and unreflecting requirements. With her death, we all lost a shining example of what it means to be a human being, a being of beauty, compassion, and vulnerability, trying to find her own voice within a community context.

Yet we must, as Earl Spencer warned in his eulogy, beware of an over-idealized characterization of Diana. We must be able to distinguish between the actual Diana and the ideal Diana, at least recognize that such a distinction exists between the human and archetypal Diana, which is difficult with such a public figure, for the reasons I have already noted. The actual Diana was dating a playboy who was no match for whom she was trying to become. She was riding as a passenger in a speeding car, wearing no seat belt. She was rebellious; she had an eating disorder; she was human. In this regard, she not only took on the sins of our times, but collaborated with those out-of-control forces that destroyed her.

Now we, the living, are left to confront our darkest nightmares, and are called, individually and collectively, to face and take responsibility for those destructive forces. To the extent that we made her carry more than her fair share, out of not realizing the Queen of Hearts adequately within and between ourselves, and to the extent that we will not let ourselves be soulfully educated by this painfully sobering tragedy, we are all implicated, and will so remain, in her death. Something in each of us also died that night. And that is why the grief, culminating in such cosmic proportions at Diana's funeral, is so broad and so deep. We all sobbed our way through that service.

Diana in Myth and in Dream

But why has this event touched us—worldwide—so deeply? Surely, only because the historical reality is woven with archetypal threads and mythic dimensions. Already, even in the popular press, Diana is linked with Arthurian legend as the Lady of the Lake, and, as queen of people's hearts, has become the Grail Queen, who transforms her own suffering into the healing of others. Were we not all, as a world, given the opportunity to release into our grief and into our love by this terribly sad occasion? The death of Mother Teresa less than a week after Diana's death, too, provided such catharsis for many, and poignantly and powerfully emphasizes the archetypal impact of these two remarkably compassionate beings, living at completely different ends of a socio-economic-mythic spectrum, yet united as perhaps two of the great mystics of our times. Their very real humanness does not detract from this fact. That these two women met during the summer, and that Diana is buried with a rosary given to her by Mother Teresa at that meeting, gives symbolic resonance to the common devotion of their incarnate lives.

From the soul's point of view, we all live out personal myths, our unique and particular or wounded version of one or several of the archetypal images, affective stirrings and behavior patternings, contained in the great universal dramas recorded in myth and sacred story from around the world. That is their appeal to us: they speak to that "other country of long ago" of Diana's favorite hymn sung at her funeral, that we re-member via different ways of knowing than we use in everyday reality, a soulscape of subtle being and longing that we nevertheless also inhabit. Dreams, visions, illness, symptoms, and the mood of reverie are often an invaluable doorway into this symbolic dimension to our everyday, otherwise ordinary, lives. Such attention to this domain often fills our life with a richness of experience and vocational depth that is not experienced easily in any other way, except in a deeply loving relationship.

But this other country of soul, though we long to embody it, is easily neglected. A being of beauty, compassion, and vulnerability, trying to find her own voice, such as I described Princess Diana above, is also an image of the soul, as told in the myth of Eros and Psyche. In this tale, the collective is so threatened by, and so envious of, such a lovely reality, that it tries to destroy it. Even the gods, or in the case of this story, the goddess Aphrodite, Queen of Heaven and Creator of all things, is so roused to fury at the possibility of being surpassed by a mere mortal, that she seeks wicked vengeance on poor Psyche. Beauty, especially beauty of soul, is always a double-edged sword—a blessing and a curse. Only through harrowing suffering, solitude, and challenge, is Psyche eventually reunited with her lover, Eros, again. Even then, the reunion takes place in the realm of the gods and goddesses, not on human turf. Are we still not yet able, either individually or collectively, to bring transpersonal love to planet Earth? Do Diana's life and death have something to say to us here?

We live in a time when books on the soul are making the bestseller lists. How we seem to long for a life lived with depth and complexity, with someone we love, united to some larger purpose. Yet, how delicate the individual human soul is, how easily it gets lost and destroyed in the context of collective forces that rail against its unique expression. Jung (1959) remarks about the soul as we have already noted that though it is older than the ego or conscious part of ourselves, and "the secret *spiritus rector* of our fate," it is also "the smallest of the small" (§257) and can be easily pushed aside. How many of us seek creative lives only to sink at the prospect of how to achieve that authenticity in the face of the rent or mortgage payment, the kids' education, the addictions of substance, people, and consumerism that meet us in every newspaper and magazine, every television commercial, every instant-fix, and the overwhelming force of traditional attitudes and opinions that come starkly into view the moment one takes the road less traveled.

Within the context of these kinds of reflections, musings, and thoughts, a dream came to me, on the Tuesday morning following Sunday's sad news, a dream that I feel addressed the mythic dimension of Diana's death, and by implication, the archetypal underpinning of her life.

> *I am with a group of women coming from all different places on Earth, assembled together to celebrate the "festival of the Bear" ceremony. The place is unknown to me, but it is where "the earth meets the ocean," and this detail of location is important in the dream. The event being celebrated has to do with the cosmo-logical meaning of Diana's death. In other words, what from the human side is a terrible tragedy, has another face from the cosmic soul's point of view, in terms of the unfolding of Earth events, as we head toward a major Aeonic shift around 2012. I have some kind of marker of this event in my possession. I do not know if it is a book, or some kind of stone plaque. I am trying to place it on that border between land and water, but the shifting sand and the encroaching tide threaten to inundate what is attempting to be remembered, and I'm afraid that it might get lost. I awake with a feeling that I must not forget the dream.*

Every dream has a personal dimension. But beyond that, this dream responds to a collective situation. It is for the sake of witnessing the larger dimensions of Diana's death that I recount the dream here. It is an ethical claim, so it is the best way for me to be *in memoriam*. This dream partly lets us know why it is that we have all been so shaken by Diana's death. Her death is an event that ripples to the heart of the soul of the world and back, to that subtle reality Jung called the col-lective unconscious or objective psyche that is the very foun-dation of our earthly and ego existence. Jung (1977) says of this realm:

The collective unconscious, it's not for you, or me, it's the invisible world, it's the great spirit. It makes little difference what I call it: God, Tao, The Great Voice, The Great Spirit. But for people of our time God is the most comprehensible name with which to designate the Power beyond us (p. 419).

As I began to unpack the dream, layer upon layer began to unfold. I would like to address four iterations of the dream, knowing in advance that what I write will be incomplete.

The Festival of the Bear

First, I will address the Festival of the Bear Ceremony, about which I knew nothing and to which I had no personal associations. The bear in mythology is connected with resurrection and new life. It is especially related to the theme of initiation and its association with rites of passage. The bear, especially the dead bear, is treated with a great deal of fear, indeed there is often a name taboo lest the bear be offended. In hero myths, the bear is solar; in inundation myths it becomes lunar, and it is also lunar when associated with moon goddesses such as Artemis and Diana.

In this regard, it is clear that the myth of Diana in our culture also has to do with an initiation and rite of passage at our time in history, emphasizing the dire need in our times for taking individual responsibility for our own soul's needs for beauty, for integrity, and for love, and that we also take on as much as we are capable of the shadow side of those desires, that is, for being aware of and taking a stand with those forces in the collective that would oppose the soul's needs. Such forces tend to keep us isolated in a fragmented world where spirit and matter, having forgotten their origins in a unified whole, remain in their degenerate state of rampant materialism and rational intellectualism. In such a world we remain devoted to an essentially unlived life of undifferentiated convention and mediocrity.

When the tragic event of Diana's death is viewed from the side of the dream, her death becomes a potential rite of passage into a rebirth for the collective in which spirit can embody and flesh become ensouled. The Festival of the Bear is a celebration of the feminine soul's aristocracy, that is, its desire for uniqueness and wild creative expression. It is a recognition that we reside in a delicately shifting place, somewhere between firm land, what we think we know and know about, and the limitless expanse of an unknown mystery that longs to be experienced. It is a vocation calling us to witness and embody this potentiality for life lived from the point of view, not of the ego's divisions, but of the soul's needs for wholeness, at this precarious turning of the Aeons.

Further, the Festival of the Bear among the Gilyaks of East Asia is instituted in honor of a recently diseased kinsman. The kin gods of the Gilyaks are human beings who have met with violent death. The festival is also celebrated for reasons of purification. The custom is an atonement offered to the species through the medium of single individuals for the loss it sustains in the slaughter of so many of its members for food.[7] So if we substitute Diana for the Bear, she is the fearsome, awesome one who is slaughtered to satisfy the (necessary?) appetites of the people. And the festival is one of atonement, for the propitiation of guilt over our way of living that kills the like of Diana. The reference here is to the ideal, not the actual Diana; though in that she had taken on the sins of our times, in her death and in her death only, she becomes real psychic food for the people in a way that in life she perhaps never could have. The idea of a certain transformation in death, a becoming available as food to others, is very present.

---

7. A kind note of thanks to the Jungian analyst Ray C. Walker, M.D., for this reference in correspondence exchanged about this dream.

The Bear and the Lunar Goddess Artemis-Diana

Secondly, the myth of the bear is associated with Artemis, whose Roman name is Diana. Artemis-Diana is a virgin goddess, noted not only for her tall beauty but also for valuing her "in-tactness," "one-in-herself." In other words, she represents not literal chastity, but a woman's independent strivings unrelated to how she is perceived by others or quite apart from the demands of any other relatedness or relationship. She belongs to no man and does what she does because it is true for her. This is an aspect of the feminine that has been denied women for centuries. It was Diana's expression of these characteristics, imaged for example in not wearing the royal glove, that placed her in trouble with the more conservative forces within the royal family.

Artemis-Diana is the protectress of the wilds, the natural order and rhythms of soul outside the civilized requirements of culture. Not being a mother herself, the goddess nevertheless aids women in the painful process of birth in which women temporarily sustain their more human aspects and become roaring forces of nature. These animal instincts are usually educated out of most nice ladies, who losing their essential selves become instead paragons of obedience, devoted to pleasing others. To actually live one's own life takes a kind of fierce commitment.

Symbolically, therefore, Artemis-Diana is the guardian of the soul and presides as midwife to both women and men in the changing requirements of the times, in the necessary breakdowns and breakthroughs of the shifting of the Aeons. She is also Goddess of the Moon, and is the divine representative of feminine values so sorely lost, and so sorely longed for, in these painfully challenging days. Princess Diana was particularly valued for making visible the sufferings of her own soul, an act that not only allowed her to identify with and represent the rejected within our culture, those who live outside the status quo, as her brother noted in his eulogy, but also released us all into our own very human feelings and failures, into our grief and into our love. Whatever the royal family's private expression of loss, it was a less hidden, more open expression of feeling that was demanded by the public. In other words, it is bringing what is concealed to the light, whether it be our feelings, our acts of creation, our dark shadows, our gravest secrets, or our visions and our dreams that long for expression; that is part of what it means to be an ethical human being today.

Artemis Requires Cruel Sacrifice

Thirdly, Earl Spencer in his eulogy spoke of the painful irony that his sister Diana, named after the ancient Goddess of the Hunt, should end her life by being hunted down. The Jungian analyst Joseph Henderson (1967) elaborates the symbolism of the bear as being the timeless carrier of secret initiation and its central meaning as a form of rebirth (pp. 223–232). Of particular interest in terms of the dream and its contemporary reference is that Artemis is not only the maternally protective, she is also a threatening mother who exacts great and savage sacrifice, whose hidden purpose nevertheless is *the power to be* in the face of the eroding civilizing influences of the cultural mother.

Something of this nuance may reside behind the story of the sacrifice of Iphigenia to Artemis in one version of Euripides' (fifth century, B.C.) play, "Iphigenia in Aulis," though the sacrifice, in this version, is freely chosen and no accident. The willing death of Iphigenia, preferred daughter of Clytemnestra and Agamemnon, assures prosperity for all Greece at the beginning of the Trojan War. In ancient times, the yearly sacrifice of the King, which was eventually replaced with a symbolic sacrificial animal, was recognized as the means of restoring human consciousness and life within its more broad and cosmic context. We no longer live at a time when the privilege of royalty goes hand in hand with an annual sacrificial act to make this kind of collective psychic energy available for the thriving of the masses, the crops, and the life of a community under the stars. Modernity is perhaps singular in its isolation from this level of consciousness. In our unwillingness to consciously sacrifice ego attitudes that keep us separate from the vast mystery of the cosmos, we remain detached from the Great Spirit to whom devotion assures the proper attitude toward that Otherness from which all life derives, and in which we are all held.

Being so thoroughly domesticated these days, we tend to be far removed from the dark, cruel, and terrifying dimensions of the ancient Goddess, such as we see in relation to Artemis. Perhaps our hubris rallies her fury and the painful sacrifice she demands. Or, lacking a conscious relation to our own coldness, chaos, and unrelatedness is why we are visited by such bloodiness so often through the back door. It should not be forgotten, though, that the car accident in which three lives were so hideously extinguished occurred on the night of the dark moon, the phase reserved for the deathly aspect of Artemis in her Hecate form. We shall perhaps never know if this was sacrifice on the part of soul, or accident; that depends, I suspect, on how one views these events. Certainly the dream takes the former attitude, though, at the same time, I cannot subscribe to the view that would suggest Diana *chose* this kind of death; that is unacceptable from a feeling standpoint. From the more broad landscape of soul, though, an election perhaps was made to suffer a fate on behalf of the many. These kinds of paradoxes or neither/nor situations, it seems to me, must be allowed to reside together, for they speak more for the complexity of truth, the darker whole, than an either/or position would.

There was a time when life-giving and death-dealing powers were inextricably bound in a view of life that was not sentimental, a knowledge that comes close to a woman these days when she is giving birth consciously. At other times, a move on the part of soul often feels like a ruthless act, ruthlessly selfish (and is often judged that way by those who have not yet descended into their own dark night), demanding not only tremendous courage but a willingness to sacrifice dearly cherished convictions and commitments. Perhaps Artemis is near when we dare to trust such moves, often made alone, even if we're surrounded by love.

Henderson (1967) stresses that, particularly for women, the Great Goddess is Mother and Maiden in one, and that "this points to an identity of girl and woman which speaks to woman's psychology in a special way—an awareness of female identity which it is the unconscious (if not conscious) desire of men to possess" (p. 232). Was this what we had to hunt down? The difference stressed by Henderson is between *knowing about* something, and *being it*. Henderson quotes Kerenyi: "'It is one thing to know about the 'seed and the sprout,' and quite another to have recognized in them the past and future of one's own being and continuation.'"[8] He also says:

> Jung emphasizes a sense of continuity with the ancestors "in such a way that these can prolong themselves via the bridge of the momentary individual into the generations of the future. A knowledge with this content, with the experience of *being in death*, is not to be despised" (p. 232).

A capacity for knowing it and being it, is the central meaning of initiation to the Great Mother. Could it be that Diana in her life and in her death was such a momentary individual, such a shaman or mystic for our culture, both linking us back to what has been so sorely lost and carrying that remembrance into the future?

"But why need there be an initiation at all?" poses Henderson (1967). He answers:

---

8. C. G. Jung and Karl Kerenyi, *Essays on a Science of Mythology*, R. F. C. Hull, trans., Bollingen Series XXII (New York: Pantheon, 1949), p. 254.

> Perhaps it is because men know it but can't experience it, whereas women experience it but do not know it. Each must learn to acquire the capacity for experience and for being conscious of that experience simultaneously. Only initiation as a rite of passage in some form can accomplish this (p. 232).

The ability both to experience deeply, and to be able to reflect on that experience, is a high achievement of consciousness, and essential if we are to become ethically responsible human beings, translating unconscious instinct into the light of awareness, before falling back into the River of Life again. A soulful life is not a perfect life; it is one that enjoys and suffers the myriad complexities that make us both vulnerable and strong. As Henderson (1967) also notes, in forms of initiation associated with the bear are found "a blend of weakness and strength—or submission combined with a spirit of independence" (p. 232). It is perhaps this appealing combination, and daring, that drew Diana to our hearts even while, not yet initiated, we tried destructively to possess it.

Cosmic Connection and Potential

In ancient Egypt, there was a belief that the King or Queen, the divine royals, became a star upon death. Within this context, it is interesting that the suggestion has been made that we rename stars or constellations of stars after Diana, Princess of Wales, as a way of remembering her. But the stellar connection is also part of the mythology of Artemis-Diana. Ursa Major, "Great Bear," colloquially called the Big Dipper (or, in England, the Plough) is ruler of the stars and protectress of the *axis mundi*, Pole of the World, marked in heaven by the Pole Star at the center of the small circle described by the constellation Ursa Major. This pole or world tree, according to the oldest traditions, was female. Barbara Walker (1983), in *The Women's Encyclopedia of Myths and Secrets*, writes that:

"the tree is the source of unborn souls," which would give birth to the new primal woman, Life (Lif) in the new universe after the present cycle came to an end. Its fruit could be given to women in childbirth "that what is within may pass out." The spring at the tree's root was a fountain of wisdom or of the life-giving fluid *aurr*, which may be likened to the "wise blood" of the Mother—that much mythologized feminine life-source likened to the Kula nectar in the uterine spring of Kundalini, as if the maternal tree upholding the universe were the Mother's spine with its many chakras (p. 60).

In many traditions, the chakras of the body, from our physical presence on Earth at the root to our most refined spiritual essence located at the crown, are the openings to our connections to the universe and the multi-dimensional world of which we are a part. It is this cosmic connection that we have lost increasingly in the last several hundred years. The rise of a rational ego consciousness divorced from body, wisdom, dream, nature, and the world has increasingly characterized our history and led us to a world that, inspite of increased technical scientific knowledge, has not made us more wise or more loving. Our new world is increasingly environmentally unsound, and wracked with suffering.

It is my deepest wish that perhaps such a dream, and such a dark initiation as Diana's death, may yet invite all of us to let our necessary grieving eventuate in a reevaluation of what, after all, is ethically required from a soulful perspective from each one of us as we move forward into a new millenium, a new Aeon, which in many traditions (Maya for example) begins not in the year 2000 but in the year 2012 (the date in the dream). In this way, the tragedy of Diana's death will not get lost, and goddess-willing, perhaps stands a chance of being redeemed. In this way, the symptomatic gestures of our collective eating disorders, whether they be of the body or of a consumer mentality, may yet find their real home in an appetite for Life, celebrating the fullness of us all—from light to dark, from controlled to wild, from generous to selfish— rooted in the *axis mundi* of a wise and loving blood line.

In a final note I want to say that in attending to this material, it struck me, again, how much the origins of depth psychology were an attempt on the part of the soul of the world once again to reconnect us to that larger Mystery with which we have so grievously lost touch. The brilliance of both Freud and Jung was in asserting the primacy of the dream, for the dream is that country of neither fact in the world nor idea of rational consciousness, that leads us into what Jung describes so well as the anamnesis of the origins. This is not just of our family of origin, but of our clan, our culture, our ancestors, and extending to the stars. We still seem so often intent on making the dream fit *our* needs. But who is the Dream Maker? Do we really know more about this Stranger after one hundred years of therapy? It is a curious paradox for me that the more I work with dreams, the more the mystery of their essential "unknownness" impresses itself upon me. Beyond what we struggle to say about it, the dream is a code or a key to this other country that longs for us to know how we are held in a much more vast vision of reality than we could ever imagine. If we miss the message, then we will have missed the opportunity of what is calling to us. My fear is that, too often, depth psychology keeps us stuck in a world that the dream is trying to get us to leave. Even sadly now among many Jungians, the practice of therapy remains too personalistic, and misses the profound invitation at its heart; the dream opens a door that connects us in a timeless way, cross culturally, to all of history, and resituates us now, in the body, as a cell in a cosmic mystery whose origins and purpose we do not know. And we are so corporate, we have forgotten Jung while we spend hours judging him.

The life and death of Diana, Princess of Wales, cruelly demonstrates that when we remain within an order of spirit so dangerously split from what matters, and do not make the necessary ego sacrifices to resituate ourselves within the mystery of a larger unknown whole, and in so doing acknowledge the presence of the goddesses and the gods, they "eat" us.

This chapter has emphasized that in becoming credal psychotherapy has lost touch with its origins and its original intention: to open that space where the chthonic and divine faces of Love and Chaos overtake us. Through the illustrations of a patient's pathos and Princess Diana's death, I have attempted to indicate that some kind of religious sensibility is what heals, because only such experiences situate us within this larger domain and vision of the Whole.

Chapter 6

LOVE AND VOCATION
Being Addressed by Voices of the Unseen World

The realization of the self also means a re-establishment of [humankind] as the microcosm, i.e. . . . . cosmic relatedness. Such realizations are frequently accompanied by synchronistic events. (The prophetic experience of vocation belongs to this category.)
—C. G. Jung (1976a), §1573

In [synchronicity], still entirely unknown to us, the macro- and microcosmos actually merge into a total psychomaterial or human-cosmic unitarian reality in that the remotest so-called chance events happening in the universe manifest themselves in meaningful connection with the inner psychic constellations in individual human beings.
—Marie-Louise von Franz (1992), p. 183

That soul is considered to be located within is a peculiar prejudice of modern Western consciousness and seems to be based on the separation of what once was a unified field of psyche and matter. Over the last several hundred years, this separation has allowed an extraordinary acceleration of knowledge: scientific, rational knowledge outside; and the exploration of the psyche with its forgotten longings and lost wisdom inside. However, the split of a differentiated ego consciousness from its foundation in a psycho-cosmic whole has also endangered our world, as we have increasingly divested the world of life and over-burdened ourselves with it.

This loss of a connection to the foundation of existence, as a matter of life and death, has required what Jung (1959) calls "an anamnesis of the origins" (§279). Jung does not mean only an anamnesis of a personal kind, but also an anamnesis of a cultural, historical, and even cosmic nature—*anamnesis* being a "recollection, a remembering of what has gone before, a recovery of a lost and forgotten wholeness." In previous chapters I have suggested that the god Eros lurks in the desire for this recovery, and that the restoration of the whole is a labor of love, an achievement of love, a surrender into love, "the work for which all other work is but preparation" (Rilke, 1954, p. 54).

Too, what is implied here is that we cannot solve the pathologies of ourselves or our patients, or our environmental problems, by the use of scientific terminology and theoretical formulations alone (such as have been developed in empirical epistemologies), for these, though easier, are inadequate to the task of transformation. What is required is a wholeness of response in relation to nature as well as a response to the expressions of the soul in the therapy room. We seek an attunement to the things of the world, a listening to the voices of the unseen realms with whom we share this beautiful planet. We seek an ensouled language, full of heartfelt images and symbols, that can enlarge our conscious attitude enough to embrace those energies both subtle and more explicit, pressing for recognition from dream, reverie, vision, and world.

Today the move toward an ecological psychology, or an ecology of soul,[1] and the establishment by the United Nations of the Earth Charter Movement may also be a move toward healing this yawning gap, this chaotic chasm that has opened up in our world in the split between psyche and matter. It may also be a symptomatic urge to resituate human consciousness in its rightful place in a larger unified cosmic field. But we need to be cautious about simply moving from inside to outside; we need to ask: Does such a move inadvertantly perpetuate the dangerous split that holds the destiny

---

1. See, for example, Roszak, Gomes and Kanner, eds., *Ecopsychocology* (San Francisco: Sierra Club Books, 1995).

of our world in a precarious balance? Not to address and respond to genuine environmental or psychological travesties might do the same. But whatever action we take, we are also addressed by the subtle world of the imaginal, its landscapes and its figures. My work focuses on this in-between space.

C. G. Jung found that his studies on synchronicity had many parallels with discoveries being made in the new physics. Synchronicities appeared to link psyche and world not in a causal way, but rather in an acausal way, by the principle of affinity or correspondence. Too, it seemed that as psychology reached toward the world and matter, physics was making an opposite move, and finding that, for example, in the influence of the observer on the observed, it must take psyche into account in its descriptions of reality.

Both psychology and physics are now facing a new challenge as they reach into the unknown: that of the nature and influence of consciousness. Beyond even this, physics in its discovery of quantum fields is facing the knowledge that some reality is structured, independently of an observing consciousness, in an acausal, nonlocal, outside-of-space-and-time dimension.[2] Quantum waves, like Jungian archetypes, exist in a transcendent domain of potential. With observation they "collapse" into being in our world.

Similarly, archetypal patternings or constellations seem to arrange both inner dream and outer event within an invisible, nonlocal field that holds them both together. Jung's famous example is of a resistant patient who at the moment she was telling a dream of a golden scarab, a real scarab beetle flew in the window, almost as if it knew its part in a mythological drama of rebirth.[3]

---

2. See, for example, A. Goswami, *The Self-Aware Universe: How Consciousness Creates the Material World* (New York: Tarcher/Putnam, 1995), pp. 59–60.
3. C. G. Jung, *The Structure and Dynamics of the Psyche* (Princeton: Princeton University Press, 1969), §982.

This reciprocal movement of psyche and nature, then, opens up a third domain, the recovery of an intermediate realm of subtle bodies, that neither/nor landscape of soul that Corbin calls the *mundus imaginalis*.

In comparing alchemical ways of knowing with contemporary discoveries in physics and psychology, Jung (1968) observes:

> But the moment when physics touches on the "untrodden, untreadable regions," and when psychology has at the same time to admit that there are other forms of psychic life besides the acquisitions of personal consciousness—in other words, when psychology too touches on an impenetrable darkness—then the intermediate realm of subtle bodies comes to life again, and the physical and the psychic are once more blended in an indissoluble unity. We have come very near to this turning-point today (§394).

In this chapter my intent is to begin a preliminary exploration of those extraordinary and unpredictable moments when psyche and matter seem to be collapsing their familiar boundaries. I will try to remain within this intermediary realm and reflect upon how we are being addressed in these happenings and what Other might be calling to us. It may be that moments of synchronicity remind us that we live in a psychomaterial or human-cosmic fullness as von Franz describes, and that we need to be restored within this wholeness, with a differentiated consciousness that can join and separate simultaneously. We need to remember that human life is but one expression of an all-pervading life force in a multidimensional vibratory universe, held together, as the ancients knew, by cosmogonic love.

SYNCHRONICITY

There are moments today when we experience a breakdown of our ego-differentiated consciousness, and fall into what Jung, using the terminology of medieval natural philosophy, calls the *unus mundus*, a world in which the duality of soul and matter seems to be eliminated, and we are addressed by something Other. These irregularly occurring and unpredictable moments Jung calls synchronistic events, and he views them as a part of a larger acausal orderedness in nature, also known to physics in phenomena such as half-life decay and the speed of light.

In synchronicity there are indications that physical energy and psychic energy may be but two aspects of one and the same underlying reality. Events seem to happen when an archetype is intensively activated in an individual, and in such an excited state the constellated field appears to extend outside the psyche into the world of matter. I gave an example of this phenomenon in the story of the hummingbird in chapter 5. This apparent extension of psyche into nature or the material world describes for Jung the psychoid aspect of the archetype, and releases the archetype from its imprisonment inside the psyche. Jung and von Franz later developed this idea into the hypothesis of psyche and matter being in a continuously mirroring relationship vis-a-vis each other.

Synchronicity involves the simultaneity of two events: one psychic as in dream, thought, or vision; the other psychophysical, occurring in the outside world. These two events are acausally yet meaningfully related to each other, and dependent on the witnessing consciousness of an observer. Moreover, the two events do not usually happen at the same time (hence they are not synchronous), but they are usually experienced as numinous and have a profound effect. They are perhaps the modern equivalents of what in former times were referred to as miracles, signs, wonders, oracular occurrences, and acts of Providence.

In synchronistic events there is a sense of another order or dimension of reality breaking through the veil of what we consider normal reality. This other reality seems to have a consciousness of events taking place in our lives beyond us, and seems to have an intention that we come to know this, and eventually be transformed by it. We feel addressed by an unseen Presence. We are called forth, invited, as it were, to step from a more confining and familiar place into a more expansive, even idiosyncratic landscape, beyond convention to a more full and creative life.

Such a presence confronts us with a vocation, an evocative word that means "to be addressed by a Voice." This Voice can take many forms and it has been imaged in a variety of ways: greater reality or conscience, god or goddess, daimon, bird-telling, angel; for we need lots of names in our attempts to evoke the reality of something essentially unknowable and unnameable. During the last half of this century, the world-wide phenomenon of extra-terrestrial encounters and space-ship or UFO sightings may be a contemporary example of how this Other is trying to make connection with us. In fact Jung (1975) in a letter comments that "the lore about Flying Saucers are effects of our dimly felt but none the less intense need to reach a new physical as well as spiritual basis beyond our actual conscious world" (p. 593). The crop circle mysteries, so prominent in England, but also appearing in other parts of the world, are also an example, perhaps from the side of matter or the spirit of Earth, of a similar Other dimension or order of reality trying to get our attention. The appearance of crop circles has also been linked with UFO sightings.

In China, the idea of a cosmic meaning is formulated in the concept of the Tao and refers to the meaningful, holistic interconnectedness of all being. In this respect, one is continuously being addressed by the Voice of Otherness, either by reading the signs of the world, or by contacting one's inner state of consciousness, for inner and outer are always considered to be in a mirror relationship with each other. This belief in the continuous reflection and union of consciousness and world is seen in the story of the Rainmaker, referred to in the first chapter. It is an attunement to this unified world of psyche and matter that increasingly seems to invite our attention, and that is most dramatically brought into view in moments of synchronicity.

Resonances to the Chinese concept of the Tao are found in the West in the Hippocratic "sympathy of all things," or

Leibnitz's idea of a pre-established harmony. Corbin's *mundus imaginalis* recalls the subtle body world of medieval alchemy in which imagination and matter are still undifferentiated and infuse each other. Today depth psychology increasingly attends to the intersubjective imaginal field—initially identified by Jung—that third body of the world which resides in the crack between sense and spirituality, in the subtle body field between patient and therapist, partaking of both but existing as an Other realm dependent on the presence of patient and therapist, yet transcending either individual or pair. This in-between world of visionary feeling is a place pregnant with wonder, a realm in which paradoxically we find our proper location in the wholeness of things, and a complete acceptance of what is—joys and sorrows, birth and death. It is a field of experience infused with cosmological love, "the more unknown," as Jung (1961, p. 354) refers to the divine, a synonym for this love. Within this field, life is restored to its sacred depths.

We know this world, too, in profound levels of loving erotic union where body, image, and affect fuse in such a way as to make spirit flesh and matter spirit, and where we see the constellations of the stars in the undulating forms of our lover's body. In these disclosures we penetrate the veil of the material world by being lovingly devoted to it, and enter that realm in which the divine and human seem to participate in an ongoing creation; each needing the other, each penetrating the other. Here our gestures celebrate and bear witness to the multiplicity of life given by God.

For the most part, contemporary people live in a three-dimensional universe, and in linear chronological time; and we act as if the laws of cause and effect are true, which they are in that dimension! If we but pause for a moment, though, we know that we are bathed in a mystery, surrounded on all sides by an invisible world, penetrated and approached by unseen presences, qualities that are clothed by the physical realities of the perceived realms, beings that we catch sight of only out of the corner of our eye.

An Image of a Unified World

*I was walking around the ancient village of Assisi, Italy, eventual-
ly going to the church built for St. Francis. At one point my husband drifted away from me as I remained transfixed by a series of
large, colorful, deeply moving wall paintings by the 14th-century
painter Giotto, depicting various scenes in the life of the 12th-cen-
tury monk, that without any words, tell his story well.*

*Particularly striking to my late 20th-century eye is that there
are almost as many panels devoted to St. Francis' life after his physical death as before it! The place of vision and dream, both in the
monk's life, and in those around him, and the ability to be in two
places at once—bilocation—are depicted as if completely normal in
the course of events. The presence and appearance of the angel, and
other non-human beings, including dark-winged devils and evil
spirits, are also seen as the quite natural accompaniment to the
human sphere.*

*The legend that it was at first a madman who recognized the
aristocrat Francis as a holy man and visionary endows what we
nowadays reduce to a pathology that requires treatment back to nor-
mality, with an integrity and vision of its own. In addition, the frescoes depicting St. Francis talking to a flock of birds at his feet and
feeding them, and commanding water from a desert rock to quench
his companions' thirst on a journey, portray a relation to life deeply
embedded within a fabric larger than the merely human, a life whose
relation to the Invisibles and Presences that inhabit our world, and
surround us in subtle as well as concrete ways, brings a richness
and depth that perhaps has become grievously lacking in our contemporary and so-called progressive, technically advanced world.*

*In this landscape the whole world is alive with spirits and dai-
mons, and the boundaries of time-space, causality, linearity, and
rationality that have become familiar to us since the 17th century
do not exist, or at least are relativized. There appears to be not a
split between spirit and matter, not an either/or, nor an inside/out-
side perspective, but rather a seamless connection between psyche
and world.*

The philosopher William James (1902/1982) in his chapter "Mysticism," writes of our rational consciousness being but one type of a multitude of potential realities that surrounds us—parted "by the filmiest of screens"—and that we can access these other forms by applying the appropriate attitude. He notes:

> No account of the universe in its totality can be final which leaves these other forms of consciousness quite disregarded. How to regard them is the question—for they are so discontinuous with ordinary consciousness. Yet they may determine attitudes though they cannot furnish formulas, and open a region though they fail to give a map. At any rate, they forbid a premature closing of our accounts with reality. Looking back on my own experiences, they all converge toward a kind of insight to which I cannot help ascribing some metaphysical significance. The keynote of it is invariably a reconciliation. It is as if the opposites of the world, whose contrariness and conflict make all our difficulties and troubles, were melted into unity (p. 388).

Let me recount a story, a "visitation" of several years ago, a parting of one of those filmy screens.

The Deer

Our house in Connecticut was situated at the end of a cul-de-sac on about half an acre of land that bordered the College Arboretum, a protected wilderness that provided sanctuary for birds, frogs, trees (some unusual ones indigenous to the area), flowering shrubs, ducks, and animals of all kinds. The boundary of our back garden was marked by a dry stone wall and five blueberry bushes, and beyond that the land sloped off into a landscape of tall uncut grass and various kinds of trees—dogwood, beech, and yew—and then steeply fell off into the Arboretum. It was so steep in fact that we rarely entered the preserve that way.

It must have been about four in the morning, perhaps a little later, but it was midsummer, so the dawn light was already begin-

ning to filter into my room. One bird, then several, and then a caca-phony of song heralded the arrival of the birthing sun—not yet seen —and a new day. It was that moment, that magical time bet-ween sleeping and waking, where one still wears the gossamer fabric of the sleeping body that does not yet wish to be clothed by the day, and in heightened sensitivity hears the sounds of the garden begin-ning to waken. It was that moment that is not quite sleep, and not yet awake, a dreamy in-between time, in-between worlds, the crack between night and day, dream and thought, darkness and light, reverie and word, a time for the unexpected to happen, reveal itself.

I was feeding my newborn daughter, seated on a gently rocking chair, near a window that overlooked the back garden. When Sarah had finished feeding and had fallen back into drowsy sleep, lips still sucking though no longer on my breast, I lifted her up and glanced out of the window at the unfolding dawn. There she was, like an apparition emerging through a misty veil, a doe, a mother deer with her own babies, two fawns, together, in the garden, eating the grass and the blueberry bushes, gentle creatures from the woods, drawn perhaps by who knows what attracting force, what strange attrac-tor, but mother to mother it seemed to me in that moment, in that crack between the worlds. She, pulled by the mother in me, me pulled by the mother in her, an act of silent, mutual recognition and regard, animal to human, human to animal, both of us in the uni-fied, magnetic field of Mother. A moment when the borders between us were dissolved into such seamless sweetness, a moment of quiet beauty and utter delight that brought tears to my eyes, and moved my soul deeply.

The only other time that I saw deer in my garden was two years later, when I had just given birth to my son, and was going through the same ancient ritual, and rising to put him back in his crib, looked, and saw the doe with her fawns eating my blueberry bushes in the early morning light.

SYNCHRONICITY AS A FIELD OF LOVE

Mystics, saints, poets, lovers, madmen, and ordinary people the world over who have had sporadic types of unitive experiences know that, as Walt Whitman (in "Song of Myself") describes, "a kelson of the creation is love" (5:14). The word kelson refers to the line of timber that fastens the ship's floor-timbers to the keel. Like the *axis mundi* of the world, the image of the kelson evokes a central pole holding the integrity of the parts in a balanced whole.

An anonymous English woman in James (1902/1982) recounts a mystical experience of the divine in which she understands that her hurt is the way in which God fulfills his revelations and that this happens "to the exact extent of my capacity for suffering." She goes on:

> While regaining consciousness, I wondered why, since I had gone so deep, I had seen nothing of what the saints call the *love* of God, nothing but his relentlessness. And then I heard an answer, which I could only just catch, saying, "Knowledge and Love are One, and the *measure* is suffering"—I give the words as they came to me (p. 393).

Another example that James (1902/1982) gives is of a Canadian psychiatrist, Dr. Bucke, author of the well-known *Cosmic Consciousness* (1901), who describes the phenomenon of "cosmic consciousness" from his own experiences (James p. 398). In such a state:

> there occurs an intellectual enlightenment which alone would place the individual on a new plane of existence—would make him almost a member of a new species. To this is added . . . an indescribable feeling of elevation, elation, and joyousness, and a quickening of the moral sense. . . . With these come what may be called a sense of immortality, a consciousness of eternal life, not a conviction that he shall have this, but the consciousness that he has it already (p. 2).

Dr. Bucke adds his conviction from such experiences "that the foundation principle of the world, of all the worlds, is what we call love, and that the happiness of each and all is in the long run absolutely certain" (p. 399). He notes that even after twenty-five years, the truths of these disclosures (that in a visionary state lasted only a few seconds) never left him, not even in the darkest of depressions.

The mystical traditions of the religions of Christianity, Judaism, Hinduism, Buddhism, and Sufism have all developed cosmic awareness methodically through yoga, meditation, or spiritual practice of various kinds, some of which focus on the energetic seats of consciousness located within the chakras of the body. Sufism and the practices of Tantra are, par excellence, supreme examples of the cultivation of ecstasy residing in the human heart, erotic love being the substance with which the divine infuses the world. Love is the divine; all else is illusion. Spiritual and meditative practices are aimed at arriving at such revelatory gnosis.

The Sufi poet Rumi (1993) writes of love's shameless excesses and risky abandonments:

> Love is reckless; not reason.
> Reason seeks a profit.
> Love comes on strong, consuming herself, unabashed.
> (p. 53)
>
> A soul which is not clothed
> with the inner garment of Love
> should be ashamed of its existence.
>
> Be drunk with Love,
> for Love is all that exists.
> Where is intimacy found
> if not in the give and take of Love (p. 69).*

The great longing in the human soul for love that is documented in the religious traditions as longing for union with the divine is mirrored in our search for soul to soul union with another in the human sphere. This is always a synchro-

---

* From Rumi, *Love Is a Stranger* (Watsonville, CA: Threshold Books, 1993). Portions of two poems, "Love is Reckless," and "The Inner Garment of Love" (pp. 53, 69) are reprinted by kind permission.

nistic matter, for we cannot make love happen. Such *coniunctio* experiences express more than any other the desire of spirit for matter, for our incarnate lives to be inspired and for the release of the quotidian confines of the ego into a larger cosmic sphere.

Today more than at any time in history, the great love experiment is underway, for we no longer have to enter a monastic order to be blissed out on God, neither do we have to deny the matter of our bodies in order to sing the great wonder of creation. A true love is never just a human affair. We are drawn into our loves by the gravitational pull of divine and chthonic eros. Cosmic consciousness and erotic human love in their natural state belong together as a union of the Great Above with the Great Below. This does not imply that all our relations are or need be sexual, but unless our relations sing some version of the songs of love, of eros, nothing much happens and the world remains rather dry and brittle, like dead wood.

For the last several years a certain shift in perspectives has been subtly underway for me, some sort of unraveling of everything I hold close to my heart, like a world cracking open asking for other realities to come forward, yet paradoxically like a return to what I have always known since the beginning. The insights of Jung's psychology experienced within the context of three analyses spanning some twelve years saved my life and brought me to this place. Yet this psychology that I have known and practiced and taught has inexplicably begun to feel like a noose around my neck, has begun to feel like a world that is constricting me, has begun to feel like an order of being that is beginning to die and fade away. I can say this while simultaneously still valuing depth psychology's immeasurable wisdom for that time in life when we need it for further self-knowledge. Individuation, however, means that we are always becoming, always changing, and this allows for further expressions and deeper experiences of the complexities of our natures to take place.

So there is another voice that calls now, something that cannot only be rationally described, something that can only be alluded to, some shift in worldview that we can tell stories about, witness, dream, and reflect on, while it is dreaming us and speaking to us in its own language. Many at this time are such witnesses to these changing realities. All we are asked to do is to tell the story in the way it comes to us, to help anchor the new vibrations of energy that come toward us from the future, seeking to reassert the integrity of our broken world.

This knowledge is not new; it is ancient. But we in the West have forgotten it. It survives in many indigenous cultures all over the world, cultures mostly reduced to Third World status by our dominant but sorely impoverished, though it is called "civilized," order. Is there a chance perhaps that before our technology, our knowledge—knowledge so divorced from feeling, wisdom, the divine and the mystery— our understanding, and our unconscionable and unethical behavior toward each other as individuals, and as nations, and toward the planet completely destroys us, that we could pause and listen and respond to what gently and urgently calls us now? Perhaps in this way our hard-won knowledge could be restored with dignity into the sacredness of life. Perhaps in this way the epiphany of chaos in our world could be received as the call into eros, and all that pains and divides us could be viewed as culture's contemporary signal that the vocation of our times is to let go of our rational, ordered consciousness as the only reality and surrender into a larger unknown presence penetrated by love.

Synchronicity and a UFO Encounter

Standing three-quarters the way up a mountain side, on a mid-May evening, in a small parking lot where the view was particularly breathtaking of the valley below—the town lit up like an ocean of gold and silver diamond stars—how could I know that my life would suddenly and irrevocably change? On that mid-May evening I was with a friend, both of us jumping up and down to keep warm in the exceptionally windy conditions. We had gone back to the borrowed car to get sweaters for further protection against the cold. The mood was light-hearted and relaxed, after an intensive 10-day ancient Mystery School retreat in the southern California desert. There was a spirit of fun and adventure and good humor, two friends having a good time.

We had turned off the road at this particular point ostensibly because the traffic was so busy on the winding mountain path, and the wind so insistent, that it made driving quite laborious and slow. Anyway we were already close to the top, and only came up for the beautiful nocturnal view of Palm Springs below.

After a few minutes of taking in the sparkling vista, we turned back toward the car to drive back down the mountain. My friend, however, stopped rather abruptly, and looking toward the mountain peak, asked me if I could see what he saw: what seemed like a large, circular, flying yet stationary object—yet it was hard to make out its exact shape—with rotating colored circular lights on its underbelly, was in midair just off to the side of the mountain top.

As I stood still to follow his gaze to where he was pointing, a most remarkable event occurred: the whole landscape shifted as if into a completely different vibration of reality. Although it was unmistakably the same geographical location, all at once the blustery wind ceased completely, and the busy stream of cars totally disappeared. We were now all alone. The darkness of the evening shifted to a dreamy moonscape, as if the land was now illumined by an unseen source. A profound stillness and calm pervaded the place where we were, a silence so pregnant that for me it was that landscape that has been described as the "still small voice," or the "still point of the turning world," that place that partakes intimately and seamlessly of both the real and the Other in a simultaneous eternal moment that has broken through the veil into time. Although at different periods throughout my life, from early in my childhood on, I had had mystical and visionary experiences, this was unlike anything I had known before.

Matthew Fox, in his book, The Physics of Angels *(1996) co-authored with Rupert Sheldrake, refers to Aquinas who "warns us that angels always announce the divine silence, the silence that precedes our own inspiration, our own words, the silence that meditation and contemplation bring" (p. 5). Could this be such an annunciation? Is this what my quiet retreat had prepared me for?*

It was as if all energy was focused in that moment between us two figures and our riveted gaze with the spacecraft, that connection itself opening up an unseen pathway between Earth and stars, between Earth and a long forgotten relationship with the cosmos, a relationship that now is longing for rebirth and remembrance, at this end of a century, this ending of a millenium, this closure of an aeon. In that mountain landscape where a meeting between human and Other took place, in that reality that was neither the material world nor the spiritual realm, yet participating in both, in that crack between the worlds where psyche and matter, no longer split from each other, re-membered the integrity of their original Oneness, their two faces merely different expressions, separate vibratory resonances, of a single unity, a soft voice spoke and called out, addressed me in the vastness of its Silence.

We did not know how long the visitation lasted. In memory, it was but a few minutes. When the door that had opened between the worlds closed again, the wind resumed its blustery force, and the busy traffic continued its course up and down the hillside. But when we returned to the home where we were guests, it was late into the night (actually about two in the morning) and everyone else was already in bed and asleep. When I looked in the bathroom mirror, I hardly recognized myself. The cells of my face looked as if they were glowing, on fire, and an energy full of rainbow light was radiating outward from my body. I couldn't quite believe what had just transpired, and might have been in danger of dismissing the whole event, had it not taken place in the presence of another person.

Though we met only briefly again on a couple of other occasions, our lives going down very different paths, we were nonetheless able to remind each other from time to time by phone that, in fact, an extraordinary event had occurred in our presence. But for now, right after the event, I felt intensely alive and full of a gentle, vibrating life force that, as if breathing itself through me, summoned me into new octaves of experience.

Returning to my home on the East Coast, I told three friends of the encounter. Two of these friends didn't believe me, thought the event at most was merely and only a product of fantasy, imagination, or dream, as if that made it more acceptable, and they ridiculed and dismissed the literalness of the event. This made me sad, and very alone with what had taken place. For what was disorientating for me was that if it had just been a dream or fantasy it would have been more understandable to me, too, but something real in the world did occur, and I myself knew that I could not deny that part of it. It was, without doubt, comforting to feel the support of my closest female friend, yet between us, the encounter still remained a mystery.

But more than either dream or literal fact was the experience that partook of both, yet was neither the one nor the other, and it was this that remained such a mystery. Why had it happened? Did it mean something? Mostly, the so-called E.T. reports that I had read about fixated on the fact that it had occurred at all, concentrated on the literal event, not on the complexity of the experience. So for several years, I seemed to forget what had happened. I put it aside, not quite knowing what to make of it, feeling that no one would believe me anyway.

But, I was not forgotten, and in time the disclosure came back to me, in a totally unexpected fashion, initiating me into a new relationship with fate, into new vibrations of reality, coming like waves from the future to our planet Earth.

UFOs AND ANGELS: THE SOUL OF THE WORLD

I'm puzzled to death about [flying saucers], because I haven't been able yet to make out with sufficient certainty whether the whole thing is a rumour with concomitant singular and mass hallucination, or a downright fact. Either case would be highly interesting. If it's a rumour, then the apparition of discs must be a symbol produced by the unconscious. . . . If on the other hand it is a hard and concrete fact, we are surely confronted with something thoroughly out of the way. . . . The phenomenon of the saucers might even be both, rumour as well as fact. In this case it would be what I call a synchronicity (Jung, 1975, p. 3).

Sardello (1994) in his article "Angels and the Spiral of Creation" writes about the Thrones, those angels who, along with the Cherubim and Seraphim, have the particular task of bridging the heavenly with the physical, material world. Sardello points out that we are used to the idea of angels as beautiful, golden-haired, winged creatures in human-like form. He writes, however, that:

> Thrones, Cherubim and Seraphim are not in this image. In Ezekiel, the Thrones are pictured as many-colored wheel-like structures. These structures are built up in such a way as to form wheels within wheels, multi-colored transparent rings, one turning within the other, the inner one with eyes; and, it is said, they rise. . . . A most complex, strange, incomprehensible picture of angels (p. 55).

Sardello (pp. 56–57) then connects this nonhuman description of angels in Ezekiel with UFO phenomena, as he claims does the Dutch angelologist H. C. Moolenburgh, and as does Billy Graham, in their respective books on angels. Further, Sardello suggests that we imagine UFOs not as material objects in space and time, but that we move more in the direction of Jung's ideas about such phenomena. Such a move would involve understanding UFOs as images of the soul of the world appearing on the threshold of space and time. On this threshold they are neither projections of the unconscious psyche, nor are they material objects "out there," but reside in that place of collapse between spirit and matter, in that in-between world that participates simultaneously in both. This is perhaps, too, the realm of the *unus mundus* or the location of the unitive experience of the mystic or the *mundus imaginalis*, the third body of the world. In physics this is described as the discontinuous, nonlocal character of the quantum world (Goswami, 1995).

Perhaps another way to describe this very powerful event is to say that if the Thrones are the angels creating matter, the beings ensouling matter, then an encounter with a UFO could be a penetration of the veil of the material world into that dimension of deepest reverence where we are privileged momentarily to glimpse cosmic thoughts being transformed into our earthly covering. Sardello (1994) describes this as follows:

> The Thrones are, in effect, envisioning the material world, seeing everything in an interior way and also manifesting that interior thought as matter-creating. . . . One of the characteristics of angels is that they visit, that is, they appear now and then in the physical. A UFO is not a physical object, but something making an appearance in the physical, at the threshold (p. 58).

The idea of UFOs-as-Thrones seems parallel to those moments of synchronicity when the psychoid nature of the archetype is at play. For example, accounts of angel encounters often emphasize the presence of a numinous sensibility quite like the experience of being communed with by a UFO in my own example.

UFO encounters do not take place in ordinary space/time, as is evidenced by the familiar accounts in such encounters of things in our world either breaking down or being interrupted temporarily: car ignitions stopping and restarting, the experience of missing chronological time, the silencing suddenly of wind and abrupt disappearance of traffic (in my example), or the debates over whether something is real or not. It is as if in the presence of these more powerful beings, our human inventions are no match for their higher vibratory reality, and we humans have to step aside, and, as Sardello (1994) says, "make way for the continuance of creation" (p. 59).

The poet Rilke describes this same effect of interruption in the presence of an angel. He writes, for example, of being addressed out of the storm by the terrible voice of the angel, and he notes how the angel's appearance would still his beating heart.[4]

Von Franz (1974) comments on a 19th-century woodcut she calls "the hole open to eternity: the spiritual pilgrim discovering another world."[5] In this woodcut there is a person, circumscribed by the arc of a circle representing this world, who leaves ordinary space-time behind and gazes through the *fenestra aeternitatis* into the timeless eternal world. M.-L. von Franz suggests that the double wheel of Ezekiel's vision is present here (p. 261), and she wonders if the timeless and temporal wheel systems are interlocked, and if in fact synchronistic events are regular manifestations of this connection of time and the eternal. She also writes that:

> *The two systems are incommensurable.* From this we can only conclude that the moments of contact occur when a spontaneous action emanates from their common center. This conclusion agrees with the empirical evidence that synchronistic events occur, as far as we can see, only sporadically and irregularly (pp. 261–262).

She continues:

> The mysterious point of contact between the two systems appears to be the center or a sort of pivot where psyche and matter meet. When an individual enters into relation with the forces of the pivot, he finds himself close to the sphere of "miracles" which seemingly could not occur without a corresponding attitude on his own part. . . . When such a constellation (the union of heaven and earth) exists and eternity breaks through momentarily into our temporal system, the primal unity actively manifests itself and temporarily unites the double structures into one, so to speak. This is how the *unus mundus* becomes revealed in the phenomenon of synchronicity. But immediately afterward the flow of events resumes its course on the track of the ordinary temporal pattern, and the timeless order falls back into a latent condition once more (pp. 263–264).

---

4. R. M. Rilke, *Duino Elegies* (New York: W. W. Norton, 1939).

5. This illustration is reproduced in C. G. Jung, *Civilization in Transition*, CW 10 (Princeton: Princeton University Press, 1970), plate VII, p. 404.

What Sardello and von Franz are indicating is that an encounter with a UFO can be imagined as an experience in which the timeless and the timebound wheels come together, as a moment when they are synchronized at that pivotal point where psyche and matter meet in the *unus mundus*, as that occasion when unity breaks through momentarily into ordinary reality, or perhaps, as the woodcut illustrates, as that occasion when we travel through the hole or window into the eternal world. This timeless world is perhaps the quantum field of the soul, an acausal, nonlocal "place" outside of ordinary space and time. It is truly a miraculous moment if one imagines oneself to be in the presence of the Angel-as-Throne, in a highly charged yet profoundly still landscape where the ordinary laws of three-dimensional reality no longer entirely apply, and the unexpected can happen so that one feels oneself blessed by the mysterious resonances of creation.

I find it no coincidence that my own encounter with a UFO took place after ten days of intense spiritual practice in which I had experienced a full Kundalini opening lasting several hours, in which I had met my soul parents and traveled extensively about the universe in a profoundly altered state of consciousness. It was perhaps because I was in such an open and spiritually expanded state, vibrating in more refined octaves of consciousness than usual, and simultaneously grounded enough not to be blown away by such an encounter, that this experience was able to happen at all.

Sardello (1994) goes on to ask what it might mean for us to imitate the activity of the Thrones, for our task as humans, according to the alchemical Emerald Tablet of Hermes Trismegistus, is to unite Heaven and Earth, the above with the below, spirit and matter such as these angels do on a much more advanced level, as it were. Sardello gives the example of Tibetan monks who use the sound vibrations of their musical instruments in combination with a prayerful attitude (the singing of mantras) to help move otherwise immovable blocks of building stone up the side of a steep cliff. Sardello asks: "Could this not be a kind of communication between the monks and the Thrones, a prayerful working with the beings of matter?" (p. 60). Might we then imagine that this is also how the pyramids or stone circles were built?

I find this question about our potential relationship to the Thrones to be a compelling one, especially in view of my own experiences and my lengthy attempts to try to listen to how I am being addressed by them. Perhaps for Earth to be restored to her place in the cosmos, and for us once again to find our place in the nature of things, we need a devotion to the heavenly within matter and of the matter-creating within the heavenly, such as Sardello suggests. This sensibility begins to find its way into our world with the awesome presence of UFOs, which, as Sardello notes, can be regarded as angels dressed in the metaphors of materialism.

L<small>IGHT</small> O<small>UT</small> <small>OF</small> D<small>ARKNESS</small>: T<small>HE</small> *Lumen Naturae*

One of the remarkable features of the UFO encounter was the shift in my experience of the landscape. Although the place was undeniably the same, the atmosphere dramatically changed, becoming profoundly still, while the dark night became illumined as if by a bright moon—it was an illumined darkness, a qualitatively different light from the brightness of the sun's rays during the day.

Paracelsus, the compassionate, medieval alchemist-physician, was particularly interested in this kind of subtle light, this night vision. He was devoted to a central alchemical image that he called the *lumen naturae*, "light of nature." This luminosity emanated from the stars and was associated with the astral body, an invisible, subtle body that was born with individuals and that survived physical death. He felt that animals, too, were attuned to this light, and so the auguries of birds, for example, could be linked to premonitions guided by the spirits of the *lumen naturae*. The idea behind this notion is that there is a wisdom hidden in the natural world, a knowledge beyond the authoritative concepts of traditional thought, that is accessible in an instinctual, intuitive, or imaginative way, based on the authenticity of one's own experience. Paracelsus claimed that this light was particularly active during sleep and was revealed in dreams or visions. He also thought of this kind of illumination as dwelling in the heart.

The central mystery of this *lumen naturae* and its emergence in alchemy had to do with its subtle quality that emanated from a luminosity not divorced from darkness, an illumination not separated from matter or nature, a new light not like any other, born of the union of male and female, feeling and spirit, and called the *filius philosophorum*. This *filius*, or son, produced by the alchemical operations, Jung linked with the archetypal image of the Primordial Man of Light, a Light Being connected with the astral body or eternal self, a being that was not separated from the dark, the hidden, and the unknown. Alchemical operations, much like Jung's individuation process today, were devoted to developing this eternal, or resurrection, body that would survive physical death.

Many years ago, during my first Jungian analysis, and before I knew about such resonance, I had a waking vision of a golden being of light who arrived with an awesome, thunderous roar out of a dark background, and whom I called "The Light Man," or "The Man of Light." This being was also linked for me with the memory of my experience in Israel, of the peculiar quality of light during a sunset over the Tiberias mountains (the account I mention in the Prologue to this book), an experience that changed the course of my life and my vocation.[6]

---

6. The "man of light" is a well-known figure from Sufi mysticism, which I did not know either at the time of my experience or when I wrote this. See H. Corbin, *The Man of Light in Iranian Sufism* (Boston: Shambhala, 1978). I develop this theme of light and the figures of light in a new manuscript in preparation.

This kind of light, enlightenment, or consciousness, is the one, too, that we know from suffering our wounds, and attending slowly to our dreams and predicaments over the years. It is not a light that comes with the clever harshness of intellectual brilliance and brittle insight. It is a light more like sunset, moonlight, or starlight, a light surrounded by darkness, clear only at nocturnal moments, hidden in the daytime, and obliterated by hurry or focus, too much sun and no shadows. It is the dark light of the unconscious, that greater Self that Jung describes as his number two personality. Or it is the light of the collective unconscious, that shadow that is visible as the invisible in all things, a light that is a blackness that has become the blues—a gnosis washed with deep pools of affect, instinct, image, and feeling.

Could it be that the UFO venue reflects this *lumen naturae* of old, signaling a call to remember knowledge that comes from nature and one's own experience, not one that comes from reading books and the traditions of men? This is a gnosis deeply seated in the body, the body as a gateway to nature and the stars. Paracelsus writes that "the true man [or woman] is the star in us," and further that "the star desires to drive [humankind] toward great wisdom."[7] This revelatory knowledge or imaginal awareness addresses us again in our impoverished and dark times, when a different kind of seeing is required, a vision that reestablishes our cosmic relatedness, a reconnection often accompanied by synchronistic events.[8]

---

7. C. G. Jung, *Alchemical Studies*, CW 13 (Princeton: Princeton University Press, 1967), §168.

8. Since writing this, I have also become interested in the phenomenon of "missing time" associated so often with these kinds of encounters. To elaborate on this phenomenon here was not integral to the main emphasis of this text; I will explore this idea in future writing.

The Human-Cosmic Connection

It is only recently that I have been able to speak about my UFO encounter. I said at the end of my account that it was not forgotten, that in time the disclosure came back to me as something that I now felt invited to bring more fully into my life, although the event itself still remains a profound and awesome mystery. It happened in the following way, beginning with a dream.

> *I'm in the wilderness, in the wilds; the landscape is very green (not dry and barren) with lots of grass growing. I'm with two other women: one reminds me of a former patient that I had worked with some years ago; the other woman is unknown to me, and remains a mystery throughout the dream. We're camping. We're on a woman's retreat or vision quest. I'm concerned about snakes suddenly appearing out of the tall grass. And in fact a snake, a huge green one, arrives, but E. (the former patient) is able to pick it up, and somehow soothe it. As I'm watching her do this, I wonder because of the shape of the tail, if the snake is a rattlesnake. She is soothing it by stroking the rattle end of the tail. She seems so unafraid of the snake, as if she has a natural affinity with it. I marvel at that.[9]*

The effect of this dream on me was that I felt I had participated in some kind of an initiation ritual. My response was to write a poem about it:

> *In the green wilderness*
> *we remain a mystery*
> *seeking visions that bring*
> *the rattlesnake goddess*
> *back into our barren lives.*

The dream brought back a fantasy that had come to me recently while meditating on an image that presented itself to me in regard to my vocation: what came before my inner vision was a serpent, a snake that—like a lightning rod—extended itself upward through my body, a snake that was surrounded by and held within a radiant sun or star.

---

9. Author's Dream Journal, November 30, 1996.

Between this experience and the dream recounted above I damaged my knee, the account of which I have recorded and described in the third chapter of this book, a wounding which reconnected me to the image of the Orphan, that presence that forges our destiny, and carries the eternal within our finite forms, our stellar identity to our earthly home. Preceding all these events, and in all likelihood initiating the whole process, was the dream of the huge mythological birds, those angels of another kind who bring with them a gnosis from the heavens to ground here on Earth.

On Christmas Eve after the rattlesnake dream I accompanied my daughter to a bookstore in town, for she wished to make bookmarks for the family members as gifts, each name inscribed in hieroglyphs. So as Sarah perused The Egyptian Book of the Dead *for the matching letters and glyphs, I sat and waited, loosely and lazily letting my eyes glance at the shelves surrounding me.*

It was one of those times in which a book literally fell off the shelf in front of me! The title was The Mayan Prophecies, *by Adrian Gilbert and Maurice Cotterell. I recognized one of the author's names from a television program I had seen in England on the relationship between the Egyptian Pyramids and their alignment with the Orion and Sirius star systems. So, as my husband and I were off to Mexico City in a few days' time, I picked up the volume and let it fall open where it would. It opened in the middle of the chapter titled, "Land of the Rattlesnake."*

Leafing quickly through the pages it seemed to my astonishment that not only was the Maya culture deeply connected to the rattlesnake, and especially to the image of the feathered serpent, Quetzalcoatl, as an image of transformed or enlightened consciousness, but in their astronomical preoccupations, the Maya were particularly fascinated with the cluster of stars called the Pleiades. Not only this, but in addition, the Maya called the Pleiades the tzab, meaning "rattle." By now I had goosebumps all over my skin! All at once, the image, the dream, the knee injury, the feeling of a period of my life drawing to a close, and last but by no means least, the totally unexpected and unanticipated out-of-the-blue memory of the spaceship encounter and experience of seven years ago, flooded my

consciousness and my body with unknown but apparently mean-
ingful links. It was one of those moments where apparently causal-
ly unrelated events, separated by time, seemed to belong together in
meaningful, but as yet unrealized ways, unified by a feeling of a
numinous mystery. Some kind of creative response to these givens
was being invited, or so it seemed to me. I bought the book!

Pyramid of the Moon

On our second day in Mexico City, we went with our guide to
Teotihuacan, that ancient and mysterious city of the Aztecs that
includes a Temple to Quetzalcoatl, priestly sanctuaries, the so-
called Avenue of the Dead, and the magnificent Pyramids of the
Sun and the Moon. Nothing is really known of this place, or how
far back it reaches into the mists of time.

I was deeply moved by the power and beauty of this sacred land-
scape. Climbing the Pyramid of the Moon, I found a quiet sunny
spot near its zenith, and lay down on the warm rocks and fell into
a deep reverie. It seemed to me that these ancient temples were
places of energy exchange, doorways where cosmic frequencies, or a
higher, more evolved or refined consciousness, became earthed and
stored; where an advanced human culture was devoted to realizing
these cosmic forces for the purposes of Earth transformation and the
evolution of consciousness on this plane. I could imagine that their
priestess, or shamanic class, in their rituals, in their speech and
song, in their spiritual or religious practices, knew about and
worked the transmuting of these energies. I felt that their gnosis
was deeply connected to their galactic origins, that their devotion to
the tremendum of the serpent power as depicted on their temples
indicated their awareness of the relationship between the human
body and a cosmic and sacred sexuality. This erotic force as that
energy that holds the universe together suggested that they knew
the secret doorways through the body into the universal octaves
where human and divine, spirit and matter, are no longer separat-
ed, but unified in a unus mundus of grace and integrity. This was
a culture for whom passion and vision, instinct and insight, feeling

and thought, though differentiated into religion and science, were seamlessly bound.

I did not know how long I lingered in dreamy reverie, but when I opened my eyes, a black butterfly with tiny golden circles along the perimeter of its wings was dancing around my head, retreating and advancing, all the while encircling me with its delicate and exquisite ritual communication. I was delighted and charmed by the appearance of this light being, this visitor from mythic realms, that came to visit me in my reverie.

On our way back from Teotihuacan to the city, the clear azure sky became quickly overcast, and it began to pour with rain. Our guide told us that it rarely rained at this time of year; he was puzzled. As we approached the outskirts of the town, it seemed as if everyone else was disoriented by the uncharacteristic display of weather. Buses and trucks were overturned on the side of the road; police and ambulance sirens filled the air; cars were chaotically spread across lanes; a general disorderliness and confusion seemed to pervade our route.

Then as we approached even closer to the center of Mexico City, a most extraordinary sight presented itself to us. The sky on the horizon in front of us began to clear, and the setting sun revealed itself as a massive wheel of light, larger than any sun I had ever seen. The rain had cleared the densely polluted atmosphere, and it was as if this clearing released waves and particles of sunlight into an expansive display of intense brilliance. Now it seemed we had entered another world, a surreal landscape somewhere between dream and reality. We turned to look out of the back of the car, and from the direction of the pyramids the sky was still dark gray and brooding, with flashes of lightning and loud outbursts of thunder. As we marveled at the contrasts of light and shadow, a stunning rainbow appeared in the sky, not one, but a double rainbow, displaying magnificent arcs of multidimensional color, a cosmic smile uniting thunderstorm and setting sun, hinting at a new relationship between Heaven and Earth, inviting us to bear witness to what we saw.

The next morning, in the garden of the hotel, with cappuccino in one hand, and pen poised over my journal to record these unusu-

al events in the other, another butterfly, similar to the one that had visited me on the Pyramid of the Moon, danced into view and alighted on the table in front of me. The visitation brought inexplicable tears to my eyes. I was touched by how this gentle creature seemed to be trying to tell me something. First, on the Pyramid of the Moon, while I was imagining the ancient and original purpose of such places; and now in the garden, as I began to write.

Later that day, during a visit to the Anthropological Museum in Mexico City, I came across a story in an art magazine in the bookstore there, a story that comes out of the soil of Mexico, a tale that actually has resonances in many other cultures, about a serpent, a snake, a rattlesnake in fact, that goes on a journey to the underworld, and after a long sojourn there—where we are not told what happens, where what happens is a secret initiation that cannot be spoken—returns as a butterfly, an obsidian butterfly, a black butterfly with tiny golden circles along the perimeter of its delicate wings.

GALAXY, GAIA, G-SPOT! COSMOS, EARTH, HUMAN!

As Maya scholar, Humbatz Men (1990), instructs us, for the ancient and indigenous Maya the letter "G" is sacred, and is found in different symbolic variants, patterns, and glyphs in their sacred texts, and on their sacred temples and pyramids, throughout the Americas. "G" was worshipped as part of elaborate rituals in a culture that, like our own Western culture long ago, did not divorce religion from philosophy, astrology, or science. Human beings were intimately connected with nature and the stars, which they patiently and keenly observed and reverenced as their Teacher. "G" referred to origins, our spiraling and swirling galactic origins in the Milky Way; "G" referred to the cosmic egg or seed from which all life emerges; "G" is the value of zero, the essence of the beginning, our essence: both the auric field, that like an egg we are embedded in and which energetically keeps us connected to our origins in the heavens. In addition, "G" is at the root of the spine, the place of the sleeping Kundalini serpent, which we know from other traditions keeps our physical reality in a sacred rootedness to Earth and all life, and which, when activated, keeps us radiantly alive to all things, all subtle vibrations of reality.

The "G" in our bodies is also that geography of sacred sexuality that is intimately connected to the Milky Way, the amrita of cosmic forces, the energy that spirals from our origins into bodily and spiritual life and which, when aroused and flowing according to the Maya, even moves the galactic core, the Hunabku, the God or energetic force, that is the origin of all things. The Maya word *gelanah* means "here I am," but when this is spoken, it serves not only to refer to one's presence here and now on Earth, but to recall galactic origins. Words in this language, therefore, enjoy multidimensional resonances, and point to a unified worldview, one that in our culture we have grievously lost with the increasing split of spirit and matter over the past several hundred years, one that calls again to us now.

What are we to make of these kinds of experiences, events that are familiar to many today—experiences such as the appearance of the hummingbird, the mythological birds of my dream, the rattlesnake numen, the deer in my garden, the silent visit of the UFO-Angel? What are we being called to at this end of a century, end of a millenium, end on an age? Are we being called beyond the limitations of our current knowledge, summoned into a new vision of reality, a new synthesis of experience, a mystery once known, forgotten, and now seeking realization again?

It seems that we are being inexorably drawn beyond ourselves if we can but respond to the hints of soul and world that speak to us sometimes subtly, sometimes more forcibly; that we are being invited into a multidimensional reality more complex, more wondrous, and more aweful than we hardly dare imagine. A new flowering of divine and numinous Life is beginning to shower its gifts upon us if we have but eyes to see, and ears to hear. Is not each of us called to do our part in witnessing this transformation, this translation of ancient eternal truths into contemporary forms. Jung (1961) writes: "The decisive question . . . is: [Are we] related to something infinite or not? That is the telling question of . . . life." Being related to the Infinite gives us values that really matter. He goes on:

> In the final analysis, we count for something only because of the essential we embody, and if we do not embody that, life is wasted. . . . The feeling for the infinite, however, can be attained only if we are bounded to the utmost. . . . Only consciousness of our narrow confinement in the self forms the link to the limitlessness of the unconsciousness. In such awareness we experience ourselves concurrently as limited and eternal, as both the one and the other (p. 325).

Listening to the voices of the unseen world—attuning ourselves to the gentle or more insistent voices in wind and water, to the nightly visitors in our dreams, to our guardians in mineral and spirit form, to the subtlety of the sounds and images of the invisible in things helps us resituate ourselves as finite creatures within a cosmic context. Listening to all those "potential forms of consciousness" lying quietly in wait all around us makes us neighbors to those parallel universes longing for us to access their gifts and their gnosis in the vast array of the beauty of creation.

EPILOGUE

We are such stuff as dreams are made on;
And our little life is rounded with a sleep.
—Shakespeare, *The Tempest*

Poetry is a metaphysics of the moment. It has to convey within the space of a short poem a vision of the universe and the secrets of a heart, a person, things—and do so all at once.
—Bachelard (1988), p. 173

What the psyche is seeking in the transition from the Piscean to the Aquarian age is the waters of Hippocrene, the milk Aganippe, of poetic madness, the source and nurse of inspiration. It is the voice of this inspired psyche . . . that creates that welcoming song to the coming guest.
—Lockhart (1987), p. 78

We live at a time of tremendous upheaval, transition, and collapse. At this time of uncertainty, when our prevailing worldview is undergoing a shift of major proportions, there is a tendency toward a chaotic outpouring of uncontained energies. When I wrote these words, the world sat poised in fear and expectation as the United Nations envoy Kofi Annan made his way toward Iraq, and I read in the newspaper that the dissolution of communism had also brought with it a white slave trade in Eastern Europe in which thousands of women were being sold into prostitution.

But we also live in a world in which an American woman has been awarded the Nobel Peace Prize for her work on behalf of achieving a global ban on the use of land mines (a movement that Princess Diana helped bring very much into public awareness); a world in which countless men and women aim to live lives of integrity; a world in which—still—at dawn as Earth, poised momentarily, moves out of its shadows toward the light, birds sing their lovely tunes with a delicacy and lightness that suggests all is right with the world.

We also live at a time in which, in spite of the specter of and potential for hideous atrocities in Iraq and Eastern Europe, Annan's visit signals perhaps a moment of restraint, as does the Albanian response to violence aimed toward them, as if somewhere in all this apparent mess there is a movement toward a more human solution—even if we fail once again.

In our field of depth psychology, we have the luxury—no, the responsibility—of being able to imagine that there are forces quite beyond the merely human that might be contributing to this kind of restraint.

In this book I have suggested that in the West chaos has traditionally been linked with order of one kind or another, but that it is precisely this ordering and structuring of reality that is undergoing dissolution and dismemberment, including perhaps the whole notion of consciousness itself, and the constraints we have placed upon it. The suggestion in this work is that we might pause a moment at such a time as ours and consider chaos's relation, not with order, but with love, imaged as Eros in some mythologies described in this work, and particularly alluded to by Freud and Jung in their later works, as offering another possibility for our all too fragmented world. This coupling of chaos and eros is also intended to point to the limitations of our acquired knowledge as power, power over the world, and to disclose a more complex gnosis that would place our ways of knowing and being in the service of love, its mysteries and shadows.

In my view, this possibility marks an exceedingly difficult challenge, for it is not possible to speak of love in our times without making space for love's shadows. To incarnate love we need to make ourselves vulnerable to the vast terrain of the soul, the complex and subtle landscape that visits in dream and encounter, and that reveals both the face of the one I would rather not be and the face of the one I am becoming, the one Life calls into being. On a less personal level, the collapse of a collective vision such as we are experiencing as we approach the millenium invites a revisioning of our place in the wholeness of creation.

In *Mysterium Coniunctionis,* one of his last works, Jung (1970b) describes both the stages of personal collapse of an individual for whom the psychic dominants no longer contain the conscious personality's life, and the devastation that happens in a civilization such as ours when the collective dominant, that is, the God-image or operative myth, is dying and in need of renewal. In alchemy, these processes are imaged as the death and renewal of the king. Jung gives two examples of the "death of the king" or the "death of God" theme: a story from Plutarch about two thousand years ago that tells of the death of the great god Pan; and its modern equivalent in Nietsche's *Thus Spake Zarathrustra,* the statement that "God is dead" (§510, including n.392). Jung (1970b) writes:

> Just as the decay of the conscious dominant is followed by an irruption of chaos in the individual, so also in the case of the masses . . . and the furious conflict of elements in the individual psyche is reflected in the unleashing of primeval blood-thirstiness and lust for murder on a collective scale . . . . The loss of the eternal images is in truth no light matter for the [person] of discernment . . . [who] knows and feels that his psyche is disquieted by the loss of something that was the life-blood of his ancestors. The undiscerning . . . miss nothing, and only discover afterwards in the papers (much too late) the alarming symptoms that have now become "real" in the outside world because they were not perceived before inside, in oneself, just as the presence of the eternal images was not noticed. If they had been, a threnody for the lost god would have arisen, as once before in antiquity at the death of Great Pan. . . . Once the symptoms are really outside in some form of sociopolitical insan-

ity, it is impossible to convince anybody that the conflict is
in the psyche of every individual, since he is now quite sure
where his enemy is. . . . When [the individual] no longer
knows by what his soul is sustained, the potential of the
unconscious is increased and takes the lead. Desirousness
overpowers him, and illusory goals set up in the place of
the eternal images excite his greed (§510).

In commenting on this important passage in *The Mysterium
Lectures*, Edinger (1995) mentions Matthew Arnold's poem
"Dover Beach" as a reflection of 19th-century lament at
the death-of-God motif. A key stanza in this poem is the following:

Ah love, let us be true
To one another! for the world, which seems
To lie before us like a land of dreams,
So various, so beautiful, so new,
Hath really neither joy, nor love, nor light,
Nor certitude, nor peace, nor help for pain;
And we are here as on a darkling plain
Swept with confused alarms of struggle and flight,
Where ignorant armies clash by night.[1]

In this poem, Arnold speaks of his love relationship with his
new wife as the only place of refuge and sanity in a world
gone mad. Edinger questions whether a personal relationship
of love can withstand the archetypal burden and weight of
transpersonal contents fallen out of a collective dominant. He
proposes instead, following his reading of Jung, that it is
rather the solitary individual who is the one in whom these
lost dominants must undergo the renewal process that both
the alchemical imagery refers to, and Christian mythology in
the form of the death of Christ and his renewal in the Holy
Spirit or Paraclete also demonstrates. In fact, here and elsewhere (for example, *The Creation of Consciousness*, 1984)

---

1. From *Major British Writers*, G. B. Harrison, ed. (New York: Harcourt Brace, 1959),
p. 619.

Edinger stresses that it is the lonely individual who contributes to the continuing work of incarnation by being a carrier of divine opposites. For Edinger this is the new myth, the myth of consciousness, the one lived and put forward by Jung that replaces a now outmoded Christianity. Edinger's final words in *The Mysterium Lectures* (1995) are these:

> But it's not beyond the realm of possibility that just one person might be enough to preserve the world. . . . I would suggest that you entertain such an idea, and furthermore, consider that perhaps you are the one (p. 326).

Edinger's attitude, which places such overwhelming significance on the individual as the carrier of differentiated consciousness (as central as this may be for the living of a responsible and ethical life), also begs the question of what, after all, is the purpose of consciousness. To what end do we become conscious, or more conscious—all that analytic work to know oneself—for what?

M.-L. von Franz (1980a) in *Alchemy* raises this issue when she speaks of the questionableness of consciousness, describing it as a dubious achievement. "Man[kind] with his consciousness is a disturbing factor in the order of nature," she writes (p. 156). It is unclear whether human beings are a "mistake," or the "crown of creation" (p. 157). She reflects that consciousness tends to make us rather wooden and not connected to nature and instincts anymore. We might go further and say that consciousness carries the danger of taking us out of relationship with each other and to the world of which we are merely a part. She suggests that after reaching the wooden state, we have to fall back into the River of Life and into a state of *almost* unconsciousness again. This almost unconsciousness she calls "a retarded spontaneity" (p. 238) or a "conscious spontaneity" meaning the achievement of a paradoxical state, "complete spontaneity yet always knowing what one is doing" (p. 239).

But interestingly, von Franz completes her book *Alchemy* (1980a) not with these critical observations and reflections, but with excerpts from an obscure text, the *Aurora Consurgens*, attributed to Thomas Aquinas, that medieval scholastic theologian-philosopher who, just before he died, in a moment of mystical ecstasy, was granted a glimpse of the cosmic radiance and love of the Divine. This experience is reputed to have transformed Aquinas from a man who knew *about* God to one who was silenced by the revelations of a deeper gnosis that all his tomes of rational theology had hardly begun to imagine. What von Franz chooses to excerpt from the account of Aquinas' visions is a marvelous celebration of this cosmic love, words that are similar in tone to that beautifully erotic text in the Old Testament, the Song of Songs. Aquinas (2000) writes:

> O, my beloved bride, thy voice has sounded in my ears and is sweet. You are beautiful. . . . Come now, my beloved, let us go out into the field, let us dwell in the villages. We will rise up early, for the night is far spent and the day is at hand. We will see if thy vineyard has blossomed and if it has borne fruit. There thou wilt give me thy love, and for thee I have preserved old and new fruits. We shall enjoy them while we are young. Let us fill ourselves with wine and ointments and there shall be no flower which we will not put into our crown, first lilies and then roses before they fade. . . . Nobody shall be excluded from our happiness. We will live in a union of eternal love and will say how good and lovely it is to live two in one (pp. 143–149).

I began chapter 2 of this book with Jung's celebration of the mysteries of eros written as part of his "Late Thoughts," reflections composed just before the closure of his life and after the completion of his monumental study, *Mysterium Coniunctionis* (1970b), which together with *Answer to Job* (1969a), *Synchronicity* (1969b), and *Flying Saucers* (1970a), formed his last published texts. And even Edinger includes Arnold's poem on love as if, for a moment, love draws him near and he is unable to resist a consideration—though passing—on the central significance of love in human life. So I wonder about Edinger's vision of the solitary individual and the task of developing consciousness. I wonder if it is too for-getful of the claims of love that draws two lovers, Earth and Cosmos, human and divine, together.

Love, however, cannot merely be the place of refuge for two individual lovers in Matthew Arnold's poem, nor should we wait till the end of our lives for its disclosure in extreme circumstances. As our mythologies suggest, and as I have tried to emphasize, love is a cosmological ray, given with cre-ation, that arrives in spite of us and that we wrestle with in one way or another throughout our lives, for even in its absence, we miss it and long for it, or suffer when it dies.

And what in any case becomes central in an analysis of any length or depth in that journey undertaken to know one-self or to become more conscious? Insight into our problems? No! These symptoms merely get us in the front door. As Freud long ago observed, it is the relationship with the ana-lyst that becomes the orienting star in treatment. And this relationship of love and its many vicissitudes becomes, with Jung's deepened understanding, the alchemical vessel that allows a fall, a fall into self-knowledge that in the ripeness of time places an ethical demand, "to become world," to use Rilke's (1954) phrase, not so that alone we might "preserve the world" as Edinger's final words to his lectures suggest; no, "to become world for himself for another's sake," (p. 54) as Rilke emphasizes, to put our knowledge and our igno-rance, our gnosis and our ability to forget it in its continual dissolution in the River of Life, in the service of love, that "difficult . . . work for which all other work is but prepara-tion" (p. 54).

Love requires a tremendous effort of differentiation of self and of refinement of Self, else it mostly remains mere senti-ment or contaminated with unexamined collective views. But the reward of falling into love's dark shadows and thereby becoming world is to participate in an abundant life where one's inner state is increasingly in harmony with the cosmos, in a world that glows with a pregnant wonder and awesome mystery. Here we are not alone, but in our solitude we are companioned by the Beloved of our soul and exist in a world that surrounds and holds us like a piece of exquisitely woven cloth sparkling the rainbow colors of creation in a gorgeous array of texture and pattern, all of it offering itself to our imagination, our beholding and contemplation.

The willingness to fall into chaos and to be undone is what allows the threads of cosmic love to knit us back together into an authentic earthy life under the stars, uniting above and below as the ancient alchemical text says so simply, with another, with an-Other. This vocation of love is what this book has tried to hint at by discrete example, by reflections that weave together other people's thoughts, clinical experience, personal encounter, vision, and dream, by the expression of those unthought thoughts at the edge where our lives are reaching into that *unus mundus* realm simultaneously extending itself toward us for definition and incarnation.

These reflections are not put forward as a new system or order. These containers are always dissolving around us in chaos. These reflections are simply presented as witness to disclosures revealed, and perhaps can be imagined best as an invitation to be present—present to your own experience—while you let the world, both real and subtle, and the Beloved that lies at its heart, reveal to you "thine original face."

FINALE—LOVE IS OUR VOCATION

Our lives are really a series of joinings and separations, a cycle of *coniunctios* and *nigredos,* falling in love, falling apart in chaos. At this moment, to honor the completion of this book, I shall dwell on a disclosure of love as a way of celebrating life in its fullest abundant offering to us. In such moments even chaos is transformed and our suffering is released into an intensely fragile yet shimmering aliveness, and we know we are part of a current, a beam of energy in which everything belongs, for everything has its meaningful place, stretching from the deep soil of earth to the farthest reaches of space. We each have moments that we treasure like this revelation of divine Eros that make the broad range of our complex nature possible to bear.

Divine Eros: Love and Its Mysteries

The two of us bundled up in warm clothes on this cold and dark November day, and made our way to Tintagel, in Cornwall, the mythic and geographically dramatic landscape of King Arthur and his medieval court. The ancient castle, now only a few stones remaining, lies on a huge rock set majestically apart from the mainland, surrounded by water heaving itself against the promontory at high tide, and accessible only by a footbridge. It was already dusk when we arrived, and the door that leads onto the castle rock was by now locked. The sky was gray and overcast; it was windy, isolated, and the damp winter night was fast approaching. A fine drizzle began to fall. We went back to the top of the mainland cliffs, and paused to look once again at the ancient site in its roaring ocean setting, in the encroaching darkness.

It seemed as if the ancient castle rock remains still linger, and the stones still hold the ghosts of stories long forgotten. Now here, now there, over the entire rock, tiny pinpoints of glowing light began to emerge out of the oncoming night. It was as if a secret life still goes on there, as if Earth stores its memories in the crystal rock and grassy knoll, tales forever available to the keen and receptive observer. Perhaps some form of Earth-life—gnome or elf-like— resides there, playing its hidden part in the integrity of the story of Earth.

Then, as if the heavens mirrored the earth we were standing on, the brooding clouds above our heads began to disperse, to disclose a brilliant starry canopy of light. Creation seemed poised in a moment of celebration and delight. The whole of nature was joining with us in singing songs of love. We stood there, poised, silent, overflowing with an array of abundant worlds, being spoken to by a vast cosmic chorus. It was now not only a cold wintry night on a deserted cliff in Cornwall, it was a disclosure of the fullness of Life, a revelation of the terrifying beauty of the mystery and vastness of the reality that surrounds us, a reality most people have sadly forgotten. The awesome presence of the Other made itself keenly felt, and we, like two stars from separate spheres, fell out of the life we had known, and into each other's orbit. We responded to what called us, to a field of Love that fuels creation, and encloses and holds the fragility of human love, in the wide expanse of its extended and limitless embrace.

Are these human unions with the wider field of creation the "signs and wonders" that herald the emergence of a new level of the differentiation of consciousness? With the dissolution of boundaries in the personal, social, incarnational, global, and cosmic spheres, are we falling into a chaotic possibility, a *participation mystique* again as we turn the corner of the millenium? The challenge, it seems to me, that this pregnant potential presents is: God(dess) willing, can we fall into a unified, ecocentric world with awareness, with ethical sensibility, with wisdom, feeling, and intuition, with a sense of beauty and high sophistication, with a willingness to be ruthlessly honest about our capacity for evil and destruction? And do we have a vital devotion to transmute that energy into "acts of creation in time"?

Can we realize that our limitations contain the seeds of eternal life, that our origins and destinies are mysteries to be walked with, dreamed on, round and round like the planets circling the Sun? Can we bear to accept that when we bind ourselves in high regard and freedom of soul to our lover, children, work, and friends, and witness in love all of creation, that we not only reach for the stars, we are the stars, and we participate in the rivers of sensuous light that in wild chaotic love permeate the dark cosmos with a deep unseen mystery, and we join in chorus with the voices of the unseen world?

Is this what we are now called to?

A PARTING IMAGE

As I approached this final chapter I had the following dream:

My husband Robert and I are inside a medieval university library, our lips embraced in a deeply loving kiss that almost flattens our faces into each other! The library stacks go up in a spiral form around and above us (the patterning reminds me of the construction of the anatomy theater at Padova that I photographed for Robert and that hangs in his office). It is quite dark inside this ancient library, but there is a source of light coming from the open door that leads to a courtyard, in the center of which is a fountain of water and a tree of life. Inside where we are, in the center, is an ancient baptismal font, an octagonal structure in stone with detailed hand-carved reliefs on it. A group of people, mostly friends of mine from Pacifica, enter the library, and are chatting and laughing.

Amen!

REFERENCES

Allende, I. (1994). *Paula*. New York: HarperCollins.

Aquinas, T. (2000). *Aurora Consurgens*, M.-L. von Franz, ed. Toronto: Inner City Books.

Bachelard, G. (1969). *The Poetics of Reverie*, D. Russell, trans. Boston: Beacon Press (Original work published 1960).

———. (1988). *The Right to Dream*. Dallas: Dallas Institute Publications.

Balmer, J. (1984). *Sappho: Poems and Fragments*. Secaucus, NJ: Meadowland Books.

Bentov, I. (1977). *Stalking the Wild Pendulum*. Rochester, VT: Destiny Books.

Bolen, J. S. (1984). *Goddesses in Everywoman: A New Psychology of Women*. San Francisco: HarperSanFrancisco.

Buber, M. (1988). *The Knowledge of Man*. Atlantic Highlands, NJ: Humanities Press.

Bucke, R. M. (1901). *Cosmic Consciousness*. Philadelphia; Reprinted Secaucus, NJ: Citadel, 1977.

Campbell, J., ed. (1990). *The Mysteries*. Princeton: Princeton University Press.

Carotenuto, A. (1989). *Eros and Pathos: Shades of Love and Suffering.* Toronto: Inner City Books.

Clow, B. H. (1991). *The Liquid Light of Sex.* Rochester, VT: Bear & Co.

Corbett, L. (1990). "The Archetypal Feminine: A Response to Betty Meador, 'Forward into the past,'" in *Dreams in Analysis.* Wilmette, IL: Chiron Publications.

Corbin, H. (1978) *The Man of Light in Iranian Sufism.* Boston: Shambhala.

———. (1972). "*Mundus Imaginalis* or the Imaginary and the Imaginal." in *Spring,* 1–19. Dallas: Spring Publications.

Downing, C. (1976). "Towards an Erotics of the Psyche." *Journal of the American Academy of Religion,* 629–638.

———. (1981). *The Goddess: Mythological Images of the Feminine.* New York: Crossroad.

———. (1992). *Women's Mysteries: Toward a Poetics of Gender.* New York: Crossroad.

———. (1996). *Myths and Mysteries of Same Sex Love.* New York: Continuum.

Edinger, E. (1972). *Ego and Archetype.* New York: Penguin Books.

———. (1984). *The Creation of Consciousness.* Toronto: Inner City Books.

———. (1995). *The Mysterium Lectures: A Journey Through C. G. Jung's Mysterium Coniunctionis.* Toronto: Inner City Books.

———. (1996). *The New God-Image: A Study of Jung's Key Letters Concerning the Evolution of the Western God-Image.* Wilmette, IL: Chiron Publications.

Eliot, T. S. (1943). *Four Quartets.* New York: Harcourt, Brace & Co.

Ellenberger, H. F. (1970). *The Discovery of the Unconscious: The History and Evolution of Dynamic Psychiatry.* New York: Basic Books.

Fierz, H. K. (1991). *Jungian Psychiatry.* Einsiedein, Switzerland: Daimon Verlag.

Fox, M., and R. Sheldrake (1996). *The Physics of Angels: Exploring the Realm Where Science and Spirit Meet.* San Francisco: HarperSanFrancisco.

von Franz, M.-L. (1972). *Creation Myths*. Dallas: Spring Publications.

———. (1974). *Number and Time: Reflections Leading Toward a Unification of Depth Psychology and Physics*. Evanston, IL: Northwestern University Press.

———. (1975). *C. G. Jung: His Myth in Our Time*. New York: G. P. Putnam's Sons.

———. (1978). *Time: Rhythm and Repose*. New York: Thames & Hudson.

———. (1980a). *Alchemy*. Toronto: Inner City Books.

———. (1980b). *Projection and Recollection in Jungian Psychology: Reflections of the Soul*. La Salle: Open Court.

———. (1992). *Psyche and Matter*. Boston: Shambhala.

Freud, S. (1930). *Civilization and Its Discontents*. New York: Doubleday/Anchor.

———. (1965). "Femininity," in J. Strachey, ed., *New Introductory Lectures on Psychoanalysis*. New York: Norton & Co. (Original work published 1933).

Friedrich, P. (1978). *The Meaning of Aphrodite*. Chicago: University of Chicago Press.

Gilbert, A. G., and M. M. Cotterell (1995). *The Mayan Prophecies: Unlocking the Secrets of a Lost Civilization*. Boston: Element Books.

Gilday, K., director (1990). *The Famine Within*. A Canadian film. Kandor Productions.

Gill, S. D., and I. F. Sullivan (1992). *Dictionary of Native American Mythology*. Santa Barbara, CA: ABC-CLIO, Inc.

Gimbutas, M. (1989). *The Language of the Goddess*. San Francisco: HarperSanFrancisco.

Goswami, A. (1995). *The Self-Aware Universe: How Consciousness Creates the Material World*. New York: Tarcher/Putnam.

Graves, R. (1960). *Greek Myths*, vol. 1. London: Penguin Books.

Guggenbuhl-Craig, A. (1995). "Reality and Mythology of Child Sexual Abuse," *Journal of Analytical Psychology*, 40 (1).

Guntrip, H. (1969). *Schizoid Phenomena Object-Relations and the Self*. New York: International Universities Press.

Harding, M. E. (1990). *Women's Mysteries: Ancient and Modern*. Boston: Shambhala.

Harrison, G. B., ed. (1959). *Major British Writers.* New York: Harcourt Brace.

Haule, J. R. (1997, May). Lecture at Pacifica Graduate Institute. Carpinteria, CA.

Hayles, N. K. (1990). *Chaos Bound.* Ithaca: Cornell University Press.

Henderson, J. L. (1967). *Thresholds of Initiation.* Middletown, CT: Wesleyan University Press.

———. (1984). "Reflections on the History and Practice of Jungian Analysis," in M. Stein, *Jungian Analysis.* Boston: Shambhala.

H. D. (1957). *Selected Poems.* New York: Grove Press.

———. (1988). *Selected Poems,* L. Martz, ed. New York: New Directions.

Hillman, J. (1972). *The Myth of Analysis: Three Essays in Archetypal Psychology.* Evanston, IL: Northwestern University Press.

———. (1983). *Interviews.* Dallas: Spring Publications.

———. (1996). *The Soul's Code: In Search of Character and Calling.* New York: Warner Brothers.

Homeric Hymns (1970). Charles Boer, trans. Chicago: Swallow Press.

Horney, K. (1967). *Feminine Psychology.* New York: Norton.

Irigaray, L. (1992). *Elemental Passions.* New York: Routledge.

James, W. (1982). *The Varieties of Religious Experience: A Study in Human Nature.* London, Penguin (Original work published 1902).

Jenks, K. M. (1992). *The Feminine in Zygote and Syzygy.* Unpublished doctoral dissertation, University of California, Santa Barbara.

Jonas, H. (1963). *The Gnostic Religion.* Boston: Beacon Press.

Jung, C. G. (1954). *The Archetypes and the Collective Unconscious.* R. F. C. Hull, trans. The Collected Works of C. G. Jung (vol. 9i). Princeton: Princeton University Press.

———. (1959). *Aion.* R. F. C. Hull, trans. The Collected Works of C. G. Jung (vol. 9ii). Princeton: Princeton University Press.

———. (1961). *Memories, Dreams, Reflections.* New York: Vintage Books.

———. (1966a). *The Practice of Psychotherapy.* R. F. C. Hull, trans. The Collected Works of C. G. Jung (vol. 16). Princeton: Princeton University Press.

———. (1966b). *The Spirit in Man, Art, and Literature.* R. F. C. Hull, trans., The Collected Works of C. G. Jung (vol. 15), Princeton: Princeton University Press.

———. (1966c). *Two Essays on Analytical Psychology.* R. F. C. Hull, trans. The Collected Works of C. G. Jung (vol. 7). Princeton: Princeton University Press.

———. (1967). *Alchemical Studies.* R. F. C. Hull, trans. The Collected Works of C. G. Jung (vol. 13). Princeton: Princeton University Press.

———. (1968). *Psychology and Alchemy.* R. F. C. Hull, trans. The Collected Works of C. G. Jung (vol. 12). Princeton: Princeton University Press.

———. (1969a). *Psychology and Religion: West and East.* R. F. C. Hull, trans. The Collected Works of C. G. Jung (vol. 11). Princeton: Princeton University Press.

———. (1969b). *The Structure and Dynamics of the Psyche.* R. F. C. Hull, trans. The Collected Works of C. G. Jung (vol. 8). Princeton: Princeton University Press.

———. (1970a). *Civilization in Transition.* R. F. C. Hull, trans. The Collected Works of C. G. Jung (vol. 10). Princeton: Princeton University Press.

———. (1970b). *Mysterium Coniunctionis.* R. F. C. Hull, trans. The Collected Works of C. G. Jung (vol. 14). Princeton: Princeton University Press.

———. (1973). *Letters, I.* Princeton: Princeton University Press.

———. (1975). *Letters, II.* Princeton: Princeton University Press.

———. (1976a). *The Symbolic Life.* R. F. C. Hull, trans. The Collected Works of C. G. Jung (vol. 18). Princeton: Princeton University Press.

———. (1976b). *The Visions Seminars,* I. Zurich: Spring Publications.

Kahlo, F. (1995). *I Painted My Own Reality.* San Francisco: Chronicle Books.

Klein, M. (1975). *Envy and Gratitude and Other Works 1946–1963.* New York: The Free Press (Original work published 1957).

Kohut, H. (1984). *How Does Analysis Cure?* Chicago: University of Chicago Press.

Kristeva, J. (1987). *Tales of Love.* New York: Columbia University Press.

Lacan, J. (1977). *Ecrits,* A. Sheridan, trans. New York: Norton.

Lamy, L. (1981). *Egyptian Mysteries.* London: Thames & Hudson.

Lockhart, R. A. (1987). *Psyche Speaks.* Wilmette, IL: Chiron Publications.

Malouf, D. (1996). *An Imaginary Life.* New York: Vintage International.

McGuire, W., ed. (1974). *The Freud/Jung Letters.* Princeton: Princeton University Press.

Meador, B. de S. (1994). *Uncursing the Dark: Treasures from the Underworld.* Wilmette, IL: Chiron Publications.

Men, H. (1990). *Secrets of Mayan Science and Religion.* Rochester, VT: Bear & Co.

Miller, J. B. (1986). *Toward a New Psychology of Women.* Boston: Beacon Press.

Millett, K. (1969). *Sexual Politics.* London: Virago.

Mitchell, J. (1974). *Psychoanalysis and Feminism.* London: Penguin.

Moi, T. (1985). *Sexual/Textual Politics: Feminist Literary Theory.* London: Routledge.

Neumann, E. (1989). "Mystical Man," in J. Campbell, ed., *The Mystic Vision.* Princeton: Princeton University Press.

Onians, R. B. (1989). *The Origins of European Thought.* Cambridge: Cambridge University Press.

Perera, S. B. (1981). *Descent to the Goddess: A Way of Initiation for Women.* Toronto: Inner City Books.

Pulver, M. (1978). "Jesus' Round Dance and Crucifixion According to the Acts of John," in J. Campbell, ed., *The Mysteries.* Princeton: Princeton University Press.

Rilke, R. M. (1954). *Letters to a Young Poet.* New York: W. W. Norton.

———. (1989). *The Selected Poetry of Rainer Maria Rilke.* Stephen Mitchell, ed. and trans. New York: Vintage International.

Romanyshyn, R. D. (1999). *The Soul in Grief: Love, Death, and Transformation*. Berkeley, CA: North Atlantic Books.

———. (2000a). "Alchemy and the Subtle Body of Metaphor," in R. Brooke, ed., *Pathways into the World: Phenomenology and Analytical Psychology*. London: Routledge.

———. (2000b). "Angels and Other Anomalies of the Imaginal Life," Kathleen Raine, ed., *Temenos Academy Review*. London: Golgonooza Press.

Rosarium Philosophorum (1550). Frankfurt.

Rose, J. (1986). *Sexuality in the Field of Vision*. London: Verso Press.

Roszak, T., M. E. Gomes, and A. D. Kanner, eds. (1995). *Ecopsychology*. San Francisco: Sierra Club Books.

Rumi, J. (1993). *Love Is a Stranger*. Kabir Edmund Helminski, trans. Watsonville, CA: Threshold Books.

———. (1994) *Say I Am You*. J. Moyne and C. Barks, trans. Athens, GA: Maypop.

Sardello, R., ed. (1994). *The Angels*. Dallas: Dallas Institute Publications.

———. (1995). *Love and the Soul*. New York: HarperCollins.

Schwartz-Salant, N. (1989). *The Borderline Personality: Vision and Healing*. Wilmette, IL: Chiron Publications.

———. (1993). "Jung, Madness, and Sexuality," in M. Stein, ed., *Mad Parts of Sane People in Analysis*. Wilmette, IL: Chiron Publications.

———. (1995). "On the Interactive Field as the Analytic Object," in M. Stein, ed., *The Interactive Field in Analysis*. Wilmette, IL: Chiron Publications.

Skafte, D. (1992, Spring-Summer). "When Ovaries Are Storm-Centers," in *Psychological Perspectives*, 26.

Spiegelman, J. M., and V. Mansfield (1996). "On the Physics and Psychology of the Transference as an Interactive Field," in *Journal of Analytical Psychology*, 41 (2).

Stein, M., ed. (1995). *The Interactive Field in Analysis*. Wilmette, IL: Chiron Publications.

Van Eenwyk, J. R. (1997). *Archetypes and Strange Attractors*. Toronto: Inner City Books.

Walker, B. G. (1983). *The Women's Encyclopedia of Myths and Secrets*. San Francisco: HarperSanFrancisco.

Wallis Budge, E. A. (1967). *The Egyptian Book of the Dead*. New York: Dover Publications (Original work published in London in 1895).

Whitman, W. (n.d.). *Leaves of Grass*. New York: Doubleday/Heritage Press.

Whitmont, E. C. (1992). *Return of the Goddess*. New York: Crossroad.

Wilhelm, R. (1977). *The I Ching*. Princeton: Princeton University Press.

Wolf, F. A. (1994). *The Dreaming Universe*. New York: Touchstone/Simon & Schuster.

Woodman, M. (1982). *Addiction to Perfection: The Still Unravished Bride*. Toronto: Inner City Books.

INDEX

and her visionaries, 35
emerging out of chaotic
  depths, 4
goddess of speech, 35
linked to Orphic mysteries, 36
Van Eenwyk, J. R., 28
Varuna, 40
virgin, 85, 92
  goddess, 165
  the initiated, 95
Vishnu, 139
vision, creative, 33
visionary
  experiences, 187
  feeling, 179
visitation, 111
visits to subtle world, 149
vocation, doubts about, 75
Voice of Otherness, 178
vulva, 94
  creation myth of, 107
  swollen, 94

W
Walker, Barbara G., 139, 140, 169
Walker, Ray C., 164
white light, 58
Whitman, Walt, 183
Whitmont, E. C., 33, 35
William, Prince, 158

Wisdom figure of Sophia, 56
wise woman, 73
witch, 88
Wolf, F. A., 2
woman/women
  descent to Other, 98
  genitals as center, 92
  gives birth to woman, 92
  individuation process of, 92
  and multidimensional con-
    sciousness, 88
  other, 85, 101
  and projections, 110
  returning from descent to
    underworld, 95
womb, 92
wonders, 177
world
  of projection, 65
  Soul, 60
  voices of the unseen, 203
world-tree, roots of, 38
  in amrita, 38
worldview, breakdown of our
  prevailing, 2

Y
yantra, 94
yoni, 36

Veronica Goodchild, Ph.D. is a Jungian-oriented psychotherapist who came to the United States from London. She is part of the Core Faculty at Pacifica Graduate Institute, Carpinteria, California. She studied theology and philosophy at London University, earned an M.S.W. from Columbia in New York City, and completed her Ph.D. from Pacifica in 1998. She lives in Summerland, California with her husband and two children. She lectures and teaches workshops.